MULTIMEDIA COMPREHENSION

Multimedia messages use combinations of texts, pictures, maps, and graphs as tools for communication. This book provides a synthesis of theory and research about how people comprehend multimedia. It adopts the perspectives of cognitive psychology, semiotics, anthropology, linguistics, education, and art. Its central idea is that information displays can be categorized into two different but complementary forms of representations, which service different purposes in human cognition and communication. Specific interaction between these representations enhances comprehension, thinking, and problem-solving, as illustrated by numerous examples. *Multimedia Comprehension* is written for a broad audience with no special prior knowledge. It is of interest to everyone trying to understand how people comprehend multimedia, from scholars and students in psychology, communication, and education, to web and interface designers and instructors.

WOLFGANG SCHNOTZ is Emeritus Professor of General and Educational Psychology at the University of Koblenz-Landau, Germany. He was a member of the Reading Expert Group for the OECD, chief editor of Learning and Instruction, and head of the DFG Graduate School Teaching and Learning. He publishes on text comprehension, multimedia learning, learning from animation, and conceptual change.

MULTIMEDIA COMPREHENSION

WOLFGANG SCHNOTZ

University of Koblenz-Landau

CAMBRIDGE
UNIVERSITY PRESS

Shaftesbury Road, Cambridge CB2 8BS, United Kingdom

One Liberty Plaza, 20th Floor, New York, NY 10006, USA

477 Williamstown Road, Port Melbourne, VIC 3207, Australia

314–321, 3rd Floor, Plot 3, Splendor Forum, Jasola District Centre, New Delhi – 110025, India

103 Penang Road, #05–06/07, Visioncrest Commercial, Singapore 238467

Cambridge University Press is part of Cambridge University Press & Assessment, a department of the University of Cambridge.

We share the University's mission to contribute to society through the pursuit of education, learning and research at the highest international levels of excellence.

www.cambridge.org
Information on this title: www.cambridge.org/9781009303217

DOI: 10.1017/9781009303255

© Wolfgang Schnotz 2023

First published 2023

A catalogue record for this publication is available from the British Library.

Library of Congress Cataloging-in-Publication Data
NAMES: Schnotz, Wolfgang, 1946– author.
TITLE: Multimedia comprehension / Wolfgang Schnotz, University of Koblenz-Landau.
DESCRIPTION: Cambridge, United Kingdom ; New York, NY, USA : Cambridge University Press, [2023] | Includes bibliographical references and index.
IDENTIFIERS: LCCN 2022034793 (print) | LCCN 2022034794 (ebook) | ISBN 9781009303217 (hardback) | ISBN 9781009303231 (paperback) | ISBN 9781009303255 (epub)
SUBJECTS: LCSH: Information visualization. | Visual communication. | Multimedia communications.
CLASSIFICATION: LCC QA76.9.I52 S35 2023 (print) | LCC QA76.9.I52 (ebook) | DDC 001.4/226–dc23/eng/20220922
LC record available at https://lccn.loc.gov/2022034793
LC ebook record available at https://lccn.loc.gov/2022034794

ISBN 978-1-009-30321-7 Hardback
ISBN 978-1-009-30323-1 Paperback

For Silke and Aaron

Contents

Preface

This book is about how people understand spoken or written texts and different kinds of static or animated pictures such as drawings, photographs, maps, and graphs. According to a widely accepted term proposed by Richard E. Mayer, these processes are referred to as "multimedia comprehension." The book focuses on multimedia comprehension because it is the bottleneck of communication and learning with multimedia. It analyzes which structures and processes are involved in multimedia comprehension and how these processes can be affected by manipulating the conditions of processing. It aims to present a coherent and consistent view of the subject matter based on empirical research during recent decades.

My interest in this topic originated from early experiments on text comprehension which I conducted in a learning research group at the University of Tübingen and as a visiting researcher at the Faculty of Linguistics at the University of Bielefeld. Later, during my time at the University of Jena and the University of Koblenz-Landau, my focus of interest was directed to the comprehension of graphics. This led naturally to an interest in the conjoint cognitive processing of texts and pictures.

While text processing has been an area of intensive research for various decades which has resulted in highly sophisticated theoretical views, research on cognitive processing of pictures is, to some extent, still in its infancy. This manifests itself in a lack of empirical research and theoretical reflection. Some commonalities between texts and pictures seem to indicate that picture comprehension can be analyzed along the same conceptual lines as text comprehension. This leads to a mindset which assumes a parallelism between texts and pictures, namely the assumption that it is possible to find correspondence between all text-related and picture-related aspects. The following examples illustrate this mindset. Because texts employ a specific, well-defined repertoire of signs (a lexicon with a specific vocabulary), this assumed parallelism would suggest that pictures also have a specific, well-defined repertoire of signs. Because words in texts are connected according to the rules of specific syntax, which ensures that sentences are well formed, this assumed parallelism would suggest that pictures also have a specific syntax which specifies how pictorial elements have to be combined in order to create well-formed pictures. Because texts are said to have a text base which grasps the semantic content of the text, an assumed parallelism would suggest that pictures have a "picture base" which grasps the semantic content of the picture. Owing to this assumed parallelism between texts and pictures, there have been discussions about whether texts can be replaced by pictures in a new age of global communication in which symbol-based communication with language will gradually be replaced with pictorial communication.

I have to admit that I have always felt uneasy about these assumptions. In the past, my impression was that we did not really understand the issue yet and that we lacked a thorough conceptual analysis. It seemed to me that the parallels between texts and pictures are very limited. We were allowing ourselves to be deceived by superficial similarities between the two kinds of representations and therefore missing the fundamental differences between them. My impression was that texts and pictures are two fundamentally different but complementary kinds of representation which serve specific and fundamentally different purposes in human communication. This view led to the development of the ITPC model (Integrative Model of Text and Picture Comprehension) which has been published and discussed in journals. The ITPC model is further elaborated in the present book. My hope is that the topic is not only of theoretical interest. Practically oriented decisions about the use of multimedia are likely to be better when they are based not only on intuition, experience, and fashionable surface guidelines but on sufficiently differentiated knowledge about the psychological processes that take place in multimedia comprehension.

It has been my great pleasure to discuss and refine my views on these issues with various people during sabbaticals and research stays at Arizona State University, the University of California Santa Barbara, Vanderbilt University Nashville, the University of Memphis, as well as the Curtin University of Technology in Perth and the University of New South Wales in Sydney. I am very obliged to Raymond W. Kulhavy, Richard E. Mayer, Mary Hegarty, Susan R. Goldman, Daniel L. Schwartz, as well as Richard K. Lowe and John Sweller for numerous fruitful discussions. I am especially grateful to Arthur C. Graesser for the stimulating exchange and intensive discussions at the Institute of Intelligent Systems in Memphis. I enjoyed these discussions very much and profited a lot from their impact.

I am also obliged to various colleagues who I have had the pleasure to cooperate with and who have contributed in various ways to this research and my own thinking on these topics. I want to mention Christiane Baadte, Maria Bannert, Beatriz Barquero, Gabriele Cierniak, Erica DeVries, Stefan Dutke, Georg Hauck, Andrea Heiß, Holger Horz, Christian Kürschner, Alwine Lenzner, Ulrich Ludewig, Christoph Mengelkamp, Katja Hartwig née Meyer, Loredana Mihalca, Phil Moore, Andreas Müller, Wieland Müller, Renate Rasch, Thorsten Rasch, Neil Schwartz, Tina Seufert, Mark Ullrich, Inga Wagner, Fang Zhao, and Thomas Zink.

I am also obliged to the German Research Foundation and the Federal Ministry of Education and Research of Germany for various grants that have supported research on the comprehension of texts and pictures, which has contributed to the present book. My special thanks go to Inga Wagner. She critically reviewed a former version of the book chapters and made numerous suggestions to improve the manuscript. I am also very grateful to Amanda Habbershaw, who ensured that it was written in smooth and readable English.

Although the book primarily has a psychological background, it is not written especially for psychologists. Instead, it is intended to address everyone who is interested in how people understand multimedia messages. As for its academic background, the book combines considerations from cognitive psychology, semiotics, anthropology, linguistics, genetics, education, and arts. So, it might be of interest for scholars from various disciplines dealing with multimedia comprehension, especially cognitive science, communication, and education. As for practitioners, the book might be of interest for web designers, human–computer interface designers, professional trainers, teachers, and artists. In brief, anyone who deals with multimedia comprehension in one way or the other. I hope very much that the book will provide a more differentiated view and contribute to a deeper understanding of multimedia comprehension. I am, of course, happy to receive comments about the book at schnotz@uni-landau.de.

CHAPTER I

Introduction

Abstract

This chapter aims at clarifying basic concepts related to multimedia: communication, comprehension, and learning. Multimedia communication is considered as the intentional creation, display, and reception of multiple kinds of signs in order to convey messages about some content. It entails two subprocesses: meaning and comprehension. Multimedia meaning is a process in which the producer of a message creates multiple external signs based on his or her prior knowledge in order to direct the recipient's mind so that the recipient understands what the producer means. Multimedia comprehension is the complementary process of reconstructing the previously externalized knowledge in the mind of the recipient. It can be seen as the bottleneck of multimedia communication. Multimedia comprehension and multimedia learning are related but are nevertheless different: While multimedia comprehension results in transient changes in working memory, multimedia learning results in permanent changes in long-term memory. Multimedia learning is a byproduct of multimedia comprehension. Further, an overview of the book is presented.

1.1   What Is Multimedia?

Multimedia is ubiquitous in modern societies nowadays. It plays an increasingly important role in education, business administration, advertising, the economy, finances, news agencies, traveling services, and numerous other fields. The ever-growing Internet is full of multimedia messages about nearly everything, including topics such as how to operate your home trainer, how to change the batteries of your TV remote control, and so forth.

In everyday communication, the concept of multimedia is frequently used in a fuzzy way. Many people understand "multimedia" to be a computer- and web-based combination of digital mass storage devices with delivery media such as computer screens, loudspeakers, headphones, tablets, or cellphones which deliver spoken or written text with pictures and sound or music. This characterization encompasses three aspects of multimedia: technology, presentation, and perception. The technology aspect refers to the delivery media which include digital networks, computers, screens, and loudspeakers. The presentation aspect refers to the format used to display information such as texts and pictures, which can be in the form of photographs, drawings, maps, graphs, and animations. The perception aspect refers to the organs of perception that receive a multimedia message, usually the eyes and the ears.

The efficacy of multimedia communication depends on all three aspects. The technology aspect is the fundament of multimedia and highly important in terms of practical reliability. Technology enables flexible combinations of different presentation formats. From the viewpoint of cognitive psychology, which focuses on how humans search, perceive, and process information, however, the technology aspect is not very important. Merely reading a text printed on paper, for example, does not fundamentally differ from reading the same text on a computer screen. Generally speaking, the comprehension of multimedia messages is only marginally affected by the technological carrier of the message. Instead, it is heavily influenced by the form in which information is presented and by the way in which a message is perceived by a recipient. Thus, cognitive psychology focuses on the presentation and perception aspects of multimedia communication.

Does multimedia require new technologies? Richard Mayer[1] defines multimedia as the combination of words and pictures. Words can be spoken or written, and pictures can be photographs, drawings, maps, graphs, as well as animations or videos. This straightforward definition of multimedia focuses only on the presentation aspect and ignores the technology aspect. This has important implications: Multimedia does not necessarily require high technology. It also includes the use of books or blackboards instead of computer screens, as well as the human voice instead of loudspeakers. From that point of view, multimedia is not a modern phenomenon. Instead, it has a long tradition which dates back to Comenius,[2] who emphasized the importance of adding pictures to texts in order to improve comprehension in his pioneer work *Orbis Sensualium Pictus* (first published in 1658). Accordingly, one can distinguish between traditional and modern forms of using multimedia.

---

[1] Mayer (2009, 2014); Mayer and Fiorella (2022).   [2] Comenius (1999).

Consider the following examples of multimedia learning. Let us assume that students have to learn about the migration of birds in Europe. To this end, the teacher presents a map of the European continent, indicating where some birds live in summer and where they spend winter. While pointing to the map, she tells the class that many birds breed in middle and northern Europe in summer, but do not stay there during winter. Instead, they fly to warmer areas in the Mediterranean area.

One of the students is assigned the task of learning about a specific migrant bird – the marsh harrier – in order to give a report to her classmates the next day. She walks into the school library and opens a printed encyclopedia of biology, where she finds a text about the marsh harrier and a picture of the bird. Furthermore, she consults the Internet and finds a text and a graph depicting the frequency of marsh harriers during different months in middle Europe. The website also features a sound button which plays the typical call of a marsh harrier near its breeding place. Altogether, the student has practiced three forms of multimedia learning: lecture-based multimedia learning in class, book-based multimedia learning in the library, and web-based multimedia learning at her computer or smart phone. Information was presented in different formats – in the visual modality (written text and pictures) and the auditory modality (oral text and sound).

Teaching and learning are different sides of a specific kind of communication which can be characterized as follows. Teachers, who have greater knowledge about a subject matter than their students, send messages about the subject matter to their students (and sometimes also about their behavior). Students send messages (explicitly or silently) about their understanding, knowledge, and interest to their teachers. Successful teaching and learning take place when the difference between the teacher's and the students' knowledge about the subject matter becomes smaller. However, as multimedia learning is merely a special case of multimedia communication, it follows that multimedia communication also comprises other variants of using multimedia. So, what is multimedia communication?

1.2 Multimedia Communication

To clarify the concepts, we will start with the concept of a medium. A medium is a means for communication that serves to convey messages from a sender to a recipient. These messages are conveyed by external signs,[3] such as flags, insignia, gestures, spoken or written words, drawings, and so forth. Does that mean the usage of signs is always related to communication? Of course not, because many signs are used outside of the context of communication. We have to remember that the world is full of causality, with causes leading to effects. Thus, effects indicate causes, which means that effects serve as signs for causes. For example, smoke indicates fire; the depth of a footprint indicates the weight of an animal, and so forth. Charles Peirce[4] calls these kinds of signs "indexes." Although we use such signs all the time for our orientation, they do not constitute a form of communication. There is no communication between a burning forest and a firefighter when he or she interprets smoke as a sign of danger and takes action. And there is no communication between a prey and a predator, who is silently following the prey's spoor in order to bring it down. We talk about communication only if signs are produced intentionally (i.e., with a goal in mind) with the aim that the recipient will understand the message and change his or her behavior accordingly. In the teaching context just described, for example, the teacher's communication goal could be to increase her students' knowledge about bird migration. In the context of advertising, the communication goal is usually to convince the addressee to buy a product.

Contrary to animals, whose communication is based on innate, relatively fixed species-specific external sign inventories, human communication is based on a much broader repertoire of powerful signs such as gesture, spoken language, written language, and pictures, which can be flexibly combined and used for all kinds of communication purposes. Many of these signs are human inventions which were created at very different times in history and can nowadays be bound together in multimedia environments.

The distinction between technology, presentation, and perception in the context of media also translates to the analysis of signs. The aspect of technology refers to the carriers of signs: clay, paper, boards, digital devices such as computers or the Internet, and even fleeting carriers such as soundwaves in the case of spoken language. The aspect of presentation refers to how information is displayed by signs such as symbols

---

[3] A sign is an object or event that indicates something else, thus representing it. Signs can exist outside of an individual, such as external objects or events. Internal processes such as pain, fear, imagery, or concepts can also function as (internal) signs. Luria (1973) argued that all higher-order cognitive functions require the use of internal sign systems, because otherwise we would only be informed about the "here and now" and could not reflect about the past or think about the future.

[4] Peirce (1932).

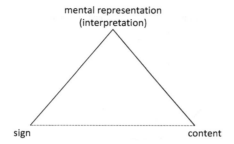

Figure 1.1   Semiotic triangle of Ogden and Richards

(e.g., words) or icons (e.g., pictures). It also refers to the way in which signs are perceived by the recipient. Once again, cognitive psychology focuses on the presentation and the perception aspects. It aims at analyzing how recipients perceive and cognitively process different kinds of signs in order to understand messages. From a psychological point of view, the carrier of signs is not important. If we follow Richard Mayer's parsimonious definition provided in Section 1.1, multimedia communication is the usage of multiple kinds of signs such as texts and pictures to convey messages. Multimedia communication is sign-based communication.

How does sign-based communication work? Signs designate something, which is equivalent to saying that they mean something or they refer to something. The word "bird," for example, refers to all elements in the whole class of birds, whereas the name "marsh harrier" refers only to a portion of this class, and "*this* marsh harrier" refers to a specific animal in the class. To clarify the relations between signs, the meaning of signs, and the content of signs, Ogden and Richards[5] introduced the concept of the semiotic triangle, which is shown in Figure 1.1. The triangle has three constituents: the sign (an external sign in this context), the designated content (also called the referent), and the interpretation of the sign. The interpretation can be understood as a mental representation or as an internal sign of the designated content.[6] The relation between the external sign and the content is not a direct one. Instead, it is mediated by two connected relations: the relation between the external sign and the mental representation and the relation between the mental representation and the designated content.

---

[5] Ogden and Richards (1923).
[6] With the term "representations," we mean any object, event, or state that stands for something else (cf. Peterson, 1996). The concept can apply both to internal structures in the mind (mental representations of some content) and to external structures referring to the content, such as external texts or pictures.

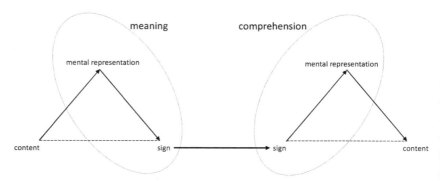

Figure 1.2   Communication considered as a combination of two semiotic triangles

Sign-based communication requires that signs are produced to be understood. In other words, sign production and sign comprehension have to be aligned as well as possible. The alignment of sign production and sign comprehension can be visualized with the help of two semiotic triangles, as shown in Figure 1.2. The sign producer starts with some knowledge about the content (i.e., a mental representation) which he or she has received from another source or from his or her own experience and which he or she wants to communicate. This can be any kind of content, for example, the visual appearance of a bird such as the marsh harrier, its habitat, or migration routes. This knowledge is then external-ized by creating external signs. When a producer creates and delivers external signs to someone, we refer to it as "sending a message" to the corresponding recipient. The signs are supposed to mean what the sign producer has in mind. Thus, "meaning" can be considered as a process that creates external signs on the basis of what the sign producer knows or intends. The producer tries to direct the mind of the recipient in such a way that the recipient understands what the producer means.[7]

Based on these external signs, the recipient tries to reconstruct the knowledge that was externalized by the producer. That is, the recipient tries to comprehend the signs. When communication encompasses multi-ple kinds of signs, the comprehension process is called "multimedia comprehension." If the communication is successful, the recipient's inter-pretation corresponds to what the sign producer meant; this is what we call "correct comprehension." If the interpretation does not correspond to the intended meaning, we call it "miscomprehension." This implies that the

---

[7] Clark (1996).

communication was unsuccessful. From a psychological point of view, correct comprehension and miscomprehension involve the same kinds of cognitive processes. However, they both differ from another kind of unsuccessful communication, namely the case where the recipient fails to come up with any interpretation at all. We call this "non-comprehension."

All in all, multimedia communication can be characterized as the intentional production, display, and reception of multiple external signs (corresponding to multiple forms of representation) in order to convey messages about a subject matter.

1.3 What Is Multimedia Comprehension?

We have characterized multimedia comprehension in Section 1.2 as a constituent part of multimedia communication, namely as the reconstruction of knowledge previously externalized by a producer of a multimedia message. This definition raises two questions: First, where does this (re) construction take place? Second, how is multimedia comprehension related to multimedia learning? To answer these questions, we need to understand the human cognitive system.

Most psychologists adopt the view that humans process information in a multiple-store memory system, consisting of sensory registers, a working memory, and a long-term memory.[8] Information from the outside world enters the cognitive system through the sensory organs. Visual information captured by the eyes is stored very briefly (less than 1 second) in a visual register. Auditory information captured by the ears is stored briefly (less than 3 seconds) in an auditory register. Information is stored in the sensory registers only long enough for it to be extracted and passed on for further processing. If attention is directed to information in the sensory registers, this information is transmitted to working memory, where it is further processed in specialized subsystems under the guidance of a central executive.[9] In the case of comprehension, cognitive processing in working memory corresponds to the construction of a mental representation of the content to be understood. The mental construction process draws on external information from the sensory registers and on knowledge of the world (i.e., internal information) retrieved from long-term memory. Due to the limited storage capacity of working memory, which comprises only five elements on average (although this can be effectively increased by chunking), mental representations have to be constructed step by step, in

---

[8] Atkinson and Shiffrin (1971).   [9] Baddeley (1986).

multiple processing cycles. By the same token, complex mental representations cannot be cognitively available as a whole at any time. However,
individuals can quickly and flexibly reactivate parts of a mental representation, if needed.[10] If a mental representation that includes new information has been sufficiently interlinked with information from long-term
memory and processed repeatedly within working memory, it is likely that
the new information is stored in long-term memory, which has a practically unlimited storage capacity. As the term suggests, long-term memory
is characterized by a very low decay of information.

Against the backdrop of these assumptions regarding the cognitive
system, we can characterize multimedia comprehension based on multiple
external signs such as text and pictures as the construction of mental
representations of what the multimedia message is about in a recipient's
working memory.

1.4   Differences to Multimedia Learning

Whereas multimedia comprehension is a transient change in working
memory, multimedia learning is a process that takes place in long-term
memory. If no change has occurred in long-term memory, nothing has
been learned. There is no way of changing an individual's long-term
memory directly, as changes must be triggered by cognitive processing in
working memory, such as comprehension. The cognitive processes during
comprehension introduce memory traces into long-term memory which
allow an individual to remember what he or she previously understood.
The individual can reconstruct previously constructed representations in
working memory provided that memory traces are still accessible.[11]
Learning strategies frequently suggest reiterating comprehension processes
systematically and at an increasingly deeper level in order to develop such
memory traces in long-term memory, because this makes mental
representations easier to reconstruct. Thus, multimedia learning can be
considered as a by-product of multimedia comprehension. Conversely, due
to the limited capacity of working memory, multimedia comprehension
can be considered as the bottleneck of multimedia communication and
multimedia learning.

---

[10] The corresponding access structures have been described as "long-term working memory" (Ericsson
and Kintsch, 1995).
[11] Cermak and Craik (1979).

This view suggests that multimedia comprehension and multimedia learning are closely related. Good comprehension is usually associated with good learning. Nevertheless, the two processes are different because multimedia comprehension results in transient changes in working memory, whereas multimedia learning results in permanent changes in long-term memory. The difference between comprehension and learning was demonstrated by the infamously striking and bizarre case of neurological surgery performed on Mr. Henry Gustav Molaison (also known as patient H. M.). After a major brain operation in 1953, patient H. M. was still able to comprehend information, but could no longer learn new declarative knowledge. Here is a short description of his deficits:

> The patient suffered from severe epilepsy and headaches. The epilepsy was localized to the left and right medial temporal lobes, which were surgically removed with most of the amygdala and the entorhinal cortex at the age of 27. The operation had no effect on his speech behavior, test intelligence, social behavior, and emotional responses. His working memory was also intact: He could easily perform tasks that required a short-term storage of information. He was also able to remember events before his operation without any problems. However, he could no longer acquire new declarative knowledge. So, he could not remember a new address after a move. He could read the same newspaper repeatedly without realizing that he had already read it. He could play with the same puzzles repeatedly, without remembering that he had already solved them. Like other subjects, he improved more and more, but said he had never done the job and had no idea how to solve it. He thus acquired automated procedural knowledge without the accompanying conscious declarative knowledge about this procedure. Thus, the patient was able to acquire new procedural knowledge in long-term memory after the operation, but he could not learn new declarative knowledge.[12]

In other words, Mr. Molaison's comprehension was still intact, but his learning was severely impaired. His deficits seemed to be caused by a blocked directed connection from working memory to long-term memory.

1.5   Intraindividual Communication with Multimedia

Comprehension is usually the starting point for further cognitive processes, further reflections, thinking, and problem-solving. When individuals think about a subject matter, they frequently externalize their ideas by talking (silently or aloud), writing, or drawing a diagram or a graph. In other

---

[12] Corkin et al. (1997).

words, they express their ideas with the help of different external representation formats. After having produced this externalization and having activated other parts of their prior knowledge, they can reinvestigate their own representations and understand the subject matter from a new perspective. This frequently leads them to other insights and new ideas. When individuals externalize their ideas by talking, writing, or drawing, and then reconsider and reinterpret their externalized ideas, they practice a kind of "communication with themselves." They switch between the roles of the sign producer and the sign recipient until they come up with a mental representation of the subject matter which allows them to answer the question they were concerned about. Thus, besides the interindividual communication described in Section 1.2, intraindividual communication can also exist. It involves individuals creating their own external representations and operating on them in order to come up with new insights, elaborate their thinking about a subject matter, and solve problems.

Whether this intraindividual communication is successful or not depends heavily on the representation formats and how these formats fit with the questions at hand. When individuals have a large scope of representation formats at their disposal, allowing them to select and combine different representations flexibly according to specific requirements, their capacity to think and reflect about a subject matter and find better solutions to problems might be enhanced. Thus, multimedia can also serve as a tool for thinking and problem-solving when self-made multiple representations are used in the context of intraindividual communication.

1.6   Overview

Multimedia technology has developed at high speed in recent years. Despite all technical innovations, however, multimedia comprehension is still constrained by the characteristics of the human cognitive system. Given the central role of working memory in the process of comprehension and its severely limited processing capacity, multimedia comprehension can be considered the bottleneck of multimedia communication and multimedia learning. The use of technologies will only be successful if the psychological laws governing comprehension processes are taken into account.

The present book is about multimedia comprehension. It deals with the construction of mental representations in a recipient's working memory based on multiple external signs such as text and pictures. The book aims at explaining general issues related to multimedia comprehension from a psychological point of view, focusing on the presentation and perception aspects of multimedia without dealing with questions of technology. Its central question is how recipients perceive and cognitively process different kinds of signs in order to understand messages.

The organization of the book is as follows. After this introduction, Chapter 2 provides an overview of the history of human sign systems used in multimedia communication, including the use of gestures and oral language. These also include early forms of writing, which were based on concepts, and later forms which were (and still are) based on phonemes (but still use hidden signs for concepts). The chapter further deals with the use of different kinds of pictures, including realistic pictures, maps, and graphs. Together, these various sign systems can be combined as tools for creating multimedia messages, which serve specific communication purposes.

Chapter 3 analyzes the principles of representation used by different sign systems more closely. Its main question is how the different sign systems and their representations are related to one another. The chapter argues that the various kinds of representation can be classified into two basic categories: descriptive representations and depictive representations. The two kinds of representation differ in terms of their representational power and inferential power. Both kinds of representation can take the form of external, physical representations and the form of internal, mental representations.

Chapter 4 deals with the comprehension of descriptive representations in the form of written or spoken texts. It analyzes the nature of the meaning of text and the creation of multiple kinds of mental representation. Special attention is given to processes of coherence formation and ways of directing the reader's or listener's flow of consciousness during text comprehension.

Chapter 5 relates to the comprehension of static or animated depictive representations which include realistic pictures, maps, and graphs. Picture comprehension is described as the creation of multiple representations through sub-semantic processing, semantic perceptual processing, and conceptual picture processing.

While Chapters 4 and 5 focus on the comprehension of texts and the comprehension of pictures separately, Chapter 6 analyzes the integrated comprehension of text–picture combinations which is at the core of multimedia comprehension. The chapter is substantiated in the Integrated Model of Text–Picture Comprehension[13] (ITPC model) which includes distinctions between descriptive and depictive representations,

[13] Schnotz (2005, 2014, 2022).

external and internal representations, and perceptual surface-structure processing and semantic deep-structure processing. Integrated processing is considered as being embedded in the human cognitive architecture, which is assumed to consist of modality-specific sensory registers, limited-capacity working memory, and long-term memory. The model covers listening comprehension, reading comprehension, visual picture comprehension, and sound comprehension.

Chapter 7 provides further and deeper analyses of the integrated comprehension of texts and pictures with a special focus on inter-representational coherence formation and mental model construction. The chapter also points out the interplay between the ambiguity of representations and their disambiguation by providing complementary representations. It further elaborates on the different, but complementary functions of texts and pictures during different phases of task-oriented multimedia comprehension.

The focus of Chapter 8 goes beyond comprehension. When multimedia comprehension has been successful, an individual can use his or her mental representation in order to infer new information or to solve problems by means of productive thinking. The chapter discusses different views of productive thinking and problem-solving. It points out that productive thinking and problem-solving make specific use of descriptive and depictive representations. In addition, it shows that the use of descriptive and depictive representations has implications, for example, for mathematics education and science education. Finally, referring to historic examples of high practical relevance, the chapter describes the use of depictive representations for data collection and statistical problem-solving based on content-related hypotheses.

Finally, Chapter 9 analyzes the conclusions that can be drawn from the previous theoretical analyses and sets out the practical implications. It provides suggestions on how developers should design multimedia messages, as well as on how recipients should process them.

CHAPTER 2

A Short History of Multimedia Sign Systems

Abstract

Human history has created a large variety of sign systems for communication. These systems were developed at different times for different purposes. While oral language has developed as part of human biological evolution, written texts, realistic pictures, maps, and graphs are cultural inventions. Human oral language might have originated from gestures supplemented by sound patterns. It is a biological anchored feature of the human species, as manifested in somatic, perceptual, and neurological pre-adaptations. Early writing systems used iconic ideograms which were gradually transformed into symbols. This made production and discrimination easier but increased the required amount of learning. Further development led to writing systems using phonograms plus orthographic ideograms. Realistic pictures are older than writing systems. They represent content by similarity but also show allegories of social relationships. Maps are realistic pictures of a geographic area facing the problem of how to present a curved earth surface on a two-dimensional surface. Graphs are visuo-spatial objects representing a subject matter based on analogy due to inherent common structural properties.

Multimedia communication uses multiple kinds of signs which draw on a large variety of human communication in different contexts: People talk to each other, using oral language, and underscore their messages with gestures. They write texts which encode the sound of oral language to some extent, but also draw on orthography which often indicates the semantic origin of written words. People also create pictures which can show concrete observable scenarios (so-called realistic pictures) or larger geographic areas (maps). Other pictures can represent abstract, unobservable relationships (graphs).

Sign systems allow specific kinds of representations to be created, which can be displayed to recipients. In multimedia environments, different sign systems can be bound together *ad libitum* in order to communicate about and represent nearly everything. However, sign systems have very different backgrounds and histories. Some of them are givens of human evolution, whereas others are cultural inventions. Some are older than several hundred thousand years; others are only a few hundred years old. It is therefore no surprise that the various sign systems differ in terms of their alignment with the human cognitive system. Some sign systems might be naturally more familiar to human cognition and more easily processed, while others might be less familiar and more difficult. The present chapter tries to provide an overview of the history of the sign systems used in multimedia. Given the limited space and the complexity of the topic, it goes without saying that, despite a considerable amount of empirical evidence, some parts of the following are necessarily "informed speculation" (but nevertheless plausible).

2.1 Gestures

Contrary to other species, our closest relatives in the animal world, chimpanzees, show considerable flexibility in their usage of signs. They do not only produce signs intentionally and interpret signs received from others; they also manage to intentionally delude each other, which implies that, beyond their knowledge about their environment, they have knowledge about what others know or do not know.

Besides using facial expressions, chimpanzees' prevalent way of communication is the use of gestures.[1] They use intentional gestures, usually with an imperative or directive intention, such as touching another individual's back (in order to get carried), presenting their own back (in order to get grooming), lifting their arm or clapping hands (to start playing), or begging with a hand gesture (to get something). Many of these gestures are learned and modified in a flexible way. If an addressee's attention is not directed toward the individual who wants to communicate, sending a message has no effect. Thus, the sender of a message has to catch the addressee's attention before he or she makes an intentional gesture. Such attention catchers involve, for example, hitting the ground, throwing an object, or slightly pushing someone.

---

[1] Tomasello (2008).

Human Gestures: Humans express their emotional states also using facial expressions and can "read" each other's faces. They also use gestures to threaten or invite others or to request certain activities from others. Human gestures can be directive (imperative) or declarative. While imperative gestures request certain activities from others, declarative gestures help to deliver information about something. A special kind of gesture is pointing, which can serve directive and declarative purposes.[2]

Pointing is an attention-directing device. It builds on the natural human tendency to follow the direction in which others are pointing or looking. Pointing gestures help to locate a relevant object (the target) in the perceivable environment[3] by specifying a straight line in space from the pointing origin to the target, provided that the addressee can see the gesture. Thus, pointing helps to synchronize the perception and consciousness of communication partners. Pointing is naturally done with a stretched forefinger, directing the attention of the addressee to a specific location. It is a communication gesture used only by humans: Other primates do not point.[4]

If the objects, events, activities, or processes that an individual wants to inform about are remote in space or time, which makes it impossible to point at them, or if there is no common language available, the informant can use iconic gestures. (We still do this nowadays in other countries if we do not command the local language and our addressee is not able or willing to speak another language.) For example, an object can be represented by a gesture showing the outlines of the object. Similarly, an activity can be referred to by using an abbreviated typical movement. Such iconic gestures implicitly invite the addressee to activate appropriate concepts and to create a corresponding scenario in his or her mind based on shared world knowledge.[5] In this way, an informant can influence the consciousness of a recipient and create a shared awareness of a remote scenario. Although it is not oral language, such communication qualifies as "talk," because it is a coordinated activity of cognitive exchange based on a common ground.

Gestures are relatively weak tools for communication compared to human language. However, it seems that language originated from the archaic gesture-based communication system. Following Michael Tomasello,[6] we can assume that our human ancestors started with gestures which were subsequently accompanied by sound patterns supplementing the message.

---

[2] Kita (2003).
[3] Bühler (1934) called this space of the environment the *Zeigfeld* ("pointing space").
[4] Povinelli et al. (2003).   [5] Kamermans et al. (2019).   [6] Tomasello (2008).

As messages became more and more elaborated, sound patterns became correspondingly more complex, leading to an integrated system of gestures and speech.[7] Eventually, the language part of the system replaced the original gesture system to a large extent. However, it never lost the connection totally, as demonstrated by people's spontaneous gestures while speaking.

Semantic Categories: We know that primates have cognitive concepts at their command.[8] Chimpanzees, for example, can choose the right tool among various artificial tools (which they have never seen before) in order to open a door. At least, some of them can. They can focus exactly on one crucial feature of the tool which qualifies the tool for a specific purpose.[9] For example, they can identify objects which could serve as screwdrivers. Thus, they demonstrate a command of the concept of a screwdriver, although they do not have a name for it. With this backdrop, it might not be too speculative to assume that our human ancestors also had concepts at their command.[10]

What kind of concepts? Step by step, they might have invented and used concepts about all kind of things relevant for their life: food, water, shelter, tools, dangers, territories, and the like. They might also have ordered things into categories which best grasped the natural discontinuities of their perceived world because this provides a maximum of orientation with relatively little cognitive effort, as described by Eleanor Rosch and her collaborators.[11]

There might have been concepts of objects (e.g., tools, prey, etc.), events (e.g., fights), activities (e.g., hunting, eating, fighting), or environmental processes (e.g., raining, flooding). Due to the importance of specific object attributes (e.g., "big" or "small," "dangerous," etc.) and of spatial and temporal relations between objects and events (e.g., "above," "beneath," "before," "later," etc.), there might also have been corresponding cognitive concepts. To communicate about relevant issues related to such concepts, our still speechless ancestors needed corresponding gestures. We can therefore assume that there were (probably iconic) gestures for objects and events, gestures for activities, and gestures for attributes and relations.[12]

Syntax: When these gestures had to be displayed in a specific order to fulfill a communication task, there might have even been preliminary forms of syntax in gesture communication. Syntactic rules are important, for example, not just to communicate who was involved in an event, but

[7] Bull (1990).   [8] Carey (2009); Murai et al. (2005).
[9] Savage-Rumbaugh and Lewin (1994); Visalberghi et al. (1995).
[10] See Dahl and Adachi (2013).   [11] Rosch and Lloyd (1978).   [12] Deuchar (1990).

also to specify who did what to whom. Gestures might have been gradually complemented and enhanced by sound patterns, which eventually attained the status of words, which could be combined into sentences. It should, therefore, be no surprise that oral language exhibits the same universals as gesture communication regarding the categorization of signs. In both cases, there is a need for signs of objects, events, activities, attributes, and relations. These sign categories seem to be universals insofar as they reflect general characteristics of human information processing based on common principles of conceptualizing the world. Accordingly, they are candidates for syntactic universals which apply both to ancient gesture communication and verbal communication.

The concept of linguistic universals is at the core of Noam Chomsky's universal grammar.[13] Chomsky assumes that all languages in the world – present, former, and future ones – follow one and the same universal rule system. This grammar claims to describe all existing languages as well as possible languages that do not exist yet but could exist in the future. Chomsky's universal grammar is disputed, as the specifics of the about 6,000 languages in the world required him to make the grammar more and more complex. In the present context, however, it is sufficient to state that Chomsky's universal grammar distinguishes between four kinds of constituents within sentences, which apply to all languages and which can be easily associated with the sign categories within gesture communication mentioned in the previous paragraph: nouns (for objects and events), verbs (for activities), adjectives (for attributes), and prepositions (for relations). The corresponding words can be elaborated to form phrases (e.g., noun phrases, verb phrases). Besides the declarative signs, there are also imperative signs and pointing signs (namely deictic expressions such as "I," "you," "here," etc.). It does not matter at this point whether these universals originate from an innate grammar or simply from universal cognitive constraints of human information processing. The important issue is that the basic constituents of today's languages (and probably all languages) can be hypothetically traced back to ancient forms of gesture communication which served as instruments for our ancestors' survival.

2.2 Oral Language

Multimedia messages can include the use of oral language, which is, after mimics and gestures, the oldest human sign system. How old is human

---

[13] Chomsky (2007).

oral language? Is there a chance of coming up with an approximate answer? Oral language seems to be a biologically anchored feature of the human species. There is no human society without an oral language. Except for heavily handicapped individuals, every human individual has the ability to learn any language spontaneously during the phase of primary language acquisition. A baby of parents from Mongolia or from sub-Saharan Africa could grow up anywhere in the world and easily learn – depending on his or her linguistic environment – Swahili, Bask, Xhosa, Chinese, or English. The child would learn the language easily without special training, "grow" into the linguistic community just by participating and speak the language as well as the other members. Contrary to humans, who easily learn to speak their primary language spontaneously and fluently, chimpanzees and gorillas are unable to produce varied speech sounds due to their different voice tract. However, they can master a non-vocal sign language such as ASL (American Sign Language), but only at the linguistic level of a 2-year-old child, even after many years of intensive training.[14] So, the use of oral language is restricted to the human species, which suggests that a biological basis should be assumed for this general feature. Humans are indeed pre-adapted to the use of any human language.[15] This refers not only to their ability to learn, but also to their genetically determined biological equipment.[16] There are somatic, perceptual, and neurological pre-adaptations.

Somatic Pre-adaptation: As a somatic pre-adaptation, the human larynx descends during the first year of postnatal development. The descent of the larynx (the human voice box) increases the pharyngeal cavity, which in turn broadens the range of possible vowel sounds. Thus, the descent enlarges the repertoire of vocal signs for oral communication. Unfortunately, this also has an important disadvantage: The trachea (windpipe) and esophagus (gullet) are no longer well separated, which can lead to the danger of choking or even suffocating over food. For this reason, humans need a well-functioning swallowing reflex. Thus, the swallowing reflex is a necessary byproduct of the development of human language. The descent of the larynx does not occur in the development of chimpanzees, our genetically closest relatives.

Perceptual Pre-adaptation: As a perceptual pre-adaptation, humans have an innate mechanism for the recognition of phonemes – the sound units used to distinguish one word from another in a particular language. Peter Eimas[17] demonstrated that babies at the age of two to four months

---

[14] Gardner and Gardner (1975); Gardner et al. (1989).   [15] Pinker (1994).   [16] Carroll (2008).
[17] Eimas et al. (1971).

are able to recognize differences between phoneme categories, not only within the particular language they are surrounded by (usually their parents' language) but also between phonemes from other languages they have never heard – both inside and outside of their mother's womb. Obviously, the classification of heard speech sounds into phoneme categories is biologically pre-determined, at least to some extent. Children are prepared from birth to distinguish between all phonemes from all languages. This ability is then further specified by learning. Depending on the particular primary language the child learns, only a subset of the possible phonemes is used. The child is trained to distinguish between these phonemes, whereas other phoneme distinctions are lost.[18]

Neurological Pre-adaptation: Neurological pre-adaption to language can be indirectly inferred from children growing up in an environment with a poorly structured language. Colonialism frequently required people from different language backgrounds such as Chinese, Portuguese, English, or Hawaiian to communicate for business. Such a mix resulted in a so-called pidgin language, characterized by a highly simplified grammar and limited vocabulary. When children grow up in such an impoverished linguistic environment, they spontaneously make language more regular, creating grammatical rules that did not exist before.[19] In this way, they generate a new language, a so-called creole language. The creation of a creole language can be considered as a process of linguistic self-organization. The new language is based on rules to the same extent as any other language and has the same capabilities to make fine-grained analytical distinctions. Apart from pidgin (which is a passing phenomenon and does not really count as a language), there are no primitive languages. All known languages – including creole languages – have complex syntactic structures and allow fine-grained differentiations. The vocabulary of a language is generally determined by the practical and cognitive requirements of everyday life. Some communities might admittedly live in less complex environments which require fewer semantic distinctions than others. A lower complexity of human life might be mirrored in a narrower vocabulary. However, this refers only to the lexicon, not the syntactic complexity of a language. When a creole language is created spontaneously, its syntactic rules are not imposed from the outside by linguistic models, because there are no such models. They originate from "inside" of the individuals participating in communications. The individuals seem to possess innate knowledge about general structural features of languages, which, according to Noam Chomsky, is stored in a hypothetical

[18] Carroll (2008).   [19] Pinker (1994).

Language Acquisition Device (LAD). It does not matter whether the innate biological ability of humans to acquire and develop languages is adequately described by Chomsky's LAD and his universal grammar or whether there are only general cognitive constraints which have been gradually implemented into our nervous system. In any case, the data suggest that humans are neuronally "hard-wired" to generate and apply well-structured linguistic expressions, following certain syntactic and morphologic rules.

Genetic Heritage: Genetic comparisons suggest that humans and chimpanzees separated from a common ancestor about six million years ago. Because it is very unlikely that the common ancestor already had a language, which was subsequently "forgotten" by the chimps, human oral language must have developed during the last six million years. If language is a biologically anchored feature of the human species, because its members are genetically pre-adapted to the use of language, this pre-adaptation must have been part of the human biological evolution. This implies that genetic variation and selection gradually led to better adaptation to the requirements of communication. In this process, individuals with a higher degree of pre-adaptation might have enjoyed higher reproduction rates, thus disseminating their DNA in the gene pool of homo sapiens more successfully than others.[20] It is self-evident that our ancestors did not start talking only after this pre-adaptation was accomplished. Instead, the adaptation took place in close interaction with the practice of communication at the possible level of the time. Given the complexity of this pre-adaptation, it goes without saying that this part of biological evolution might have required a considerable amount of time.

In and Out of Africa: Paleontological and genetic data suggest that our human ancestors left Africa between 70,000 and 100,000 years ago and dispersed gradually to Asia and Oceania, Europe, and eventually to the Americas.[21] On their different trails, they inevitably lost contact with each other. In this way, the overall human gene pool was split up. This allowed minor physical adaptations to different climates and local life conditions, leading to different races. These minor modifications did not (and still do not) impair intra-human fertility. Thus, they did not affect the identity of Homo sapiens as a biological species in any way. They also did not affect the universal ability to spontaneously learn any language during primary language acquisition described at the beginning of this section. As it is very unlikely that the same pre-adaptation to language use evolved independently (in parallel) in the peoples following different tracks across the

[20] Dawkins (1976); Mayr (1976).   [21] Cavalli-Sforza (1996).

world, we have to conclude that this pre-adaptation had already taken place before our ancestors left their African home continent. The adaptation must have already been encoded in the gene pool carried along on the different human tracks.[22]

Does this mean that oral language is at least between 70,000 and 100,000 years old? Of course not. Before leaving Africa, our human ancestors had already undergone a lengthy development. Due to the huge size of the continent, the gene pool might have been split up into different groups much earlier before leaving Africa. The dispersion of humans within Africa allowed adaptation to different environmental conditions. Comparative studies have revealed that the genetic differences between native sub-Saharan Africans are considerably bigger than the genetic differences between Europeans and Chinese or Japanese.[23] Estimations based on genetic data suggest that the development of these intra-African differences required at least about 250,000 years.[24] However, despite their physical differences, these groups do not differ regarding their pre-adaptation to the learning and usage of any language. Once again, because it is very unlikely that the same pre-adaptations took place independently across the different human tracks, we have to conclude that pre-adaptation had already been completed before dispersion. Accordingly, we can infer that humans used oral language already about 250,000 years ago or even earlier. We can, therefore, assume that our human ancestors, when they spread out across the world, already had fully developed languages at their disposal, which they could use to communicate about anything in a differentiated way based on conceptual systems referring to objects, events, activities, processes, attributes, and relations. Thus, natural oral language (whichever it may be) can be considered the most natural, reliable, and powerful tool for communication.[25] Accordingly, natural oral language is especially privileged as a communication tool in multimedia environments.

2.3 Conceptual Writing

About 8,000 years ago, advantageous conditions in some areas enabled high-density settlements of humans such as, for example, in ancient Egypt and in the emerging city-states of Mesopotamia. This required an increasingly complex organization of the economy. For example, delivery of merchandise had to be documented, and receipt of goods had to be

---

[22] Mayr (1976).   [23] Cavalli-Sforza (1996); Cavalli-Sforza et al. (1988).   [24] Stringer (1992).
[25] Clark (1996).

acknowledged. Property, dues, orders, agreements, and specific obligations had to be recorded. Laws and general rules had to be made available across time for all members of society. Messages had to be conveyed across large distances without sending an emissary, and so forth. This demanded tools for documentation and communication and the use of signs on durable sign carriers, contrary to the fleeting sounds of oral language. The problem was solved through the invention of writing systems and durable sign carriers such as wax, clay, wood, or stone.

Ideograms: Although humans had a highly differentiated oral language at their command, the first writing systems were unrelated to oral language. Instead, they used signs of the corresponding concepts from their world knowledge. At the beginning of this development, the signs were of an iconic nature. The hieroglyphs used by the ancient Egyptians, for example, were icons representing concepts, therefore serving as ideograms. Signs were related to their concepts through their similarity to a typical member of the corresponding category.

For instance, a picture of a bird represented the concept "bird," a picture of a fish represented the concept "fish," a picture of a jar the concept "jar," and so forth. Additional determiners were used to specify superordinate categories in order to constrain the meaning of ambiguous hieroglyphs. There were determiners for males and females, mammals, plants, rivers, abstract concepts, gods, and so forth. There were hieroglyphs designating concepts of objects, which corresponded to nouns in the spoken language and could therefore be considered as noun-equivalents. There were also hieroglyphs designating concepts of activity, which could be considered as verb-equivalents. For example, the picture of a kneeling man raising his hand to his mouth could represent the concept "eat," "drink," "speak," "give advice," or "stay silent" – all related to the mouth. The picture of a pair of legs represented the concept "walk," the picture of an ear represented the concept "hear," and the picture of a stretched arm with a hand holding an object represented the concept "offer." Finally, there were hieroglyphs for attributes serving as adjective-equivalents, such as the picture of a bowed man signifying the concept "old" or the picture of a little bird signifying the concepts "small" or "weak." Examples of hieroglyphic writings are shown in Figure 2.1.

Hieroglyphs were primarily used in monumental buildings or temples and retained their pictorial character in this context. For everyday usage, however, the ancient Egyptians used a cursive writing system derived from hieroglyphs, the so-called hieratic writing system, which was then further simplified and standardized, leading to the demotic writing system. As the

Figure 2.1   Examples of hieroglyphic writings

signs had to be written quickly again and again, they became more and more abstract and schematized.

Gradually, they lost their similarity with the typical category member. In other words, they lost their iconic character and became symbols. Figure 2.2 shows a comparison between a set of hieroglyphs and the corresponding hieratic signs.

Trade-offs: The gradual change of signs just mentioned took place under multiple constraints. Ferdinand De Saussure[26] pointed out that a sign is defined by the characteristics that make it different from other signs. This leads to a first constraint: Signs should be easily distinguishable. A second constraint follows from the writer's perspective: Signs should have a simple structure which allows them to be produced quickly and easily. A third constraint refers to the process of reading: Signs should be easily perceived and understood with no or little prior learning. Of course, these constraints operate in opposite directions. Icons are easy to learn due to their similarity with the objects of the reference category. However, they usually do not have a simple structure, are not easy to discriminate, and are more difficult to produce. Symbols, on the contrary, have no similarity with the objects they refer to. Their meaning is based on a convention. Symbols, therefore, require higher learning efforts in order to master them. When the system has been learned, however, discrimination and production of signs is generally easier.

The trade-off between these constraints is illustrated by the example shown in Figure 2.3. The sign on the far left was found on a clay tablet from Uruk, a Sumerian city-state in Mesopotamia. It originates from 3100 years

[26] De Saussure (1922).

Figure 2.2   Hieroglyphs and corresponding hieratic signs

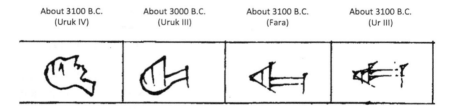

Figure 2.3   Example of the development of an iconic sign into an abstract cuneiform sign
(from Damerow et al., 1994)

BC, shows a human head (originally drawn upright), and also meant "head." Because of a change in the writing direction for technical reasons, the signs were turned by 90° to the left. Due to their frequent use and production, the signs became more and more schematized, as can be seen from the later variants shown in the figure, until the sign was transformed into a highly schematized cuneiform sign in about 2100 BC.

Similar developments can be found for the Chinese writing system, which was slightly modified by the Japanese, leading to their Kanji system. At the beginning, iconic signs were used to represent specific concepts.

Figure 2.4   Development of the Chinese sign for "elephant" (象)

Then, these signs were gradually transformed into more and more abstract symbols until their pictorial character had largely disappeared. Figure 2.4 illustrates this with the Chinese sign for "elephant."

For all of these different examples, a historical process of abstraction removed more and more of the pictorial details from the original sign. This process of abstraction and schematization decreased the similarity between the pictorial sign and the designated object. Simultaneously, discrimination between different signs became easier due to progressive schematization. Due to the increasing abstraction and simplicity of signs, writing also became easier. But because signs had lost most of their similarity with the typical referent of their category and the process of schematization was associated with standardization, the corresponding conventions had now to be learned by the users of the system. As a result, the effort required to master the sign system had increased. It goes without saying that humans were not biologically pre-adapted to use writing systems because the time period of 8,000 years was much too short. Furthermore, only a few individuals knew how to read and write. Therefore, while every human individual learns a language spontaneously and largely effortlessly, learning to use a writing system is hard work and requires extensive, time-consuming training.

It should be emphasized that the hieroglyph writings and the hieratic or demotic writings derived from them as well as the Chinese writings were not written languages. They were ideograms: written sequences of concepts. Although the original hieroglyphs and the Chinese graphic signs had an iconic character, messages written with these sign systems were far from being pictures of the communicated content. The icons served only as signs for activating specific concepts. Thus, written messages consisted of sequences of icons, resulting in sequential activation of the corresponding concepts. The messages were conveyed through ideograms representing specific concepts rather than through pictures of the communicated content. The stepwise transformation of icons into symbols by abstraction, schematization, and simplification did not affect their nature as ideograms.

Ideogram writing seems to be cumbersome, but it has an important advantage. As soon as one knows the relevant concepts and how these concepts are graphically encoded, it is possible to convey messages to other individuals without speaking their language. The Chinese and Japanese, for example, use fundamentally different languages and are usually unable to understand each other with oral communication. Nevertheless, the Japanese can read a limited amount of Chinese writings, and vice versa. The Chinese and Japanese also use their sign systems in modern multimedia environments and have found a way to handle them with digital devices.

However, other nations followed another route. As more and more concepts had to be communicated, more and more signs had to be introduced. This increased the required effort for learning signs and made it more difficult to discriminate between signs. To address these problems, other writing systems were created based on the establishment of connections to the well-functioning oral language.

2.4   Written Language

The ancient Egyptians gradually started using hieroglyphs to represent sounds (consonants) of the existing oral language. In other words, besides their function as ideograms, hieroglyphs were also used as phonograms. A similar development took place in Asia, where the Japanese simplified some of their kanji (which they had borrowed from the Chinese) and created signs for syllables (consonant–vowel combinations) of Japanese words, the so-called hiragana, and signs for syllables of foreign words, the katakana. In this way, they added phonograms to their ideogram writing system. However, the hiragana did not replace the kanji. Educated Japanese still use mainly kanji in their written correspondence, while the hiragana serve only an auxiliary function.

In the Middle East and in Europe, in about 1300 BC, the Phoenicians invented an alphabet with only 22 signs for consonants, and the Greeks added another 5 signs for vowels. In this way, they created a phonogram writing system which is now about 3,000 years old and still used in the writing systems of modern Western cultures with only minor modifications due to the specifics of single languages. In this system, the written signs no longer represent ideas, but are associated with the auditory representation of these ideas in spoken language.

At first appearance, phonogram writing systems seem to tremendously reduce learning requirements for mastering the system because learners generally have a very good command of their native oral language. Pre-school children who have just learned the alphabet usually practice pure phonogram writing for their first letters. However, in addition to writing phonetically understandable messages, they are later expected to follow orthographic rules and to know how words are spelled correctly.

A closer look reveals that the writing systems used today in the Western cultures are not pure phonogram systems, but a mixture of phonograms and hidden ideogram elements. In oral language, homophones (words with the same pronunciation, but different meanings) can usually easily be disambiguated due to the context. In written language, however, homonyms are often written differently, and the different graphemic patterns enable distinction between the meanings of "cell" and "sell," "dear" and "deer," "peace" and "piece," and so forth. Thus, beyond the phonogram function of letters, the specific orthography of words provides additional graphical hints on the meaning of words. Frequently, orthography also provides hints on the ancestry of words such as, for example, the French and Latin origin of "queue," "fragile," and "ratio." All in all, today's widespread writing systems combine phonogram writing with ideogram elements in terms of orthography. Achieving full command of these combined writing systems with correct orthography and a broad vocabulary still requires a considerable amount of learning. Nowadays, this sign system of written language is primarily used for written text, including of course multimedia messages.

2.5 Realistic Pictures

Long before humans invented writing systems, they already created other kinds of enduring visual signs: Pictures, which can be either drawn, painted, engraved, or carved. The oldest known rock paintings, estimated to be about 44,000 years old, were recently detected in Borneo (Indonesia). Other rock paintings have been found in the caves of Altamira, Pasiega, and Nerja in Spain. Figure 2.5 shows a picture of a buffalo from the cave of Altamira. These paintings are estimated to be between 15,000 and 40,000 years old.[27] Most of them show hunting scenarios and might have played a role in hunting magic. The paintings demonstrate not only extensive manual skills, but also an excellent memory for shapes and visual details, because they were painted in dark caves.

Later, pictorial skills were also used to glamorize emperors and other potentates by painting glorifying pictures. These pictures usually showed the heroics of the ruler, his victories, his conquest of other peoples, and

---

[27] Cave paintings older than 64,000 years were recently found in different sites in Spain. The paintings are from Neandertal origin, because modern humans arrived in Europe only 20,000 years later (Hoffmann et al., 2018).

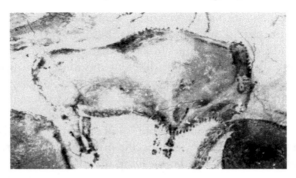

Figure 2.5   Picture of a buffalo from the cave of Altamira

Figure 2.6   Relief image of Emperor Constantine's victory in the Battle of the Milvian
Bridge

so forth. The ruler and the peoples conquered by him were made identifiable with the help of their heraldic symbols. So, the pictures did not
display snapshots over the course of time but showed a condensed allegoric
representation of complex social relationships. Accordingly, to understand
these pictures, it did not suffice to recognize the drawn objects and the
depicted spatial scenario. It also required knowledge about the sociopolit-
ical background (which is nowadays usually presented by a museum
guide). Figure 2.6 shows an example of such a glorifying pictorial display
from the Arch of Constantine in Rome built around 315 AD. It represents
the emperor's victory in the Battle of the Milvian Bridge with a relief

Figure 2.7   Jacques Louis David's painting of Napoleon Bonaparte on the
Great St. Bernhard Pass (from Wikimedia Foundation)

image, which can be considered a $2^{1/2}$-dimensional picture.[28] A later
example is the famous carpet of Bayeux in France, made in 1080, which
has a length of 68 meters showing scenes from the conquest of England by
William the Conqueror. The picture in Figure 2.7 shows Napoleon
Bonaparte riding his horse on the Great St. Bernhard Pass. It was painted
in 1800 by Jacques Louis David and was meant to depict Napoleon's claim
that, by occupying Italy, he became the successor of Charles the Great.

During the Age of Enlightenment, pictures were also used to inform
about the visual appearance of unknown animals or hidden objects, such as
the human organs. A famous example is Albrecht Dürer's (1471–1528)
woodcut of a rhinoceros from 1515, shown in Figure 2.8. Dürer had never
seen the animal, but created the picture based on a friend's description.
Other examples originate from Leonardo da Vinci (1452–1519), who
dissected corpses (secretly, ignoring the church's prohibitive rules) and
produced detailed drawings of the inside of a human body. A few decades
later, Flemish anatomist Andreas Vesalius (1514–564) dissected corpses
publicly and created illustrations of human organs which he published in
his textbook of anatomy. Figure 2.9 shows an illustration of the muscular
system of an adult male from this textbook.

---

[28] The "1/2" indicates that the relief's depth dimension was shortened.

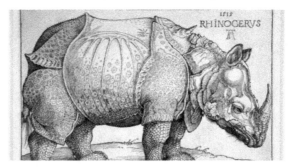

Figure 2.8   Albrecht Dürer's woodcut of a rhinoceros
(from Robin, 1992)

Figure 2.9   Illustration of an adult male's muscular system by Andreas Vesalius
(from Robin, 1992)

We will call these kinds of pictures "realistic pictures." The term "realistic" does not mean that these pictures cover each and every detail of an object in a manner that is as lifelike as possible. It simply means that these pictures represent the depicted object based on visual similarity. Similarity between a picture and the represented object implies that the representing and the represented attributes are the same: length is represented by length; height is represented by height; depth is represented by depth. In this way, the relations within the picture correspond to the spatial relations within the object.[29] For example, if there is a 2:1 relation between the length and height of a depicted object, the relation between length and height should also be 2:1 in the picture, modified of course according to the requirements of the central perspective.

Correspondence between attributes can also include characteristics such as color, hue, brightness, and so forth. However, similarity is not all-or-nothing. Similarity can vary gradually, based on the number of corresponding relations and attributes, and one has to define which attributes and which relations are to be taken into account and which are not. Line drawings usually include only the outline of an object and ignore color altogether. Andy Warhol's portraits of Marilyn Monroe in different colors ignore this aspect altogether, with infinite variations, as Marilyn's face was never any of the colors in the portraits. Nevertheless, we can see similarity between her and the pictures. Political caricatures usually exaggerate specific spatial configurations within a portrayed face, but there is still enough correspondence to recognize who has been portrayed.

So, what visualizations – such as line drawings, relief images, naturalistic paintings, photographs, and caricatures – have in common is that they refer to their depicted objects with a sufficient degree of similarity. This is why we refer to them as "realistic pictures."[30] In order to recognize objects shown in a realistic picture, no special training is required. Even children who are deliberately kept away from all kinds of pictures during their first few years can easily and spontaneously identify familiar objects (such as a horse, a dog, a cat, etc.) when they see them drawn or painted in the first picture they see in their life. This applies not only to static pictures but also to animations visualizing changes in the appearance of and the relations between objects.

---

[29] Gentner (1983).

[30] Sometimes, these pictures are also referred to as "representational pictures." However, this seems to be less adequate because other kinds of pictures (such as graphs) also have a representational function.

2.6 Maps

Maps can be considered as realistic pictures of a geographic area because they are similar to what they represent. However, as they are associated with specific representational problems which do not occur with other realistic pictures, it seems justified to dedicate special consideration to them. While we can nowadays directly perceive similarities between a map and the depicted geographic area with the help of satellite pictures or aerial photographs, this was not possible in ancient times. Nevertheless, the accuracy of old maps (i.e., their degree of similarity with the geographic area) was often surprisingly high.

One of the first maps of the Earth (including Eurasia and Africa) was drawn in the third century BC by Greek scholar Eratosthenes, as shown in Figure 2.10. Although many distances are highly distorted, some topological relations are displayed correctly, revealing some rudimental similarity with the Earth. A much more sophisticated map was carved in 1137 AD in China, showing the tracks of Yü the Great, as displayed in Figure 2.11. The map used a grid system based on precise knowledge about longitudes and latitudes with a distance between the grid lines of 100 li (about 50 km). This resulted in remarkably accurate drawings of the river systems and the coastal line. It is a convincing example of how advanced Chinese

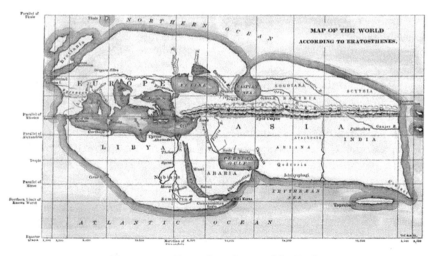

Figure 2.10   Eratosthenes' map of the Earth
(from North Wind Picture Archives, Alamy Stock Foto)

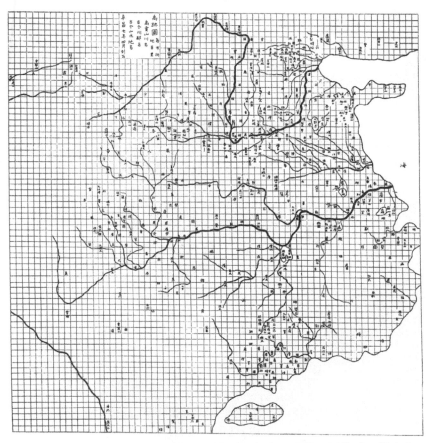

E. Chavannes, "Les Deux Plus Anciens
Spécimens de la Cartographie Chinoise,"
*Bulletin de l'École Française de l'Extrême
Orient*, 3 (1903), 1–35, Carte B.

Figure 2.11   Map of the tracks of Yü the Great
(from Tufte, 1983)

cartography was compared to European religious maps of cosmography of
the time. Due to its accuracy, the similarity of the map to the shape of the
country was close to perfect.

Creating maps of the Earth raises the problem of how to represent the
Earth's curved surface on a flat, two-dimensional plane. Cartographers have
developed projection techniques which transform each point on the curved
reference surface of the Earth into Cartesian coordinates representing

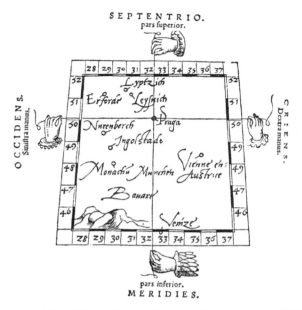

Figure 2.12 Map of Central Europe from the Cosmographica of Apianus
(from Tufte, 1983)

positions on the two-dimensional surface. For example, the Earth's surface projected onto a map wrapped around the globe as a cylinder produces a cylindrical map projection known as the Mercator projection. This technique, which was developed by Flemish geographer Gerardus Mercator in 1569, has become the standard projection for navigation, because any traveling course with a constant bearing is presented as a straight line. The Mercator preserves the shapes of small objects, but it inflates the size of big ones. Inflation is very small near the equator but increases with higher latitude and becomes infinite at the poles. Thus, landmasses close to the poles appear to be far larger than they really are compared to landmasses near the equator.

Figure 2.12 shows a map from the *Cosmographica of Apianus* (published in 1546), which presents a part of Central Europe.[31] The map is combined with two quantitative scales at the top and bottom and two quantitative scales on the left-hand and right-hand sides, from which the longitudes and latitudes of the depicted cities can be read. The map can be seen as a realistic

[31] From Tufte (1983).

picture, as the spatial relations between the dots on the map correspond to the spatial relations between the depicted cities as required by the principle of similarity. However, with only a few steps of abstraction, the map could also be considered a master copy for the creation of graphs for statistical data. If the longitude and latitude scales were replaced by any other quantitative scales at an interval level (e.g., family income per month and number of children) and if the depicted cities were replaced by other entities (e.g., families), the map would turn into a scatterplot. Historically, however, as we will see in Section 2.7, this step of abstraction needed two more centuries.

2.7 Graphs

It was only about 250 years ago that British economist William Playfair invented a new kind of picture, which allowed visualization of complex quantitative relationships. Omnipresent today, these pictures are usually called "graphs," "diagrams," or "logical pictures." Playfair's pioneer work revolutionized the display of statistical data. One of the many examples from his work is shown in Figure 2.13. The line graph shows the changes in the national debt of Britain from the revolution to the end of the war with America. Beyond revealing the different amounts of national debt, the graph clearly shows that national debt increased dramatically during the three wars in the time period covered by the graph, whereas it decreased during the periods of peace in between the wars.

Another example is shown in Figure 2.14. This line graph presents British exports and imports to and from Denmark and Norway from 1700 to 1780. Because the two lines enclose two areas representing different balances between the two countries, the line graph allows immediate perception and comparison of the balance against England and the balance in favor of England during different time periods.

The idea of visualizing qualitative and quantitative relations with the help of visuo-spatial displays has been further elaborated during the last two centuries, eventually leading to the use of conventionalized graph formats. These conventionalized formats include structure diagrams (e.g., for visualizing the structure of an organization), flow diagrams (for visualizing temporal sequences), pie charts (for visualizing the breakdown of a quantity into components), bar graphs (for visualizing the relations between qualitative and quantitative variables), line graphs (for visualizing determinist relations between quantitative variables), and scatter plots (for visualizing non-determinist, stochastic relations between quantitative variables). These graph formats have stood the test of time as they have proved

Figure 2.13   William Playfair's visualization of Britain's national debts from 1688 to 1784
during war and peace
(from Tufte, 1983)

to be most useful for quick and easy communication of qualitative and quantitative data. They can be considered as "ready-mades" for most kinds of data visualization task.

Thus, graphs are visuo-spatial objects that represent a subject matter based on an analogy that has inherent common structural properties. They have no similarity with what they represent. They usually visualize subject matter which is not perceivable such as national debt, export, and import. Whereas visuo-spatial attributes in realistic pictures are used to represent the same spatial attributes of a depicted object (e.g., height is represented by height), visuo-spatial attributes in graphs can be used to represent qualitatively totally different attributes of a subject matter such as debt, exports, or imports. In the line graphs shown in Figures 2.13 and 2.14, a specific spatial distance, namely the height of curves (i.e., their distance from the zero-line of the abscissa), at some point in time represents a specific

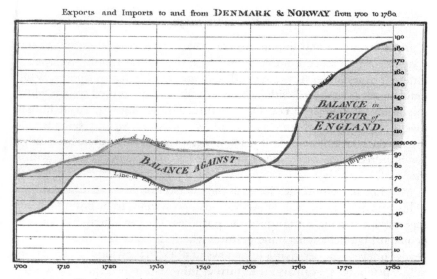

Figure 2.14　William Playfair's visualization of British exports and imports to and from
Denmark and Norway from 1700 to 1780
(from Tufte, 1983)

value of debts, exports, or imports at this specific time. By the same token, an increase or decrease in the height of the curves represents a real increase or decrease, and so forth. Accordingly, a graph is characterized by a specific set of inherent quantitative spatial relations, which are used to represent a corresponding set of quantitative relations within another domain. Thus, there is structural equivalence between the representing graph and the represented subject matter. Represented attributes and representing attributes can be different, while the quantitative spatial relationships within the graph and the quantitative relationships within the domain are the same.

The pictures mentioned – realistic ones, maps, and graphs – can be flexibly combined and complemented by verbal information – words, sentences, short text paragraphs. Such integrated visual representations of verbal and pictorial information are known as "infographics." They are frequently used to visually summarize information. As infographics are composed of multiple kinds of pictures and language, they are not a specific type of picture on their own but can be seen rather as a hybrid form of visual information display.

2.8   Takeaways

Human evolution and human history have created a large variety of sign systems for human communication. These sign systems were developed at different times under different conditions and for different purposes. While oral language combined with gestures is a biologically rooted system which might have existed since Year One, pictures and writing systems are human inventions. Some of them – such as realistic pictures, writing systems, and maps – date back thousands of years. Others – like graphs – date back only a few hundred years, while animations have become widely used only within the last few decades.

Multimedia communication is at the intersection of these different lines of historic development. It allows various sign systems to be bound flexibly together for specific communication purposes. We can watch and listen to people using oral language and gestures when they take the role of "talking heads" or eyewitnesses giving interviews or of experts giving a presentation. While listening, we can also read further information presented by written text or we can look at pictorial amendments in the form of realistic pictures, maps, or graphs in order to understand the conveyed messages.

The different sign systems are tools for creating multimedia messages which are to be understood by recipients. Appropriate use of sign systems requires differentiated knowledge about their strengths and weaknesses in order to tailor adequate combinations to the communication purposes at hand. The strengths and weaknesses of sign systems and their associated representations will be dealt with in Chapter 3.

Basic Forms of Representations

Abstract

Sign systems help to create descriptive and depictive representations. Descriptive representations operate on symbols. They are based on conceptual analyses identifying objects or events as well as attributes and interrelations. Attributes and relations are ascribed by predications to entities according to syntactic rules resulting in so-called propositions ("idea units"). These propositions can be integrated into coherent semantic networks. Propositional representations are considered as mental structures which can be externalized in the form of spoken or written texts. Despite their informational incompleteness, descriptions have high representational power. Depictive representations are based on inherent commonalities between a representing object and the represented subject matter. The inherent commonalities can be based on similarity or analogy. These representations are complete with regard to a certain class of information. Due to their completeness and consistency and because information can be read off directly, depictive representations have high computational efficiency.

Sign systems are used to create messages. These messages include representations of a subject matter to be conveyed by the producer of a sign to the recipient of a sign.[1] In view of the different sign systems described in chapter 2, the question arises as to how these systems and the messages created with them are interrelated. Are there "families" of sign systems whose members are more closely connected than they are to others? How many such families can be distinguished, and which system belongs to

---

[1] "Representation" means any object or event that stands for something else (Petersen, 1996). The concept can apply both to internal structures in the mind (mental representations) and to external structures used as signs (Markman, 1999).

which family? Such questions are relevant for semiotics and cognitive science, including psychology and even art.

External representations can be described in terms of various features, such as the sensory modality they address or their usage of symbols or icons. Although it is tempting to use such features to classify representations, such an approach ignores important distinctions. Gesture, written text, realistic pictures, maps, and graphs generally use the visual modality but not necessarily in all cases. Written text can also be written in braille, which addresses the haptic modality. Pictures can also present objects by engraving their outline, also requiring tactile perception.

Whether icons or symbols used within representations is not crucial for the categorization of sign systems. For example, inserting a symbol into a map in order to clarify what a specific graphical entity stands for does not change the representational principles used by the map. Whether the location of Paris in a map of France, for instance, is indicated by a pictogram (icon) of the Eiffel Tower (its most famous landmark) or by the word "Paris" does not make a difference for the map's representational principles. When rivers are drawn in blue color (although they are never blue in reality) and federal highways are drawn in yellow (although they are gray in reality), these visual attributes are conventional symbols. However, this does not affect a map's characteristics either.

Note that inserting the word "Paris" into a map is in no way a description of the city. It is just an act of naming, which allows mapping between a graphical entity and a geographic entity. Similarly, a thematic map showing the "blue states" and the "red states" in the United States uses a visual attribute (color) to specify political governance. However, the use of color to convey further information about entities does not turn a map into a description.

Conversely, written text can include schematized pictures (icons) which then also function as symbols. The upper panel of Figure 3.1 shows an example of an advertisement encouraging tourists to visit the city of Pisa in Italy, in which a picture of the leaning tower is both an icon and a symbol (the letter "I"). The lower panel shows the word "tunnel" with an inverse "U" visualizing the referent of the word. Once again, this does not change the character of the representation. By the same token, an ideogram text (produced by conceptual writing) can use icons and symbols, but this does not affect its character as an ideogram text, because the signs represent concepts anyway.

Texts and pictures have some features in common which make them appear similar, but these commonalities turn out to be unimportant for a

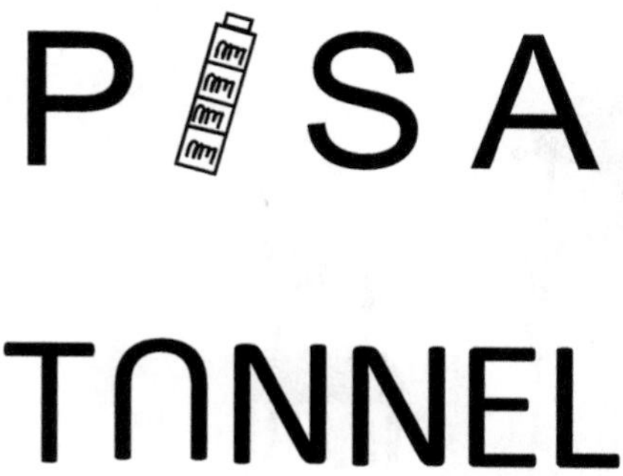

P S A

TNNNEL

Figure 3.1   Examples of icons serving simultaneously as symbols

theory of representation. For example, texts and pictures are generally well structured according to certain conventional rules. Unfortunately, this can stimulate the misleading claim that pictures, like texts, need to be well structured based on a specific pictorial syntax – an imaginary "syntax of pictures." The frequent talk about the "language of pictures" is another example of a misguiding view regarding equivalence between pictures and texts.[2]

Various sign systems and their corresponding representations have different features and differ fundamentally in how they represent content. In addition, there is no easy and straightforward answer to the question of how sign systems and their different kinds of representations are related to one another and how they can be best categorized from the view point of representation theory.[3] Answers can be expected from various disciplines such as philosophy, semiotics, and cognitive science. Stimulation for finding answers can also come from art, as can be seen in Section 3.1.

3.1   One and Three Chairs

In 1965, Joseph Kosuth (born 1945), a pioneer of conceptual art, created a piece of art that he entitled "One and Three Chairs." Conceptual art is promoted by an international group of artists who redefined the object of art. Accordingly, the ideas in a work of art should take precedence over

---

[2] Partial equivalence of texts and pictures is also assumed by the well-known proverb "A picture can be worth more than 10,000 words," which implicitly suggests that the two kinds of representation can replace each other (Larkin & Simon, 1987).

[3] Markman (1999).

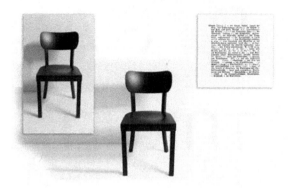

Figure 3.2   Joseph Kosuth: "One and Three Chairs" (version A)

technical and material concerns. In other words, the artist works with ideas and with meaning, rather than with objects such as the canvas that carries the painting, the figures painted on the canvas, the colors used in the painting, and so forth.

Kosuth's artwork is shown in Figure 3.2. Kosuth used common functional objects (such as a chair). He presented a full-scale photograph of an object to the left of the real object and a photostat (which is in itself a picture!) of the object's definition from a dictionary to the right of the real object. Accordingly, "One and three chairs" consisted of a physical chair standing in front of a wall, a photograph of the chair, and a text taken from a dictionary with a definition of the word "chair." Everything observers saw when looking at the object had to be the same as in the photograph. So, each time the work was presented with a new installation, a new photograph was needed. Figure 3.3 shows another example. As Kosuth explained, the artwork was basically the idea behind it, whereas the single realization and its formal components were less important.

In Kosuth's scenarios, a short definition of "chair" could be the following:

> "A chair is a raised surface used to sit on, commonly for use by one person. Chairs are most often supported by four legs and have a back."

A more elaborate definition would also be possible:

> "A chair is a raised surface used to sit on, commonly for use by one person. Chairs are most often supported by four legs and have a back. However, a chair can have three legs or a different shape. A chair's design considers its intended usage, ergonomics (how comfortable it is for the occupant) as well

Figure 3.3 Joseph Kosuth: "One and Three Chairs" (version B)

as non-ergonomic functional requirements such as size, stackability, fold-ability, weight, durability, stain resistance, and artistic design. Its intended usage determines the desired seating position."

It should be noticed that both descriptions are incomplete with regard to the real chair presented in the artwork. They focus on specific features and ignore others, which is not coincidental. Even the most elaborate description of a chair would still ignore some of the countless (albeit mostly irrelevant) features of a specific chair. The artwork shows that, because descriptions of natural objects are always inherently selective, they are informationally incomplete.[4] The incompleteness of the previous descriptions of a chair (even of the more elaborate one) allows the description to fit very different chairs, as the examples in Figure 3.4 demonstrate.

The artwork further demonstrates that a picture is always information-ally complete with regard to some class of information. One cannot draw a triangle without drawing a specific triangle, which then implicitly includes all the information characterizing that triangle: all side lengths, all angles, its area, and so forth. Similarly, the real chair used in Kosuth's work is necessarily a specific chair and its photograph necessarily includes all information about its physical shape, albeit from a specific perspective.

---

[4] Complete descriptions of objects are only possible for ideal objects such as in mathematics (e.g., triangles, squares, etc.).

Figure 3.4   Examples of different chairs

In this respect, the artwork suggests that, despite various similarities, texts and pictures are fundamentally different kinds of representations. In the following, we will argue that texts and pictures are just specific instances of two more basic forms of representations operating according to fundamentally different principles: descriptive and depictive representations.

3.2   Descriptive Representations

Oral language, conceptual writing, and written language are the most widely used tools to create descriptions (see Chapter 2). However, they are not the only ones. Special domains have developed their own language and notational systems to create descriptions. Mathematicians, for example, use expressions such as $V = s^3$ to describe the relation between a cube's size s and its volume V (whereby they call the term s^3 "s raised to the power of 3"). Physicists use the formula $F = m^* a$ to describe the relation between force, mass, and acceleration according to Newton's Second Law. All these are examples of descriptive representations.

3.2.1 Conceptual Analysis: Propositions

What does it mean to describe something? Descriptions result from an interaction between analysis and synthesis. Analysis means that the subject matter is cognitively segmented into its components based on conceptual knowledge and that attributes of entities and relations between entities are recognized. Synthesis means that entities, attributes, and relations are integrated into propositions which then serve as the building blocks of descriptions. Propositions can be further synthesized into a coherent semantic network serving as an overall description of the subject matter.

Depending on the individual's world knowledge and his or her goals, this analysis can be coarse- or fine-grained. Specialists such as sailors, pilots, mine workers, and other professional groups have incredibly rich conceptual knowledge about their domain and, accordingly, elaborate terminology in the respective domain. However, the principle of ana-lyzing things is not bound to a specific domain. It always follows a general procedure which involves distinguishing entities, attributes, and relations.

Entities: Segmentation leads to the identification of entities in space and in time. Segmentation in space leads to the identification of objects and segmentation in time leads to the identification of events. Identified entities are cognitively subsumed under corresponding concepts. For example, an object can be recognized and categorized as a bird, a mouse, or a lizard, and an event can be recognized and categorized as the catching of a prey.

Attributes: The identified entities can possess specific attributes. Describing a subject matter requires attributes to be ascribed to corre-sponding entities. For example, a bird (such as the marsh harrier) can have the attribute of being a bird of prey that feeds on small mammals (such as mice) and reptiles (such as lizards). The bird could also possess the attribute of being a migrant species, which means that it breeds in the middle and northern areas of Europe but winters further south in tropical marshes and swamps.

In order to ascribe attributes to entities, cognitive scientists have used formalisms borrowed from predicate logic. In these formalisms, the attribute (e.g., being a bird; being migrant) takes the role of a predicate of an expression, and the entity (e.g., the marsh harrier) takes the role of a so-called argument in this expression. The ascriptions of attributes to entities are also called predications.[5] For example, the following two predications

IS-A-BIRD (MARSH HARRIER)

IS-MIGRANT (MARSH HARRIER)[6]

specify that the marsh harrier is a migrant bird. Predicates used as attributes can represent states and their internal structure. Such so-called structure predicates apply when the entity's attributes remain relatively stable within a specific time frame of interest (such as "small," "tired," or "asleep"). Predicates used as attributes can also represent processes. They are referred to as "event predicates." Event predicates specify temporal and causal relations between different states, whereby the entities' attributes vary within the time frame of interest (such as "falls," "flows," or "grows").

Relations: Two or more entities can be connected by relations which create more complex conceptual structures. Such relations are expressed by predicates which take two or more arguments. Depending on the kind of relations, the connected entities can play different roles. A widely used category of relations expressed by multi-argument predicates is the concept of activity, which means a process initiated intentionally by some agent. The main semantic roles of entities within activities are the agent (i.e., the initiator of the activity), the patient (i.e., the entity affected by the activity), and the instrument (i.e., the entity used by the agent as a means to follow his or her intentions). For example, the predications

FEEDS ON (agent: MARSH HARRIER, patient: SMALL MAMMALS)

CATCHES (agent: MARSH HARRIER, instrument: TALONS)

express the fact that the marsh harrier (which is, as we know, a bird of prey) feeds on small mammals which it catches with its talons. Another widely used relation is the concept of causality, which can be applied also to processes not initiated by somebody's activity.[7] For example, the predications

CAUSALITY (cause: WINTER, effect: LOW TEMPERATURES)

CAUSALITY (cause: LOW TEMPERATURES, effect: BIRD MIGRATION)

---

[5] Engelkamp and Zimmer (1994).

[6] The use of upper-case letters indicates that reference is being made to the cognitive concepts, not the words of language.

[7] Note that archaic thinking has frequently associated causality with some mystical agent whose actions caused the effects in question.

express the fact that winter "causes" (in a broad sense) low temperatures which, in turn, results in bird migration. There are numerous other relationships between objects and events – including spatial, temporal, intentional, functional, and other relationships – which can connect entities to other entities.

Internal Descriptive Representations: The various predications result in internal (mental) structures composed of concepts. These conceptual structures, which can be more or less complex, are called "propositions" or "idea units."[8] In the previous examples of information about the marsh harrier, these idea units could represent the following facts:

- The marsh harrier is a bird of prey.
- The marsh harrier feeds on small mammals (such as mice).
- The marsh harrier feeds on small reptiles (such as lizards).
- The marsh harrier catches its prey with its talons.
- The marsh harrier is migrant.
- The marsh harrier breeds in middle and northern Europe.
- The marsh harrier winters in North Africa.

Propositions are complex conceptual structures which serve as the building blocks of descriptions. Based on a conceptual analysis, a subject matter can be described by synthesizing the corresponding propositions into a coherent whole, a so-called semantic network. The basic idea of coherence among propositions within a semantic network is visualized in Figure 3.5. It should be remembered at this point that a propositional semantic network is meant to be an internal mental structure which is different from its externalization by a graphical structure, as shown in Figure 3.5, or its externalization by a written text. Thus, the semantic network is a complex internal conceptual structure which consists of interconnected propositions, providing an internal overall description of a subject matter.

The analysis of subject matter by identifying conceptual structures, as portrayed above using examples of information about the marsh harrier, is of course a gross oversimplification. There are many more fine-grained conceptual distinctions that can be made and many more different semantic roles that can be differentiated into highly complex relationships. However, the basic principle remains the same: The subject matter is segmented into entities. These entities are identified by subsuming them under corresponding concepts which are part of prior knowledge.

---

[8] Chafe (1970).

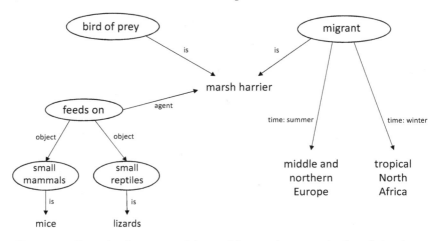

Figure 3.5   Example of a conceptual (semantic) network representing knowledge about the marsh harrier

The analysis proceeds by recognizing attributes of entities and by recognizing relations between the entities. Predications are made, ascribing specific attributes to entities and relations between entities. This results in propositions which serve as the building blocks of descriptions. The synthesis of the propositions into a coherent semantic network then serves as an internal overall description of the subject matter.

Hypothetical Mental Language: As demonstrated in the examples presented in Section 3.2.1, predicates of propositions usually require a specific number of arguments and specific kinds of argument for their various semantic roles. For example, a predicate signifying an activity requires concepts for the role of the agent, the object, and the instrument. Thus, propositions are composed of concepts according to specific syntactic rules. If concepts are considered as mental symbols, propositions can be seen as complex mental symbols – similar to the sentences of natural language. Accordingly, propositional representations can be considered as internal descriptions in a hypothetical mental language – a "language of the mind." This mental language is assumed to operate directly on concepts and seen as closely related to natural language.

External Descriptive Representations: In order to transmit messages that include descriptions of a subject matter, internal conceptual descriptions have to be externalized and made accessible to others. Natural human language (oral or written) is perfectly suited for this purpose, because it provides a toolbox for expressing predicates and arguments. The entities to be described (i.e., objects and events) by predications can be named by nouns. Nouns are frequently the names of categories under which the entity has been subsumed, but the name of an individual can also be a noun. The attributes to be ascribed to entities can be named by adjectives, providing further specification of objects or events. The relations between entities used for the predication of activities or processes can be named by verbs. Finally, spatial, temporal, and other relationships can be named by prepositions. In the example of the marsh harrier, the externalization could be a simple short text such as the following:

> "The marsh harrier is a bird of prey which feeds on small mammals such as mice or reptiles such as lizards. The bird is a migrant. It breeds in middle and northern Europe but winters in North Africa in order to avoid excessively low temperatures."

Given the central role of natural language for the externalization of conceptual descriptive structures, it seems that the universal categories proposed by Chomsky's universal grammar – noun phrases, verb phrases, preposition phrases, and adjective phrases – mirror universals of human cognition and, therefore, provide the necessary tools for externalizing conceptual structures and, thus, describing any kind of subject matter. The details of the proposed grammar do not matter at this moment. The point is that during human evolution the cognitive requirements of human life might have been relatively steady for a long time. Under these conditions, universals of human cognition might have become gradually "hard-wired" into our central nervous system, because some innate a priori knowledge corresponding to these requirements provided an evolutionary advantage. Similarly, a priori knowledge about the general structures of natural languages might have become "hard-wired" into our central nervous system during the process of evolution, because such innate a priori linguistic knowledge enhanced language learning and provided an evolutionary advantage. As a tool for communication, natural language is also an instrument for internalizing conceptual structures, namely when the listener or reader understands a spoken or written description and reconstructs the same conceptual structure in his or her mind.

3.2.2 Representational Power

Descriptions draw on concepts. Thus, individuals creating a description have a full range of concepts – from concrete to abstract – at their disposal. More importantly, these concepts include concepts of relations. At the level of conceptual analyses, which lead to internal (mental) structures in the form of

Figure 3.6   Depictive signs of "Smoking not allowed" and "No pets please"

propositions, the predicates of propositions with two or more arguments represent concepts of relations. At the level of externalized structures in the form of language, relational concepts manifest themselves in the use of verbs and prepositions, which serve as symbols for relations. In domains like mathematics or physics, signs such as "=" (is equal), ">" (is bigger than), "<" (is smaller than), "$\geq$" (is equal or bigger than), and so forth are used as relational symbols. The availability of specific signs that signal specific relations allows descriptions to be explicit about how specific entities are connected.

Relations can have pre-defined properties. For example, the relations "is-a," "is-in," and "bigger than" (">") are transitive. If a dog is a vertebrate and a vertebrate is an animal, then a dog is an animal. If Peter is in the room and the room is in the house, then Peter is in the house. If A > B and B > C are true, then A > C is also true. The transitivity of these relations is pre-defined. Because relations have pre-defined properties, the relational characteristics of descriptive representations can be regarded as being "built into" relational signs.[9]

As descriptions rely on concepts, they have higher representational power in terms of abstraction than depictions. For example, it is no problem to express general negatives in natural language such as

"Smoking not allowed"

or

"No pets please."

Communicating the same message using pictures causes considerable difficulties. Figure 3.6 shows an example (in the shades of grey). The left-hand picture shows a cigarette combined with a prohibitory sign. However, the message refers not only to smoking cigarettes, but to smoking in general, including cigars, cigarillos, pipes, and hookahs. Similarly, the right-hand picture shows a dog with the "no" symbol, but it does not only refer to dogs (or refers even less only to terriers), but to any other

---

[9] Palmer (1978) therefore called such representations "extrinsic."

animals as well. People usually do not misunderstand such signs, because they reinterpret them as indicating abstract concepts and representing correspondingly broader categories. In doing so, however, they treat the icons no longer as pictures, but as signs of more abstract concepts. In other words, they interpret the icons as ideograms.

Realistic pictures can represent categories only up to a certain abstraction level, but not beyond. In her pioneer work on categorization, Eleanor Rosch showed that in a hierarchy of increasingly abstract concepts, a medium level of abstraction allows the best discrimination of a category from its neighbor categories.[10] Rosch called concepts at this level "base concepts." For example, "chair" is a base concept, whereas "kitchen chair" and "furniture" are not. "Dog" is a base concept, whereas "terrier" and "carnivore" are not. The base concept level is the highest level in an abstraction hierarchy at which the superimposed pictures of an object's contour lines can still be recognized as a visualization of the concept. When the outline drawings of different chairs (from a canonical perspective) are laid on top of each other, the observer is still able to recognize an outline corresponding to the category "chair." However, if the outline drawings of a chair, a table, and a cupboard are laid on top of each other, the observer is unable to recognize the category "furniture." Thus, it is possible to draw a recognizable picture of an average chair or a picture of an average kitchen chair, but it is not possible to draw a recognizable picture of an average item of furniture. Similarly, it is possible to draw a recognizable picture of an average dog or a picture of an average terrier, but it is not possible to draw a recognizable picture of an average carnivore. The use of realistic depictions is restricted to entities up to the abstraction level of base concepts.

Figure 3.6 demonstrates further limitations of depictions, namely regarding the expression of negations. It is possible to destroy a picture, thus making it "non-existent," but it is not possible to negate the pictorial content of a picture. Negation requires special symbols which have a conventionalized meaning which needs to be learned. This is why prohibitory signs have to be combined with icons in Figure 3.6 in order to specify the meaning of the message.

Because descriptions can include relational concepts, they can also easily express logical disjunctions, usually signaled by the connective "or" in natural language. For example, it is no problem to say

"This seat is reserved for old or disabled persons or for parents with infants."

On the other hand, it is much more difficult to convey the same message pictorially. A picture of an old person and a disabled person and

---

[10] Rosch and Lloyd (1978).

Figure 3.7   Depictive signs of "This seat is reserved for old or disabled persons or for parents with infants"

a parent with an infant could be misunderstood as meaning that only a group of these people could occupy the seat. In the subway in Vienna (Austria), the problem is solved by a series of pictures, as shown in Figure 3.7. The series includes a picture of an old man, a picture of a disabled man, and a picture of a mother with a small child. To avoid gender discrimination, the same pictures featuring an old woman, a disabled woman, and a father with a small child are displayed, resulting in a total of six pictures.

Descriptions are usually selective because they emphasize specific entities (instead of others) and emphasize specific attributes and relations with the help of adjectives, verbs, and prepositions (while ignoring others).[11] For example, the description of a triangle including the length of two sides and the angle between the two sides determines the triangle perfectly well, but is nevertheless highly selective because it does not include the third side, the other angles, the area, and other features.

---

[11] Mathematics deals with ideal objects, such as straight lines, triangles, squares, etc. If these ideal objects are assumed to possess only a limited set of pre-defined features, a complete description of such an object seems to be possible. However, this is usually not the case with natural objects, as they possess a practically unlimited number of features.

Thus, the description determines the triangle completely, but is informationally incomplete because much information about the triangle is not explicitly stated.

Further information could be added to complement the description of the triangle. However, this might result in the overall information about the triangle becoming inconsistent. If, for example, the description includes the size of all the three angles and these angles do not add up to exactly 180°, the description has become inconsistent. This leads to another characteristic which makes descriptions different from depictions. As they are selective, descriptions are not only informationally incomplete, they can also be inconsistent, whereas depictions cannot.

3.3   Depictive Representations

While descriptive representations rely on concepts, depictive representations rely on objects. Photographs, paintings, and drawings, which we called "realistic pictures" in Chapter 2, are the most common depictive representations in everyday life. However, the category of depictive representations is considerable broader.

First, there is no reason to restrict the term to two-dimensional objects. Three-dimensional objects such as sculptures or $2^{1/2}$-dimensional objects such as reliefs, as shown in Figure 2.6, are also depictive representations. Likewise, a miniature model of a building or a wax statue in a Madame Tussauds museum are depictive representations. Second, depictive representations do not need to share similarities with what they represent. Some of them have no similarity with their referent at all. A line graph or the deflection of the pointer in a tachometer share no similarity with what they represent but are nevertheless depictive representations. This category includes even such strange things as so-called analog computers. Analog computing means that some physical system (e.g., electric circuitry or a hydraulic system) is used as a model for a totally different object of knowledge, because the functioning of the model can be described by exactly the same mathematical equations as the functioning of the knowledge object. Computation thus means manipulating the model, measuring the outcome, and transferring the result from the model to the object of knowledge.

Accordingly, the category of depictive representations includes not only realistic pictures such as photographs, paintings, and drawings, but also maps and graphs, either static or animated. As far as gestures include iconic elements, for example, gestures showing the shape of an object or imitating an activity, they can also be considered as depictive representations.

3.3.1   Structural Commonalities

What do depictive representations have in common? The answer is that they are all based on inherent structural commonalities between the representation and the represented referent. This is why Palmer[12] called them "intrinsic representations." Contrary to descriptive representations, which have "built-in" structural characteristics through relational signs (which makes them "extrinsic"), depictive representations have inherent structural properties which are used for representational purposes. There are two forms of structural commonality: similarity and analogy.

Similarity: Realistic pictures and maps have spatial structures which correspond to the spatial structures of the depicted content. That is, length (if considered) is represented by length, width (if considered) by width, height (if considered) by height, and so forth. In other words, represented attributes and representing attributes as well as the inherent spatial relationships within the representation and within the represented object are the same. Such correspondence between spatial structures constitutes similarity.

The correspondence between the attributes and spatial structures of a represented object and a realistic picture was described by Renaissance architect Leon Battista Alberti (1404–1472), who developed a theory that considered painting as an imitation of reality. A painting was seen as a surrogate for a real window, providing a view on an external reality (hence called "Alberti's window"). The painter has to select a particular viewpoint from which he or she looks at the scenario to be painted. With the help of a grid, every point within the scenario can thus be exactly projected onto one point of the image area. Thus, when one looks at the painting, one sees a three-dimensional world as if one were looking through a window. Painters such as Canaletto and Spitzweg were famous for their skills in capturing subject matter with such a level of accuracy and detail that it gave the observer an illusion of looking upon reality through a window. Albrecht Dürer visualized Alberti's theory in the picture shown in Figure 3.8. The picture includes an object to be painted (a lying woman), a painter, and the technique used to project points from the object to points in the picture. Alberti's idea of painting as an imitation of reality is also at the core of Gibson's definition of a picture:

> "A picture is a surface treated so that it yields light to a particular station point which could have come from a scene in the real world."[13]

---

[12] Palmer (1978).   [13] Gibson (1954).

Figure 3.8 Alberti's theory of pictures as a simulation of windows illustrated by Albrecht Dürer's "The Drawer of a Lying Woman" (from Robin, 1992)

Figure 3.9 Specific faces and general faces (from McCloud, 1993)

The definition is essentially saying that (realistic) pictures are objects that "simulate" depicted scenarios.

Because pictures essentially provide the same sensory input as direct perception, it is no surprise that recognition of what is presented in a realistic picture does not need to be learned. Even very young children who have never seen a picture before are immediately able to recognize well-known objects such as dogs, horses, cats, flowers, and so forth in a picture. As substitutes for reality, such pictures can also make a common ground available for communication partners who can refer to a picture instead of the real situation.

However, as mentioned in Chapter 2, similarity is not an all-or-nothing issue. The features that are incorporated in a similarity have to be specified, because not all features of reality are represented in a picture and not all features of a picture have a representational function. Thus, similarity can be higher or lower, depending on how many and which attributes and relations have been included in a representation. Figure 3.9 demonstrates this with a set of different drawings of a human face. The set ranges from a detailed photograph on the left-hand side and less detailed drawings in the middle through to the face of a stick man on the right-hand side. The detailed photograph on the left portrays a single specific individual. When more and more details of the face are left out through schematization, the picture becomes less and less specific. Accordingly, the number of people who appear to look similar to the picture increases more and more, and the similarity is lower and lower. The face of the stick man on the right-hand side is a picture of everyone, but its similarity to a real human face is minimal.

This reduced similarity which is common between pictures and reality is also an issue with maps. Whereas geographic maps are usually accurate in terms of distances between localities (except for large areas due to the Earth's curvature), road maps frequently preserve the distances between cities, but simplify ("idealize") the course of roads. Subway network maps often preserve neither the distances between stations nor the course of subway lines. Instead, they retain only information about connectedness among stations. Therefore, similarity needs to be specified in order to clarify which pictorial attributes can and cannot be interpreted.

Analogies: Contrary to realistic pictures, where the represented attributes and the attributes representing them are the same, other depictive representations do not require equivalence between represented and representing attributes. This is true, among others, for graphs such as bar graphs, line graphs, pie charts, or scatterplots. They share no similarity with what they represent, and they visualize states of affairs which are not even perceivable, such as the development of foreign trade, national debt, or pandemic infection rates. Graphs are objects with visuo-spatial attributes which are used to qualitatively represent totally different attributes of a subject matter. Nevertheless, graphs are depictive representations because they represent a subject matter based on inherent structural commonalities. Such structural commonalities are referred to as analogies.[14]

Analogies are based on a common description (usually specifying quantitative relations) which holds both for the represented object (the subject matter) and the representing object (in this case, the graph). An analogy holds as far as (and because!) this common description is true on both sides. Accordingly, a graph is an analog two-dimensional model which represents specific relations related to a subject matter by means of corresponding visuo-spatial relations. The line graphs drawn by William Playfair shown in Figures 2.13. and 2.14 are examples of analog visuo-spatial models. The

---

[14] Gentner (1983).

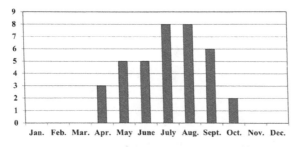

Figure 3.10   Bar graph of the marsh harrier's observation frequency in a Middle European habitat

same is true for bar graphs, as shown, for example, in Figure 3.10. The graph visualizes the marsh harrier's observation frequency in a Middle European habitat. The height of the bars corresponds to the number of marsh harriers observed in a habitat during the corresponding month, and the sequence of the bars corresponds to the sequence of months during the year. Like a similarity, an analogy has to be defined: Not all attributes of the displayed subject matter have to be represented, and not all attributes of the representing object need to have a representing function.

Analogy plays an important role in the interpretation of hybrid realistic pictures in which a spatial dimension represents time instead of space.[15] An example is given in Figure 3.11. The picture shows the life cycle of *Popillia Japonica Newman* (also called the "Japanese beetle") by representing time periods (months) through pictorial spatial slices.[16] Other examples can be found in the pioneer work of physiologist Étienne-Jules Marey on the chrono-photography of movement, who integrated overlapping pictures from different points in time – for example, of a bird's wings during flight – into a single pictorial display.

3.3.2   *Inferential Power*

Completeness: While descriptive representations are always selective, depictive representations are (as mentioned in Section 3.1) always informationally complete with regard to a certain class of information: If we draw a triangle, we necessarily draw a specific triangle. Note that the triangle is also necessarily a complete triangle: It entails the complete set of information about that triangle. With the help of appropriate

---

[15] Torralbo et al. (2006).   [16] From Tufte (1983).

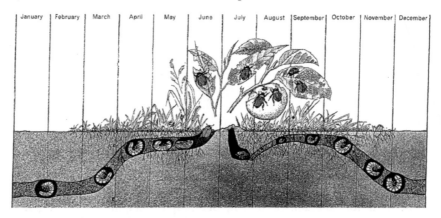

Figure 3.11   Example of a hybrid realistic picture in which a spatial axis was replaced by a time axis. The picture shows the lifecycle of *Popillia Japonica Newman* (the Japanese beetle) (from Tufte, 1983).

measurement procedures, information about these features can be directly read off from the figure. The complete set of information is initially only implicit. The measurement procedure (in this case, reading off from the figure) makes the information explicit.

Similarly, if we draw an object, we draw not only its shape, but necessarily also its size and orientation. A picture of a bird of prey eating a mouse includes not only information about the shape of the bird and the shape of the mouse, but necessarily also about their size, their orientation in space, about how the bird holds its prey, and so forth. In a description, on the contrary, one can specify the form of an object without mentioning its size or orientation. This is what Leibniz might have had in mind when he considered that a drawing was a useful "tool against the uncertainty of words." Admittedly, specific features can be included in a depictive representation or not (such as color or details producing a finer-grained resolution, as shown in Figure 3.9). This can broaden or narrow the available classes of information. However, there is always a certain class of information that is completely available. Thus, depictive representations have a high computational efficiency because the information that has to be inferred (i.e., "computed") can be directly read off from the representation.

This feature of depictive representations is also at the core of Philip Johnson-Laird's theory of thinking about the construction and manipulation of mental models.[17] According to this theory, so-called logical

---

[17] Johnson-Laird (1983).

Figure 3.12   Maurits C. Escher's picture of an "impossible" building, entitled "Concave and Convex".

inferences are not based on internal rules of logic. Instead, the individual is assumed to mentally construct an internal model of the state of affairs described in the premises and then to read off new information from this model. The mental model is a hypothetical analog representation of the subject matter and, thus, an internal depictive representation. According to the theory, the individual takes advantage of the direct accessibility of the required information. Errors occur mostly when the full range of possible mental models has not been taken into consideration.

Consistency: Depictive representations can be correct or incorrect. However, because an object cannot contradict itself, information read off correctly from a depictive representation is never incompatible. In other words, a depictive representation is necessarily consistent. Admittedly, some pictures seem to contradict this claim, pictures of so-called "impossible objects". These pictures indeed seem to be contradictory. An example created by mathematician and graphic artist Maurits C. Escher is shown in Figure 3.12. The left half of the picture seems to present a building from above and the right half seems to present it simultaneously from below, which is clearly contradictory. However, if we remind ourselves of Alberti's theory of pictures, which requires that a painter selects a particular viewpoint from which he or she looks at the scenario to be painted, we come to see that Escher's viewpoint violates the concept of a picture (which is of course a constituent of his art). The same follows for Gibson's definition of a picture mentioned in Section 3.3.1 which specifies that a picture yields light to a particular station point. Of course, an observer cannot be simultaneously above and below a displayed building. The seemingly contradictory picture is in fact an assembly of two pictures with a perfectly hidden interface.

No Signs of Relations: Within communication, depictive representations such as realistic pictures, maps, and graphs act as signs of what they represent. Such signs are naturally complex and can of course include other, embedded signs. These embedded signs can be icons (based on similarity) and symbols (based on convention). The use of symbols is very common in maps, where words such as the names of cities are used to designate specific elements, as representatives of the corresponding specific locations in reality. The same is common in graphs, where symbols are used to designate parts of the graphical structure, allowing them to be mapped onto specific entities or variables.

It should be emphasized that this kind of symbol use in depictive representations serves only to perform element-to-element mapping. The symbols help to identify the entities drawn in the map or in the graph, usually by naming them. However, depictive representations do *not* include *symbols for relations*. More specifically, there is no single, discrete element in a depictive representation that uniquely signifies a specific relationship. A picture can provide a large range of relational information (e.g., about different sizes or locations of objects in space), but does not include any distinct and unique sign, neither as symbol nor as icon, which would express by itself the fact that an entity is bigger than another entity or that the two are equal. Such relational signs can be found universally in natural language in the form of verbs and prepositions. They can also be found in the language of mathematics where relational signs such as ">," "=," or "<" are common in mathematical terms (i.e., descriptive statements). However, they cannot be found in depictive representations. If such expressions are written on a picture (which is very possible), then they are not a part of the picture, but descriptions occupying some space of the picture area. The fact that depictive representations do not include single, discrete elements that uniquely signify specific relationships implies that they do not describe their referent but rather display the referent based on inherent structural commonalities.

3.4   Takeaways

The specific mental representations created in multimedia communication with different sign systems can be classified into two basic categories: descriptions and depictions. The different mental representations are associated with different mental structures and different mental operations.

Descriptions require conceptual analysis. Conceptual analysis involves identifying entities and predications, which includes ascribing attributes to entities and connecting entities via relations. The analysis results usually in a coherent internal conceptual structure which consists of propositions (i.e., idea units). Propositions are composed of concepts according to specific syntactic rules and can be considered as "internal sentences" formulated in a hypothetical mental language, a "language of the mind." For communication, such internal conceptual structures must be externalized by speaking (as oral language) or by writing (either as conceptual writing or as written language).

Descriptions have high representational power because they have the full range of concepts at different levels of abstraction at their disposal and because they include signs indicating specific semantic relations such as negations, logical connectives, and others. Descriptive representations are selective and therefore usually incomplete. This allows them, on the one hand, to fit with many entities of a category (such as a large variety of chairs). On the other hand, they can be inconsistent when incompatible information is added to them.

Depictions represent a subject matter based on inherent structural commonalities between the representation and the subject matter, either in terms of similarity (same relations, same attributes) or in terms of analogy (same relations, different attributes). Depictive representations include realistic pictures (such as photographs, paintings, and drawings), sculptures, maps, and graphs. Realistic pictures are based on similarity, simulating the appearance of what they represent. Thus, recognition of what is presented in a realistic picture requires no learning, as demonstrated by very young children. Graphs are based on analogy.

Depictive representations are informationally complete with regard to a certain kind of information. Depending on their level of detail, they can be more specific or more general. Depictions are limited in their representational power: They do not include signs of semantic relations and (what refers to realistic pictures) their abstraction level is limited, because, at the utmost, they can represent base-level concepts.

Accordingly, descriptions and depictions are useful in different ways for different purposes. Descriptions have higher representational power than depictions, because they allow logical operations according to semantic relations such as negations and logical connections and because they can use concepts beyond the base level. However, as they are selective, they can be (and usually are) incomplete with regard to certain classes of information about the represented subject matter, and they can be inconsistent.

Depictions have lower representational power, because their degree of abstraction is limited to the base concept level and because they do not provide signs for negations, disjunctions, and other semantic relations. Instead of describing reality, they simulate it. Information can be read off from a depictive representation with appropriate procedures and is necessarily consistent. The relative completeness, consistency, and direct accessibility of information allows high computational efficiency and makes depictions a useful tool for drawing inferences.

CHAPTER 4

Comprehension of Text

Abstract

Spoken or written texts are coherent sequences of sentences. Text comprehension is equivalent to the construction of multiple mental representations in working memory. It is based on an interaction between external text information and internal prior knowledge information stored in long-term memory. Mental representations include a text surface representation, a propositional representation, and a mental model. They are characterized by different forgetting rates. As speakers and authors omit information which can be easily completed by listeners and readers, text comprehension always includes inferences. Listening and reading comprehension use the same lexicon and the same syntax but qualitatively different text surface structures. Due to local and global coherence of texts, comprehension is also a process of mental coherence formation. Limitations of working memory require focused attention on the construction of topic-specific mental models which are carried along from sentence to sentence by a flow of consciousness. Speakers and authors can direct this process through topic information within the text surface.

Coherent sequences of sentences are referred to as "text." Texts are the most prevalent kind of descriptive representations in everyday life, business, administration, science, and other domains. They can guide cognitive processing of any content, including descriptions of complex dynamic physical or social scenarios or descriptions of causalities in order to explain previous events or to predict future events and so forth. Texts can be presented in the form of oral language (as spoken texts) or written language (as written texts).[1] Text comprehension can therefore take place as listening comprehension and reading comprehension.

Spoken and written texts can be "translated" into each other: Written texts can be read aloud (spoken) and spoken texts can be written down. However, translation into another presentation modality changes the conditions of comprehension. Spoken text allows the use of prosody, pauses, and pitch as comprehension aids.[2] However, the carriers of spoken language (sound waves) are fleeting, requiring the listener to pay permanent attention. Written text does not include prosody, pauses, and pitch. However, the graphemic signs are relatively stable, providing the reader with more control in processing the text.[3] Furthermore, written text can use orthographic signs to provide additional hints toward the meaning of words, which are not available in spoken text, as described in Chapter 2. Thus, translations of spoken texts into written texts or vice versa usually ignore some subtle communication aids that were used in the original text. Despite these differences, however, there is also a basic commonality. Spoken text and written text use the same language, the same lexicon, and the same syntax, which makes comprehension processes similar. This commonality justifies treating the comprehension of spoken text and the comprehension of written text together first before turning to their differences in due course.

4.1   Where Does Text Meaning Come from?

Texts consist of sentences. Sentences consist of words, and words have meanings. So, it seems reasonable to assume that word meanings combine to form the meaning of a text. However, this view can be easily challenged based on the following text fragment from a study by Bransford and Johnson.[4]

> "The procedure is actually quite simple. First you arrange items into different groups. Of course, one pile may be sufficient depending on how much there is to do. If you have to go somewhere else due to lack of facilities that is the next step; otherwise, you are pretty well set. It is important not to overdo things. That is, it is better to do too few things at once than too many. In the short-run this may not seem important but complications can easily arise. A mistake can be expensive as well. At first, the whole procedure will seem complicated. Soon, however, it will become just another facet of life . . ."

---

[1] We will bypass texts written with conceptual sign systems such as Chinese or Japanese (see Chapter 2), because they play only a minor role in Western countries and because there is currently only little psychological research on them.
[2] Danks and End (1987).   [3] Ferreira and Anes (1994).   [4] Bransford and Johnson (1972).

Most people find this text difficult to understand. When asked to recall the text, their performance is poor. But why is the text difficult to understand? Its sentences are short. There are no complex embedded sentences and the words are well known to adult readers. The problem is not in the sentences or in the words. The problem is that one does not know what the text is about. Although readers have rich world knowledge about many different domains, they do not know which facet of their prior knowledge should be activated in the present case. However, when Bransford and Johnson presented the text with the headline "Washing Clothes," the comprehensibility ratings and recall performances improved dramatically. Under this condition, the participants could activate their domain-specific knowledge about washing clothes, which helped them to make sense of each sentence and interpret the text.

The study nicely demonstrates that text meanings do not originate from the text. Text meanings are actively constructed by the individual through an interaction between external information from the text and internal information from the individual's prior knowledge. However, this interaction between text information and prior knowledge has to take place immediately during the comprehension process. In other words, the relevant prior knowledge has to be activated at the very moment that the text information is processed. This was demonstrated by Bransford and Johnson in an experimental condition in which the participants learned about the topic only after reading the text. Under this condition, the comprehensibility ratings and recall performances were low because the participants had not seen the headline before being exposed to the text.

According to a widespread view held in cognitive science, individuals' prior knowledge about the world is comprised of so-called cognitive schemata stored in long-term memory. These schemata correspond to the way in which concepts are implemented in the mind. They are hierarchically organized internal mental structures which represent general and typical relationships within a domain of reality. Cognitive schemata serve as prior knowledge packages which can be activated bottom-up by empirical data and top-down by expectations. Following this view, text comprehension is based on a continuous interaction between bottom-up and top-down activation of cognitive schemata triggered by information in the text. During this interaction, the schemata do not only guide the construction process by adding information from long-term memory. They also help to inspect and evaluate the previous construction process by checking for consistency and plausibility. Eventually, the interplay between bottom-up and top-down activation results in a specific configuration of the activated schemata that qualifies as the best interpretation of the text.

Inferences: While the text about washing clothes was artificial insofar as it was designed to demonstrate the importance of prior knowledge for comprehension, "normal" texts also require considerable prior knowledge to be understood. Consider the following example:

> "Joanna was invited to Peter's birthday party. She wondered whether he had binoculars. She went into her room and shook her piggybank, but could not hear anything."

Young children in secondary schools usually have no problem understanding this text. They can easily answer questions such as the following:

> Why did Joanna shake her piggybank? Why did she wonder whether he had binoculars?

They know that Joanna needs a gift to take to Peter's birthday party. They know that if Peter already has binoculars, Joanna should not bring him binoculars as a gift, and they know that Joanna knows this. They also know that Joanna needs money to buy binoculars for Peter and that money is frequently kept in a piggybank. Further, they know that if a piggybank is silent, it means that there is no money in it. In short, they know that Joanna has a problem.

What is remarkable here is that none of the above is stated in the text. The information is added by the reader based on his or her prior knowledge about conventions regarding birthday parties, about conditions of buying, and about habits of storing money. Such additions are called inferences. Inferences are an integral component of text comprehension, because the author of a text omits information which can be easily completed by the reader. Due to the limitations of working memory, however, a reader cannot draw all possible inferences. So, the question arises as to which inferences are drawn in normal text comprehension and which are not. Research indicates that if a text with only local coherence[5] is read fast by a reader with low prior knowledge, he or she draws only a minimum number of inferences.[6] On the contrary, if a locally *and* globally coherent text is read slowly for pleasure or knowledge acquisition by a reader with high prior knowledge and high comprehension standards, he

---

[5] In a text with only local coherence, successive sentences are semantically related but without an overarching thematic connection. In a locally and globally coherent text, successive sentences are connected and there is an overarching thematic connection.

[6] McKoon and Ratcliff (1992, 1995).

or she draws considerably more inferences, such as causal inferences (explaining events by other events) or motivational inferences (explaining events by the actions of protagonists) in order to establish global coherence.[7] A lot of inferences are triggered by presuppositions: "Joe has stopped smoking" presupposes that Joe used to smoke; "Donald did not win the election" presupposes that Donald was a candidate; "Liz could not forget being attacked" presupposes that Liz was attacked, and so forth. The use of presupposition is not only a tool for efficient communication. It can also serve as a manipulative tool to silently convey invalid information.

4.2 Mental Representations in Text Comprehension

Text comprehension has been intensively studied in cognitive psychology under the perspective of information processing for nearly half a century. This research has led to numerous highly sophisticated theoretical models. After hundreds of experiments, it is now widely agreed that text comprehension includes the formation of at least three kinds of mental representations: a text surface representation, a propositional representation, and a mental model (sometimes also referred to as a "situation model").[8] These representations correspond to different levels of processing.[9] They are qualitatively different insofar as they are based on different representational principles, serve different functions in the process of comprehension, and have different forgetting rates.[10] In order to characterize differences between representations in the following, we will describe "thought experiments" under extreme conditions and analyze what kind of behavior results from such conditions.

Text Surface Representations: The mental representation of a text surface includes all linguistic details of the text, its verbatim formulations, phrasing, and the syntactic structures of sentences. Because texts are external descriptive representations, mental representations of the text surface are also descriptive representations. If readers (or listeners) create only a mental representation of a text surface, they only know what has been said (or written) without understanding it. In order to experience such a strange situation, imagine hearing someone say:

„Eki wa, doko des' ka."

---

[7] Graesser et al. (1994); Graesser and Zwaan (1995).   [8] Schmalhofer and Glavanov (1986).
[9] Cermak and Craik (1979).
[10] Kintsch and van Dijk (1978); van Dijk and Kintsch (1983); Graesser et al., (1997).

Like most people, you probably do not understand what has been said. However, you have no difficulties in repeating the sentence verbatim. You just do not know what the sentence means – unless someone tells you that it is Japanese and means "Where is the railway station?" Similar situations might sometimes happen to opera singers who have to perform arias in a language they do not understand. The example demonstrates that a text surface representation allows verbatim recall of what has been heard (or read) even without understanding it. Such a representation allows only a superficial level of processing. The standard situation is, of course, that the listener (or reader) understands the language. The text surface representation serves as the basis for constructing another mental representation which carries the meaning of the text: the propositional representation.

When learners read expository texts with the aim of constructing a mental model of what the text is about, they have high forgetting rates for surface representations, as generally found by previous research. Learners seem to use the surface structure representation merely as a means to extract the semantic content and encode it in a propositional format. However, because text comprehension is a strategic process, individuals can also adapt their processing to their specific goals.[11] Actors or singers learning a text can intentionally concentrate on the exact phrasing and store a verbatim representation of the text surface in long-term memory where forgetting rates are low.

Propositional Representations: When listeners or readers understand the language, they usually create a propositional representation of a text's meaning based on the text surface representation, which is sometimes also referred to as the "text base." The propositional representation grasps the semantic content of the text with the help of propositions ("idea units") as described in Chapter 3. Remember that propositions are complex hypothetical mental symbols resulting from predications which ascribe features (attributes and relations) to entities (objects or events). Attributes and relations are represented by so-called predicates; entities are represented by so-called arguments. Propositions are descriptions that denote conceptual structures and follow a specific syntax. By transforming sentences such as

> "The marsh harrier feeds on small mammals. It migrates from Europe to North Africa in winter."

into propositions such as

---

[11] Vidal-Abarca et al. (2010).

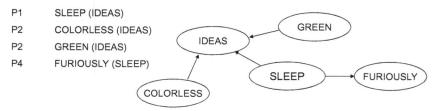

P1	SLEEP (IDEAS)
P2	COLORLESS (IDEAS)
P2	GREEN (IDEAS)
P4	FURIOUSLY (SLEEP)

Figure 4.1   Propositional representation of Chomsky's famous sentence "Colorless ideas sleep furiously"

FEED ON (agent: MARSH HARRIER; object: MAMMALS)
SMALL (MAMMALS)
MIGRATE (agent: MARSH HARRIER; from: EUROPE; to: NORTH
  AFRICA; time: WINTER),

it can be seen that nouns (e.g., "marsh harrier," "mammal," "Europe," "winter," etc.) translate into arguments, while adjectives (e.g., "small," etc.), prepositions (e.g., "on," "in," "to," etc.), and verbs (e.g., "feed," "migrate," etc.) translate into predicates. Propositions represent text meanings without embracing the specifics of linguistic description. What propositional representations can do and what they cannot do in text comprehension is also demonstrated by the following famous sentence used as a borderline case to show that the process of comprehension is blocked at some point:

"Colorless green ideas sleep furiously."

This sentence became famous when Noam Chomsky introduced it into scientific discussion in order to demonstrate that the linguistic knowledge of native speakers is not based on myriads of linguistic experience, as learning theorists had assumed. Although native speakers had never heard the sentence before, they could judge it as syntactically well-formed, although admittedly semantically bizarre. Due to its bizarreness, the sentence has often been qualified as meaningless.

However, the latter statement is false. The sentence does indeed have meaning. As shown in Figure 4.1, its meaning can easily be decomposed into a list of propositions which can be transformed into a semantically equivalent semantic network. Based on this propositional representation, one can answer questions such as the following:

What is the sentence about? Answer: Someone sleeps.
Who sleeps? Answer: Ideas.
What kind of ideas? Answer: Colorless ideas.

Do the ideas have any other features? Answer: Yes, they are green.
How do they sleep? Answer: Furiously.

The example demonstrates that it is possible to understand what has been said in a sentence or text without understanding what the sentence or text refers to. The problem with Chomsky's bizarre sentence is not that it has no meaning. The problem is the incompatibility of its semantic constituents with the real world and any possible world. It is not possible to find a colorless green idea that sleeps furiously in the real world, and it is also not possible to imagine such an idea in any world. In other words, there is a description but there is no referent for the description in our real world or our mental world. The description does not fit to anything.

Sentences or text about colorless green ideas are artificial utterances which do not occur in usual communication. However, it is also possible in everyday life that a reader or listener can only construct a propositional representation, but further comprehension is blocked because he or she cannot imagine what the author or speaker is referring to. This can happen with very difficult texts, for example, texts in philosophy or in the natural sciences such as physics. Such texts frequently leave the reader or listener in a situation where he or she has only understood what has been stated without understanding what it refers to. A propositional representation corresponds to a medium level of processing, which is associated with a medium forgetting rate. It allows an individual to recall and paraphrase what has been said or written, even without knowing what it refers to. In ordinary communication, of course, comprehension does not stop at this point. Instead, propositional representations serve as a basis for constructing mental models.

Mental Models: The process of comprehension is only complete when the reader or listener has constructed a mental model of what the author described in a text. Following Philip Johnson-Laird,[12] we consider a mental model as an analog representation of what a text is about, a kind of internal "quasi-object" or internal image.[13] For example, a mental model that represents the information that marsh harriers migrate from Europe to North Africa in winter could be a cognitive map of Europe and North Africa displaying the birds' movements. Mental models are

---

[12] Johnson-Laird (1983).
[13] The idea of mental models as referential representations was further developed for narrative texts in the event indexing model (Zwaan et al., 1995). According to this model, events of a story can be interrelated according to different dimensions including *space, time, causality, motivation,* and *common entities* (objects and persons).

constructed on the basis of text information and information from prior knowledge, for example, about the geography of Europe and North Africa or about washing clothes. When listeners or readers have constructed a mental model, they have not only understood what was said or written about the subject matter but can also imagine the subject matter: They know what the text refers to. A mental model corresponds to the deepest level of processing, and it has the lowest forgetting rate.

A mental model enables inferences about the represented subject matter and it allows the text content to be freely recalled by re-describing the mental model in one's own words. Contrary to the descriptive nature of text surface representations and propositional representations, which are closely related to the text, mental models are depictive representations which are closely related to the structure of the subject matter. However, for a mental model to be constructed, the referent does not have to exist in the real world. Architects can imagine and draw pictures of a building that does not exist yet or that has been destroyed. We can also easily imagine a unicorn, and painters have created numerous pictures of unicorns without ever having seen one. It does not matter that they will never encounter a unicorn in the real world. It is sufficient that a unicorn is a possible referent in a possible world that they can think of.

4.3 Listening Comprehension and Reading Comprehension

Based on the distinction between different levels of mental representations involved in text comprehension, we are now in a better position to consider the differences between listening and reading comprehension. It goes without saying that a comparison between the two kinds of comprehension only makes sense with regard to sufficiently literate individuals. It is also no surprise that younger individuals and those with less schooling have a higher preference for listening than for reading, whereas individuals of medium or older age seem to prefer reading to listening.[14]

If listening and reading comprehension involve creating multiple levels of mental representation as described in Section 4.2, their surface representations must be qualitatively different. Spoken text is processed via the auditory sensory system and written text is processed via the visual sensory system. Accordingly, the surface representation of spoken text includes all the processed auditory information, while the surface representation of written text includes all the processed graphemic information. Both representations

---

[14] Kürschner et al. (2006).

should include linguistic details such as wording and syntactic structures as well as physical features of the spoken or written language.

While the surface representations of listening and reading comprehension are clearly different, it is not so obvious as to whether the two kinds of comprehension differ also in terms of higher-order cognitive processing, which leads to the construction of propositional representations and mental models. In empirical studies, short and simple verbal material (word lists) were remembered better when presented in the auditory than in the visual modality. However, this advantage disappeared with more complex material.[15] For difficult texts, reading was more advantageous than listening.[16] Other studies with complex texts found that readers were better at remembering details of the content, whereas listeners were better at understanding the main points of a text.[17]

Due to the stability of written text, readers obviously have better control of their cognitive processing, which allows them to choose different processing strategies and to concentrate also on details. Listeners, due to their lower control of processing and the fleeting nature of auditory information, have to concentrate on the main ideas (i.e., on macro-propositions) and extract the gist of the text as soon as possible. The difference in processing control might be the reason why some texts are intentionally formulated to be listened to and others to be read. Whether modern interfaces for playing audio files give listeners sufficient control of the presentation speed and allow easy repetition of specific information in order to compensate for the fleeting nature of auditory text remains to be seen.

As already stated in this section, listening comprehension and reading comprehension differ in terms of the sensory quality of their text surface representations. Beyond that, however, there are no indications that listening and reading differ qualitatively at higher levels of mental representations. Listening and reading comprehension use the same mental lexicon and the same syntax. They also seem to use the same kinds of higher-order cognitive processing. Nevertheless, the different conditions for processing in listening and reading can lead to differences in the detail and content of the propositional representations and mental models. These differences should be quantitative rather than qualitative. They originate from processing conditions at the text surface level rather than genuine qualitative differences regarding propositional representations and mental models. A fleeting external text requires other processing strategies than a text that

---

[15] Crowder (1993).   [16] Green (1981); Sanders (1973).
[17] Hildyard and Olson (1978); Rubin et al. (2000).

is permanently available. Thus, one can expect differences between listening and reading regarding the information that is selected and passed on to the higher representation levels. In this way, the higher-order representations created in listening and reading comprehension can be qualitatively the same but differ quantitatively in terms of the represented information and detail.[18]

Combined with other representations such as pictures, listening is of course extremely advantageous when a text provides verbal guidance on when to look, where to look, and what to notice. Listening avoids splitting visual attention , which is inevitable when texts have to be read.[19]

4.4   Coherence Formation in Text Comprehension

Up to this point, text comprehension can be characterized as the construction of multiple mental representations through an interplay between bottom-up and top-down activation of cognitive schemata, which function as building blocks of the reader's or listener's prior knowledge. Bottom-up activation is text-driven, meaning that the construction process is fed with external information. Top-down activation is knowledge-driven, meaning that the construction process is fed with internal information from prior knowledge. As full understanding involves constructing a mental model in which possible mistakes during comprehension are corrected as far as possible, text comprehension can also be characterized as the construction, evaluation, and (if needed) revision of a mental model of the subject matter described in the text.

Local and Global Coherence: What makes a text different from an arbitrary collection of sentences is its coherence. The text's sentences are semantically related and can be integrated into a coherent whole. There are relations at a local level between adjacent sentences, which contribute to so-called local coherence, and there are relations at a global level between larger segments of the text, which contribute to so-called global coherence. Readers (and listeners)[20] have to reconstruct the local and global text coherence in their minds.

Mental coherence formation is usually enhanced by special signals in the text surface, indicating the kind of relations between sentences and larger text segments. These signals are called "cohesive devices." Cohesive devices

---

[18] Kürschner and Schnotz (2008).   [19] Mayer and Moreno (1998); Moreno and Mayer (1999).
[20] For simplicity, we will only refer to readers in the following, although we assume that listening and reading comprehension do not fundamentally differ at higher levels of processing.

encompass, for example, the use of pronouns and connectors in the text surface. Pronouns are generally used for anaphoric (i.e., backward) references. The use of a pronoun signals to the reader that a noun for the same referent has already been introduced in the text surface and that its referent is (most likely) still in the reader's focus of attention.[21] Connectors are words that indicate the semantic relation between text segments such as "and," "or," "then," "because," "thus," "but," "although," "nevertheless," and so forth. Connectors enhance coherence formation because they specify how to semantically connect sentences and larger text segments.

Coherence Formation Processing: Walter Kintsch and Teun van Dijk developed a very influential model of coherence formation in text comprehension.[22] The model explains how propositions delivered (or stimulated) by a text are connected into a coherent network. Due to the limited capacity of working memory, the authors assumed that coherence formation occurs in multiple processing cycles. In each cycle, a certain number of propositions are read and fed into working memory, where they are integrated into a kind of network (a "coherence graph") based on certain characteristics of coherence such as common arguments between propositions or the embedding of propositions into other propositions. A certain number of previously processed propositions are stored in a working memory buffer and carried across to the next cycle, where they serve as connection points for integrating the new propositions with the previously read propositions.

Depending on whether possible connection points for new propositions are still in working memory or not, or on whether such connection points have to be inferred first with the help of prior knowledge, processing is more or less fluent. Coherence formation is easy if a new proposition can be directly connected to a previous proposition that is still accessible in working memory. Coherence formation is more difficult if the previous proposition is no longer in working memory and therefore has to be retrieved from long-term memory. Coherence formation is most difficult if the proposition serving as a connection point first has to be inferred with the help of prior knowledge. Although this model focuses primarily on local coherence formation, it has proved to be rather successful in predicting reading difficulties.[23]

The construction–integration model of text comprehension proposed by Walter Kintsch analyzes the integration of text information and prior knowledge in more detail. Processing of sentences is assumed to consist of

[21] Garrod and Sanford (1983).   [22] Kintsch and van Dijk (1978).   [23] Graesser et al. (1997).

a construction phase and an integration phase. In the construction phase, the reader creates in his or her working memory a local propositional network based on text information and inferences resulting from a process of spreading activation within prior knowledge. When the network is large enough, the integration phase begins. Excitatory and inhibitory connections adjust the network to produce a stable state representing the final meaning of the sentence.[24]

Recent investigations have revealed that individuals' cognitive resources are allocated differently to lexical access, assembly of propositions, integration of propositions, and mental model construction during re-reading as compared to initial reading. When re-reading a text, individuals tend to allocate proportionally more cognitive resources to text-level integration and model construction because proposition assembly is easier than during initial reading.[25] In this process, good readers make better use of re-reading to update their mental model than poor readers.[26]

Topic and Comment: Functional linguists have pointed out that two information components can be distinguished – the topic and the comment – in each sentence but also in each larger unit of text.[27] The topic specifies what the sentence or text unit is about, whereas the comment includes what is said about the topic. If a comment is seen as a message, the topic can be considered as an address where the message is to be delivered. If text comprehension involves constructing a mental model, the topic tells the reader on which part of the mental model he or she should currently focus, whereas the comment provides directions for further constructing the model.

If text is globally coherent, there is an overarching topic across all paragraphs and sentences which integrates them into a unitary whole. This global topic can usually be subdivided into sub-topics which refer to parts of the text. These sub-topics can be further subdivided into sub-sub-topics which refer to smaller text segments until one arrives at the sentence level of the text. The resulting topic hierarchy functions as a framework for coherence formation. An example of local and global coherence is presented in the following fragment of a text about ecosystems:

> "The exchange of matter and energy in ecosystems occurs for the most part in food chains. At the outset of the food chains are the producers. The producers convert light energy into nourishment. They are mainly plants. Plants create organic compounds from inorganic compounds with the help of solar energy. During this photosynthesis, plants create oxygen which they

[24] Kintsch (1988).   [25] Millis et al. (1998).   [26] Millis and King (2001).
[27] Halliday (1994).

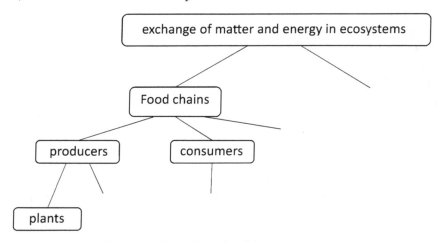

Figure 4.2   Topic hierarchy of the ecosystem text

emit to the environment. The continuation of the food chains is made up of the consumers. The consumers are unable to create organic compounds from inorganic compounds. They live on other living organisms, on producers, or on other consumers . . ."

The hierarchical topic structure of this text fragment is shown graphically in Figure 4.2. The overall superordinate topic is "The exchange of matter and energy in ecosystems." A first-order subordinate topic (which can be followed by further topics at this level) is "food chains." This topic is then subdivided into two second-order topics: "producers" and "consumers." The producers are then subdivided into plants (besides other, non-specified living things) as a third-order subordinate topic, and so forth.

Flow of Consciousness: As mentioned in Section 4.2, at the highest representational level, text comprehension involves constructing a mental model of the subject matter described in the text. Due to the limited capacity of working memory, this model can of course not be constructed all at once. Instead, the reader needs to focus on the current topic at the time of processing. That is to say, he or she constructs a topic-specific mental model. This mental model is carried along from sentence to sentence while it becomes further elaborated as long as the corresponding topic is not changed. The corresponding passing on of semantic structures from sentence to sentence has been called the "flow of consciousness."[28]

---

[28] Chafe (1979).

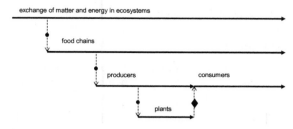

[The exchange of matter and energy in ecosystems] occurs for the most part in food chains. • At the outset of [the food chains] are the producers. • [The producers] convert light energy into nourishment. → [They] are mainly plants. • [Plants] create organic compounds from inorganic compounds with the help of solar energy. → During this photosynthesis, [plants] create oxygen which they emit to the environment. ◆ [The continuation of the food chains] is made up of the consumers. • [The consumers] are unable to create organic compounds from inorganic compounds. → [They] live on other living organisms, on producers or on other consumers ...

Figure 4.3   Sequential processing of the topic hierarchy of the ecosystem text

Global coherence formation implies that topic-specific mental models are constructed step by step and finally integrated into a coherent overall model. Because the different topics in a text are hierarchically organized, they are located at different hierarchy levels. This implies that, during global coherence formation, the flow of consciousness has to take place simultaneously at different topic levels.

For the previous example of a text about ecosystems, the sequential processing of hierarchically organized topics is shown in Figure 4.3. Accordingly, the flow of consciousness occurs at four topic levels. When a subordinate topic is introduced, the superordinate topic is still carried on. For example, when the topic "food chains" is introduced, the superordinate topic "exchange of matter and energy in ecosystems" is still implicitly maintained. When the text introduces plants, it is still implicitly talking about producers, about food chains, and about the exchange of matter and energy in ecosystems. So, besides the explicit topic at hand, there are also superordinate implicit topics which are silently carried on. In this way, the flow of consciousness through successive mental model construction can take place simultaneously at multiple levels of the topic hierarchy.

Topic Continuity: A text including multiple topics will require some topic changes in due course. However, these topic changes should be kept to the necessary minimum as far as possible. In other words, the average topic continuity of a text should be as high as possible because this enables a continuous flow of consciousness. Figure 4.3 illustrates the principle of how to ensure high topic continuity:

> At each level of the topic hierarchy, an introduced topic should not be interrupted before it has been completed. It should then be replaced by the next topic, which should be treated in the same way, and so forth.

Otherwise, the reader would have to abandon an unfinished topic which then has to be reactivated later. Unnecessary retrieval or reactivation of previously constructed topic-specific mental models imposes not only a high cognitive load on the reader's working memory[29] but also runs the risk that the retrieved or reactivated model is informationally incomplete, because the reader has forgotten some aspects of it. Topic discontinuity due to unnecessary topic changes should therefore be avoided. Topic continuity enhances global coherence formation, whereas topic discontinuity is likely to spoil it.

Figure 4.3 further illustrates how the degree of topic continuity varies across a text. The sentence topics are indicated by [rectangular brackets]. Topic changes between consecutive sentences can vary from soft to hard. For each transition from one sentence to another and for each level of the topic hierarchy, one can investigate whether the topic at this hierarchy level has changed or not. Regarding the transitions between the first six sentences of the text presented in Figure 4.3, there is a new topic either at only one subordinate level or there is no topic change at all. In other words, there are only soft topic changes (indicated in the figure by the symbol "●"), or there are no topic changes at all (indicated in the figure by the symbol "→"). In other words, topic continuity is high. Between sentences six and seven, there is a change at two levels. The topic "plants" is finished and the topic "producers" is replaced by "consumers." This can be considered as a medium topic change (indicated in the figure by the symbol "◆"). In other words, topic continuity is medium. If the text was continued and a topic change involved more hierarchy levels, a hard topic change would occur. Generally speaking, topic continuity at a specific point in a text is lower when more topics in the hierarchy are terminated at this point and replaced by new topics.

4.5 Directing the Flow of Consciousness in Text Comprehension

Even if a text describes highly complex content with a sophisticated network structure, it is nevertheless restricted to a linear presentation. It

---

[29] Sweller et al. (2011).

is expected that the text is read word by word and sentence by sentence, thus conveying a sequence of propositions. In the course of comprehension, these propositions are gradually integrated into a coherent conceptual structure which serves as a basis for a coherent overall mental model. In this way, the text leads the reader through the conceptual structure. The sequence of propositions expressed by the sequence of sentences stimulates the reader's flow of consciousness and should therefore be carefully planned. As explained in Section 4.4, it should allow high topic continuity and be mindful of the inherent prerequisites of comprehension, for example, the fact that A cannot be understood without knowing about B, which requires that B is presented before A.

Focus Tracking: However, the sequence of sentences by itself only provides a rough guide for the flow of consciousness. We have seen in Section 4.1 that texts cannot be understood without activating relevant prior knowledge. We have also seen that this relevant prior knowledge has to be activated at the very moment that the text information is processed. Due to the limited capacity of working memory, only a small part of prior knowledge can be activated at a particular time. This is why the reader has to know exactly what the author is talking about all the time in order to activate the corresponding prior knowledge. Thus, text comprehension requires cooperation between the author and the reader. The author has to direct the reader's flow of consciousness and the reader has to follow the author's directions. If the author moves to another topic, the reader should immediately recognize this move and follow it by shifting his or her focus of attention accordingly. This process is called "focus tracking." A smooth and easy flow of consciousness needs to be fine-tuned by effective mechanisms of focus tracking. This fine-tuning of the flow of consciousness is done by shaping the topic information of text sentences.

When a new sentence is processed, readers first identify the topic information. If the topic information is compatible with the previous topic, they assume that the former topic is being maintained, which implies topic continuity. If the topic information is not compatible, it means that the topic has changed. When authors want to move on to a new topic, they should therefore avoid using a topic description which is compatible with the former topic because readers might not recognize the move.

When readers notice a change in topic, they conduct a mental search for a corresponding entity in their mental representation (or they construct such an entity based on their world knowledge from long-term memory) and focus on this entity as the new topic. If a text is well-written, the reader receives subtle information about relevant search parameters from the topic information in its sentences.[30] First, the reader is informed whether the topic has changed or not. Second, the reader is informed whether a small or a big shift of attention is required depending on whether a soft or a hard change of topic has taken place. Third, the reader receives information about where the new entity can be found and, fourth, the reader receives a profile for searching for the entity. This information is conveyed through

- marking of the topic information,
- differential use of nouns and pronouns, and
- focus tracking in multiple mental representations.

Marking of the Topic Information: Figure 4.4 shows three pairs of consecutive sentences. The second sentence of each pair always conveys the same information about the same topic. In all three cases, the topic of the second sentence is the marsh harrier, and the comment is always that the bird is usually found in wetlands. What is different between the three cases is how the topic information is presented in the second sentence. The topic information ranges from "it" via "the marsh harrier" to "what refers to the marsh harrier." Each of the three variants of topic information refers to the same referent – the marsh harrier – but the markedness of the topic information is different. Using a pronoun such as "it" is the lowest possible marking of the topic information. The noun phrase "the marsh harrier" represents medium markedness, and the phrase "what refers to the marsh harrier" represents high markedness of the topic information.

Remember that Figure 4.3 showed that topic changes can vary from soft to hard depending on the number of topic levels involved. Soft topic changes, where the new topic is still close to the previous one and where the reader has to perform only a small topic shift, are signaled by low topic markedness. Hard topic changes, where the new topic is relatively far away from the previous one and where the reader has to perform a bigger topic shift, are usually signaled by high topic markedness. Conversely, low markedness is interpreted by the reader as a hint that the previous topic is being maintained or has only shifted slightly. High markedness is interpreted by the reader as a hint that a hard topic change has taken place and a big shift of attention is required.[31]

Differential Use of Nouns and Pronouns: New topics can always be introduced with nouns or noun phrases, which give no hints as to whether the referent has been mentioned already or not. Thus, the referent has to

---

[30] Sidner (1983).   [31] Givón (1983); Fletcher (1984).

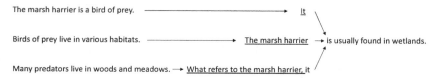

The marsh harrier is a bird of prey. ⟶ It

Birds of prey live in various habitats. ⟶ The marsh harrier ⟶ is usually found in wetlands.

Many predators live in woods and meadows. ⟶ What refers to the marsh harrier, it

Figure 4.4 Examples of differently marked topic information in different contexts

be searched for within a larger range of possibilities. However, a noun phrase provides an elaborated search profile for identifying the referent. The use of a pronoun as topic information, on the contrary, affords a very lean search profile as it includes only the grammatical gender (male/female/ neutral) and number (singular/plural). Thus, a pronoun signals that no or only a minor change in topic has taken place. Because a pronoun provides only a very lean search profile, it can only be used when the gender and number are sufficient for the reader to identify the referent. As illustrated in Figure 4.4, using a pronoun also signals to the reader that the corresponding noun was already mentioned explicitly in the text surface before, so that the corresponding referent is likely to still be in working memory. Accordingly, the search area for a pronoun is very small, which enables focus tracking with minimal topic information.

Focus Tracking in Multiple Mental Representations: Authors can shape the topic information of sentences so that the mental search for the new topic is easier or more difficult, depending on which kinds of mental representations are included in the search profile. Figure 4.5 shows three variants of a text which differ in terms of how the topic of the last sentence is described.

In the first variant, the term "marsh harrier" as topic information was already used before in the text surface. Furthermore, the concept of a marsh harrier was introduced into the propositional representation and a corresponding entity was added to the mental model. Thus, the term "marsh harrier" used in the first variant allows the reader to find the referent of the topic information at all three representation levels: text surface representation, propositional representation, and mental model.

In the second variant, the term "predator" as topic information was not used before in the text, but the previously used term "bird of prey" might have triggered the concept "predator" at the propositional level. Furthermore, a corresponding entity might have been inferred at the mental model level. Thus, the term "predator" used in the second variant allows the reader to find the referent (the marsh harrier) at two representation levels: propositional representation and mental model.

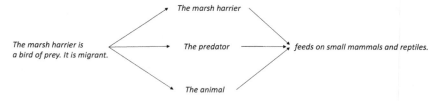

Figure 4.5   Examples of different topic information items employing different mental representations

In the third variant, the term "animal" was not used before in the text, and the term is not sufficiently distinct at the propositional level. However, if the marsh harrier was the only animal mentioned before, the general term might suffice for the reader to identify the topic. A distinct entity which can be referred to as "the animal" would then be found by the reader only at the mental model level.

These different variants of topic information which refer to one and the same referent demonstrate that the mental search for a new topic can be more or less difficult. The difficulty hinges on how many representation levels are involved in the mental search process, which depends on the profile provided by the author.

All in all, directing the reader's flow of consciousness in the process of comprehension is a highly important task for authors and requires a skill which can be described as "cognitive empathy" with the reader. Authors have to align the topic information with the expected mental state of their addressee. This alignment requires fine-tuning by adequately using subtle hints. The following questions provide guidance on how to achieve such alignment:

- What is in the reader's current focus of attention?
- Which prior knowledge is currently activated?
- In the case of a new topic, is a small or a larger topic shift required? In other words, how far is the new topic away from the former one?
- Does the markedness of the topic correspond to the required topic shift?
- Has the search area in which the new topic is to be found been sufficiently specified?
- Is the description of the new topic sufficiently specific for the reader to identify the new topic within the search area?

Answering these questions adequately seems to be key to activating the readers' relevant prior knowledge at the very moment when the comment's information is processed in order to enable successful comprehension. Of course, the search parameters need to be well coordinated. The larger the search area and the more entities within it that are similar to the referent, the more specific the search profile has to be in order to allow successful identification of the new topic.

4.6 Communication Context and Meta-comprehension of Texts

Communication requires cooperation between a speaker or author and a listener or reader. In order to convey a message about some content to an addressee, the speaker or author tries to direct the listener's or reader's cognitive processes by formulating the text in such a way that the recipient understands what the speaker or author means. This requires some (mostly unconscious) cooperation and a division of labor between both partners. The speaker or author provides conceptual guidance for the mental construction processes, but also expects the listener or reader to contribute by making inferences. The recipient follows the speaker or author, but expects the text to be adjusted to his or her prior knowledge and cognitive skills to achieve clarity and comprehensibility.

The implicit assumptions of ideal cooperation between communication partners was described by Grice in terms of so-called conversational maxims.[32] According to these maxims, the speaker or author in an ordinary, nonmanipulative conversation or text communication is silently expected to be as informative as necessary, to say only what he or she considers to be correct, to denote presumptions as such, to concentrate on what is relevant for the recipient, to be as coherent as possible, and to avoid long-windedness. Listeners and readers are usually not aware of these conversational maxims. Following the maxims is, therefore, largely automatized. Many readers do not even consider the possibility that an author could write manipulative texts expressing false, contradicting, or irrelevant ideas.

Real-world communication does not always follow these maxims.[33] On the one hand, readers and listeners have personal goals; for example, they might want to acquire general information about a subject matter or prepare themselves for specific tasks. They use the text to accomplish these goals by focusing their attention on specific goal-relevant information.[34] They select some information as more important than other information and use certain strategies to process the text information in a specific way

[32] Grice (1967).   [33] Carroll (2008).   [34] McCrudden and Schraw (2007).

which aims at constructing task-appropriate mental representations.[35] On this account, readers of newspaper articles, for example, focus more on mental model construction than readers of literary texts, who focus more on the text surface.[36]

It is not only readers and listeners who have goals. Authors and speakers also have goals. They prepare their texts or speeches to communicate specific ideas to their readers and listeners. Teachers intend to convey knowledge about a subject matter. Politicians may try to persuade their addressees to join or vote for a specific party, and advertisers encourage their target group to spend money on a specific purpose or to buy a specific product. Alternatively, salespersons may sometimes not be sufficiently informative about the adverse features of their product, thus manipulating their clients. All in all, it goes without saying that the goals of authors and speakers do not necessarily coincide with those of their readers and listeners.

Sophisticated readers and listeners, especially those from communication professions such as journalists, politicians, and scientists, are usually sufficiently skilled to recognize what the author or speaker wants to communicate. They try to check the professional expertise, the credibility, and sincerity of the text author or speaker, and evaluate whether or to what extent the goals of the author or speaker correspond to their own goals.[37] In this way, readers and listeners construct a mental representation of the overall communication, including the aims, expertise, credibility, and sincerity of the producer of the message.[38] The creation of a mental representation of the overall communication between the author and reader (or speaker and listener) can be characterized as a kind of "meta-comprehension" (i.e., comprehension of the present communication process). This meta-comprehension is likely to affect the reader's or listener's willingness to adopt the conveyed messages and views of the writer or speaker.

4.7   Takeaways

Texts are not carriers of meaning. Instead, they trigger processes whereby multiple coherent mental representations are constructed through an interplay between text-driven bottom-up and knowledge-driven top-down activation of cognitive schemata. As texts have local and global coherence, text comprehension includes local and global mental coherence formation. Mental representations include representations of the text surface

---

[35] Guthrie et al. (2007); King (2007).   [36] Graesser et al. (1997).   [37] Rouet et al. (2017).
[38] Rouet and Britt (2022).

structure, propositional representations of the text meaning, and mental models of the text content. With respect to the latter, text comprehension can be characterized as the construction, evaluation, and (if needed) revision of a mental model of the subject matter described in the text.

Text comprehension can take place as listening comprehension or reading comprehension. The two kinds of comprehension differ in terms of the sensory quality of their surface structure representations. As they use the same lexicon, the same syntax, and the same prior knowledge, however, they are not expected to be qualitatively different in terms of their higher-order mental representations. Due to the different conditions for processing a fleeting text versus a permanently available text, there can be quantitative differences in terms of content, the amount of detail, or emphasis on the main ideas.

Coherence formation is enhanced by signals at the text surface, called "cohesive devices." For each text unit (sentence or larger text segment), topic information specifies what the unit is about, whereas comment information provides further information about the topic. The topic information tells the reader on which part of the mental model he or she should currently focus. The comment information conveys what additional construction steps should be made. Due to the limited capacity of working memory, coherence formation takes place as a stepwise flow of consciousness, in which topic-specific mental models are constructed and carried along from sentence to sentence as long as their corresponding topics are maintained in the text. Due to the hierarchical organization of topics and subtopics, the flow of consciousness takes place simultaneously at different topic levels. Depending on how many levels in the hierarchy are affected by a change of topic, either a small or a big shift of focus to the new topic is required.

A continuous flow of consciousness with a minimum number of topic changes enhances mental coherence formation, whereas frequent changes in topic require readers to undertake abundant focus tracking activities. If an author abandons a topic temporarily, he or she has to reactivate it later. This requires the reader to retrieve the previously processed information from long-term memory, and the retrieved information will frequently be incomplete. Accordingly, topic discontinuity imposes an unnecessary cognitive load on working memory.

The flow of consciousness in coherence formation is directed by the author via the topic information, which in case of a topic change triggers mental search processes for the new topic in multiple mental representations. When the author proceeds to a new topic, the topic information conveys various search parameters which the reader can use while searching for the new referent. Due to the critical role of topic information in triggering mental search processes in the course of focus tracking, the author has to specify it very carefully in order to allow successful focus tracking. The search parameters naturally need to be well coordinated. The larger the search area and the more entities that are similar to the referent, the more specific the search profile has to be in order to allow successful identification of the referent.

CHAPTER 5

Comprehension of Pictures

Abstract

Pictures are two-dimensional depictive representations. They include static pictures and animations. The latter are defined as pictorial displays that change their structure or other features over time and trigger perception of a continuous change. Static and animated pictures can display static as well as dynamic content. Both can have an envisioning, explanatory, orientation, organizing, and argumentative function. Picture comprehension entails sub-semantic perceptual processing, semantic perceptual processing, and conceptual processing. Sub-semantic perceptual processing is primarily pre-attentive and data-driven. It results in viewer-cantered and object-cantered visual representations. Semantic perceptual processing is attentive and data- as well as knowledge-driven. It results in object or event recognition. Conceptual processing is attentive and primarily knowledge-driven. It creates complex propositional structures and mental models in working memory. Picture comprehension is based on analog structure mapping under the guidance of perceptual and conceptual representations.

Pictures are two-dimensional depictive representations including realistic pictures (drawings, paintings, photographs), maps, and graphs. Contrary to text, they do not describe their referent, but serve as a substitute for it, as explained in Chapter 3. They differ also from text in terms of processing constraints and in terms of information access structure.

Due to their linear[1] structure, texts have an inherent prescribed order of processing. By default, they are expected to be read word-for-word and

---

[1] The concept of hypertext as a so-called non-linear text seems to contradict the inherent linearity of text. In fact, a hypertext replaces only a single linear text sequence with multiple linear text sequences without questioning linearity as such.

sentence-for-sentence. Several pictures can also be presented and processed sequentially, but within a picture there is no such prescribed order of processing. The perceptual salience of graphical entities or directive signs can, to some extent, affect what will be focused upon first, but the order of picture processing is mainly up to the observer. Furthermore, pictures deliver information in a more compact way than texts. In a picture, entities are presented just once; when described in a text, they are usually mentioned several times. Accordingly, thematically related information can be packed more closely together in a picture than in a text. As a result, the search path required for finding a specific piece of information among the two-dimensional information displayed in a picture is on average considerably shorter than for linear, one-dimensionally displayed information in a text.[2] In brief, due to the shorter search paths, pictures provide faster and more flexible access to specific information than texts.

5.1 Static Pictures

For a long time, pictures were created on rigid sign carriers such as stone, wood, canvas, and paper, which is why most of them are still static today. That is, their structure and other features remain stable over time. This does not imply that they cannot represent dynamic subject matter. The pictogram of a tennis player shown in Figure 5.1 is a static picture, but observers automatically draw inferences that the player is in motion.[3] In another example, which was shown in Figure 3.11, the horizontal time axis in a graph was used to represent the life cycle of the Japanese beetle. Similarly, sea maps can show water currents through arrows of different lengths indicating the direction and speed of movement. A further technique for presenting movement in static pictures was developed by Étienne-Jules Marey,[4] who displayed a series of superimposed snapshots taken at regular time intervals in order to show the different states within a movement.

---

[2] For the purpose of illustration, assume that pieces of information are randomly distributed across 100 slots. In one case, the 100 slots are linearly organized in a 1 × 100 one-dimensional array. As backward reading is not possible, information is searched for linearly, always beginning from the first slot. The average length of the most direct search path required to find a specific piece of information is 49.5. In another case, the 100 slots are organized in a two-dimensional 10 × 10 array. The information search always starts in the middle of the array. The average length of the most direct search path required to find a specific piece of information is only 4.45.

[3] Miller (1990).   [4] Marey (1895).

Figure 5.1   Pictogram of a tennis player

Static pictures can serve different functions including envisioning, explanation, organization, spatial orientation, argumentation, and others. Realistic pictures can have an envisioning function when they inform others about the appearance of an unknown object. An example was provided in Figure 2.8, which showed the appearance of a rhinoceros as imagined by Albrecht Dürer. Realistic pictures can also have an explanatory function when they provide visual help for following cause–effect chains related to the operation of technical devices such as pulley systems or for understanding natural processes such as the formation of volcanoes. Realistic pictures can also have an organizing function. A somewhat bizarre example is presented in Figure 5.2. The figure shows the cover picture of a medical handbook published by Hans von Gersdorff in 1517. The book is about the surgery of war wounds inflicted in the sixteenth century. The picture shows the weapons and the injuries caused by them. In other words, it serves as a pictorial list of contents. Nowadays, a mouse click or touch on a screen could provide access to the required medical information.

Maps provide spatial orientation about a geographic area by reducing it to a pictorial space. They display information about what is located where in the corresponding geographic area. The what-information is conveyed by signs: icons or symbols. For example, a pictogram of the Eiffel tower or the word "Paris" can indicate the capital of France. The what-information can also refer to invisible entities such as isobars (lines of equal atmospheric pressure) on weather maps, water currents on sea maps, or environmental variables such as air pollution or average rainfall

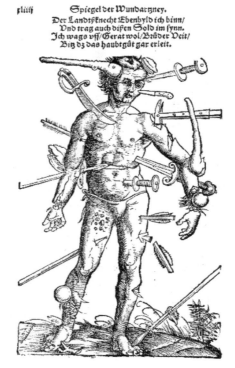

Figure 5.2   Cover page of Hans von Gersdorff's handbook about surgery of war wounds
published in 1517
(from Robin, 1992)

per year on thematic maps.[5] The where-information is conveyed by the location of the corresponding signs within the pictorial space of the map.

Maps can display distances between locations and provide information on how to get from one location to another. However, such orientation functions need certain specifications because only some features of the map have a representational function, while others do not. For example, a map of a larger geographical area based on a Mercator projection inflates the size of objects that are remote from the equator due to the curvature of the Earth. Such a map can, therefore, only precisely display spatial structures and distances within limited geographical areas. The size of larger areas on the map that are remote from the equator are not representative of the size

---

[5] Tufte (1990).

of the corresponding geographic areas. Accordingly, the structural correspondence between cartographic relations and geographical relations needs
to be made specific with well-defined analogy relations. The user of the
map has to keep the specific relationships in mind in order to interpret the
map correctly and to avoid incorrect readings.

Another example of a map which uses only a limited set of features for
representation purposes is presented in Figure 5.3; a map showing a
segment of the New York subway network. The map is designed for
subway users who want to find the shortest way from one location to
other locations, identify which lines to use, and establish where to change
trains. Other geographic information is omitted from the map in order to
avoid distraction.[6] Thus, it would be a mistake to relate distances on the
map to real distances.[7] It would also be a mistake to assume that all the
subway connections proceed exactly in North/South and East/West directions (or in Northeast/Southwest or Northwest/Southeast directions). By
the same token, the fact that the distances between subway stops on the
map are equal does not mean that the stops are really at equal distances
from each other.

Graphs display relations among quantitative variables or between quantitative and qualitative variables, whereby they can serve explanatory and
argumentative functions. A famous historic example has already been
shown in Figure 2.13: William Playfair's line graph presenting the national
debt of Britain from the revolution to the end of war with America. In this
graph, quantitative variables (national debt and time) are combined with a
qualitative variable (war versus peace) to demonstrate that British national
debt increased during war and decreased during peace. Provided that the
aim of policy was to minimize national debt, the graph could support the
argument that peace was more beneficial for Britain than war. It was, thus,
meant to serve as a "visual argument" for a specific view.

The widespread use of graphs to display data has led to conventional
graph formats which can be used as "ready-mades" for all kinds of visual
data communication.[8] Figure 5.4 gives an overview of the most frequently
used graph formats in terms of the variables, data, and relationships.[9] The
leftmost panel shows a common visualization for relations between nominal variables, the so-called structure diagram. The second panel, which
consists of a vertically arranged group of three graph formats, shows
common visualization formats for combining discrete independent

---

[6] Berendt et al. (1998).   [7] Fabrikant and Montello (2008).   [8] Kosslyn (1994a).
[9] Zelazny (1985).

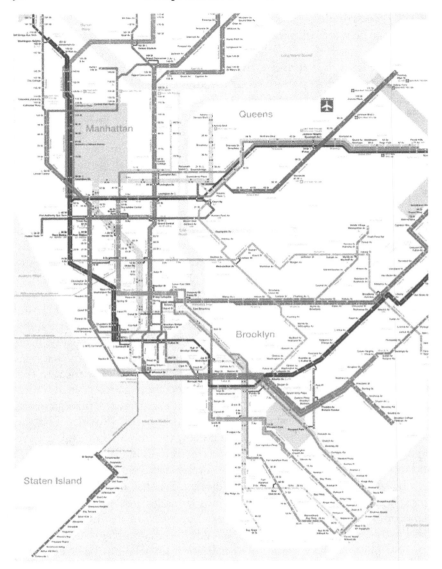

Figure 5.3   Map of a segment of the subway network of New York

variables and a determinist relationship with a dependent variable. If the independent variable is at nominal level, the most common format is a vertical or horizontal bar graph. Whether vertical or horizontal bars are

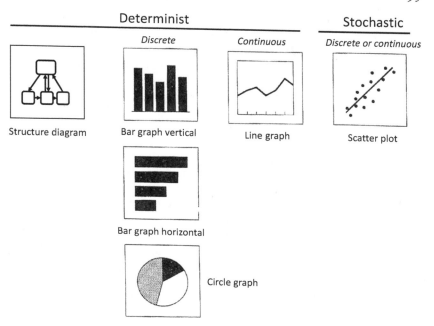

Figure 5.4   Overview of the most frequently used graph formats for the visualization of determinist and stochastic relations between qualitative and quantitative information

used depends on the metaphorical use of space. Horizontal bars seem to be naturally associated with measures such as the stopping distances of cars or the range of airplanes, because cars move horizontally and airplanes largely fly horizontally. Vertical bars might be more closely associated with measures such as production numbers or profits, because these are considered as high or low. There is no prescribed order for the bars, but it is common to arrange them according to usage-related variables such as importance, frequency, or the alphabet. The lengths of bars represent the values of the dependent variable.[10] If the graph shows the breakdown of a whole into its parts (which implies that the values of the dependent variable add up to 100 percent), a circle graph can be used instead of a bar graph. The third panel in the figure shows a common format for visualizing determinist quantitative relationships: the line graph. Such a graph uses a Cartesian coordinate system to display the relationship

---

[10] Isotype graphs, invented by Austrian-born philosopher and political economist Otto Neurath, use a number of content-related pictograms instead of abstract bars to represent quantities.

between an independent variable (x-values) and a dependent variable (y-values) for a theoretically unlimited number of values. If the relationship between the independent and the dependent variable is stochastic, the relation can be graphically presented by a scatterplot, as shown in the right panel of the figure.

5.2 Animations

Moving pictures became a possibility through advances in technology: the invention of film in 1895, followed by video, and then finally by computer-generated animations. As viewers can hardly see differences between the types of moving picture anymore, the technology used to produce them no longer has essential psychological relevance. We will therefore use "animation" as a general term to refer to moving pictures. We define an animation as a pictorial display that changes its structure or other features over time and triggers perception of a continuous change.[11] This definition includes not only the presentation of moving objects, but also the continuous presentation of static objects from different perspectives or the presentation of how a static object is assembled from its parts. There is no one-to-one relationship between the static or dynamic characteristics of the represented content and the use of static or animated pictures. Not only can static pictures display both static and dynamic content, but animations can also display static and dynamic content. The two kinds of pictures differ insofar as animations give observers the possibility to perceive changes within dynamic content directly from external representations, whereas static pictures of dynamic content require observers to infer these changes. Thus, animation is not another kind of picture. It just adds the aspect of change to pictorial displays.

Animation can be integrated into all different kinds of pictorial displays: into realistic pictures, into maps, and into graphs. Animated realistic pictures can show movements of an object such as the gallop of a horse, the jump of a kangaroo, or the functioning of a car brake. As mentioned at the start of this section, they also allow us to present objects continuously from different perspectives and to demonstrate how a complex object is assembled from its parts. Animated maps can show the movement of local or global weather systems or large-scale movements of humans such as, for example, the Völkerwanderung (Migration Period) or today's movements

[11] Schnotz and Lowe (2008).

of refugees. Animation can also be integrated into graphs in order to illustrate trends or to visualize covariation between variables.

Animations can serve two basic functions: representation and direction of processing. As for their representation function, animations can, among others, serve to visualize causal relations. Causal relations in the real world become apparent through the directed co-variation of attributes. Specific changes in certain attributes of an entity systematically result in specific changes in attributes of another entity. Changes can include changes in the position of entities in space or changes related to the attributes such as their size, shape, color, and other aspects. Because directed co-variations occur over time, they can be displayed by an animation. Such an animation has an explanatory function.[12]

As for their function in directing processing, animations can guide the observer's visual attention to specific entities by increasing the perceptual salience of these entities.[13] This can be done with cueing techniques such as flashing or zooming. Visual cueing in an animation is also possible through manipulation of the dynamic contrast, namely the extent to which the movements of an entity differ from those of its surroundings. These techniques increase the perceptual salience of entities, making them perceptually more dominant so that they are more likely to attract the viewer's attention. Due to the fleeting nature of animations, it is essential that cueing techniques direct the observer's visual attention to the right place at the right time.

Animations can be run at different speeds, which affects their perceptual processing. The sensitivity of human visual perception is limited not only for spatial patterns, but also for temporal patterns. Humans have a high general sensitivity for perceiving movements, but this sensitivity operates only within a very specific speed range. Outside of that range, we are unable to observe dynamic information. For example, we cannot see that a plant is growing unless its growth is speeded up in an animation. Conversely, we cannot see a chameleon "shooting" an insect with its tongue within a few hundredths of a second unless the process is slowed down. The "temporal zooming out" for excessively slow events and "temporal zooming in" for excessively fast events serves to transpose processes into the human eye's range of sensitivity to change.

Dynamic systems include changes at different levels. High-level changes refer to global systems, for example, global meteorological weather conditions moving across a continent. Events at this level can be called "macro-

[12] Lowe et al. (2022). [13] Lowe and Boucheix (2011).

events." Low-level changes are local, for example, local meteorological events such as thunderstorms or tornados as parts of global weather conditions. Events at this level can be called "micro-events." Animations can emphasize different levels of a system's dynamics through different speeds of presentation.[14] If the speed of presentation is high, macro-events tend to be more salient than micro-events and, thus, the macrostructure of the dynamic information is emphasized. Conversely, if the speed of presentation is low, micro-events become more salient than macro-events and, thus, the microstructure of the dynamic information is emphasized.

5.3   Sub-semantic Perceptual Processing

The process of seeing starts with sensory cells in the retina and continues in the primary visual cortex, where specific groups of neurons react on specific stimuli such as lines with different spatial orientations. Secondary fields of the visual cortex are responsible for extracting more complex information patterns representing specific features of objects such as their form, size, color (hue, saturation, lightness),[15] texture, spatial orientation, or movement. Jacques Bertin calls these features "retina variables."[16] Size and color are distinct attributes which are processed separately. Hue, saturation, and lightness of color are integrated attributes which are processed jointly.

These primal perceptual processes are based on automated visual routines which are executed in parallel. They allow graphical elements (dots, lines, and areas) to be noticed, discriminated, and identified and also allow these elements to be grouped into specific configurations. This processing is primarily data-driven (bottom-up). Accordingly, it is largely independent of the observer's prior knowledge and goals. Because conceptual prior knowledge does not play a role at this stage, this processing is sub-semantic. Because it is not cognitively penetrable and cannot be affected by the observer's conscious attention, processing is pre-attentive.

The pre-attentive nature of sub-semantic processing can be demonstrated with visual illusions such as the well-known Müller–Lyer illusion shown in Figure 5.5. The upper horizontal line seems to be longer than the lower horizontal line, although they are the same length. Even if we know

---

[14] Lowe (1996).
[15] Hue refers to the tone of the color (red, yellow, green, blue, or any mixture of them). Saturation refers to how little white, black, or gray is mixed in, and lightness refers to how much white versus black is mixed in a color.
[16] Bertin (1967).

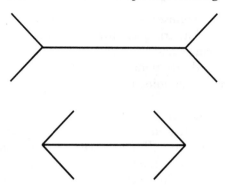

Figure 5.5   The Müller–Lyer illusion: The horizontal lines are the same length, but seem to be different

Figure 5.6   Perception of a non-existing figure: There is no white triangle

that they are equally long based on our own measurement, we are still unable to see the two lines as equivalent. This false judgment results from pre-attentive automated visual routines, which are hard-wired into our visual system. The error is unavoidable because cognition cannot penetrate a perceptual judgment. Another illustration demonstrating the automated nature of pre-attentive processing, which cannot be cognitively penetrated, is shown in Figure 5.6. The figure presents what is called Kanizsa's triangle:[17] We see a white triangle superimposed on three black circles

---

[17] Kanizsa (1955).

and another triangle circumscribed by black contour lines. We also see the contour lines of the white triangle. However, although we perceive them, there is no white triangle and there are no contour lines of this triangle. Once again, hard-wired pre-attentive automated routines which cannot be cognitively penetrated determine perception.

According to David Marr's[18] computational theory of visual perception, seeing a real object entails creating three types of internal visual representations: an initial representation, a viewer-centered representation, and an object-centered representation.[19] The initial representation is Marr's primal sketch, which includes only intensity changes across the visual field. The viewer-centered representation includes the spatial arrangement of visible surfaces from the viewer's position. The object-centered representation includes the object's shape, its surfaces, and its spatial relations with respect to other objects. The latter representation is independent of the viewer's position. Because realistic pictures simulate the depicted scenario, these visual representations are also created when an observer perceives a picture of an object.

Figure and Ground: The viewer-centered representation of objects is based on pre-attentive segregation of the perceived world into figures and ground, whereby figures qualify as possible objects. The segregation of figures from the ground implies the transformation of complex visuo-spatial structures which include multiple elements into a perceptual representation consisting of only a few entities on an undifferentiated background. The distinction between figure and ground is usually unequivocal, although ambiguities can sometimes occur. A well-known example of such an ambiguity is shown in Figure 5.7, called "Rubin's vase." The visual pattern presented in the figure can be seen as a white vase in front of a black background or as the silhouette of two black heads in front of a white background. People see either one figure–background combination or the other. Their pre-attentive visual processing decides for one or the other option.

Figure–ground distinction is enhanced by surroundedness, convexity, size, contrast, symmetry, and granularity. Areas surrounded by other areas (such as an island surrounded by water) are likely to be seen as a figure. Convex shapes (such as a peninsula) are more likely to be seen as a figure than concave shapes (such as an embayment). The smaller of the two areas is more likely to be seen as a figure than the larger one. The higher the visual contrast of an area to the surrounding area (including dynamic contrast), the more likely that it is seen as a figure. An area with a

[18] Marr (1982).   [19] We follow the terminology of Ellis and Young (1996) in this context.

Figure 5.7 Example of an ambiguous figure–ground distinction: A white vase or two black faces?

Figure 5.8 Maurits Escher's artwork "Sky and Water I."

symmetric form is more likely to be seen as a figure than an area with a non-symmetric form. For two adjacent areas, the area with the more fine-grained pattern is more likely be seen as a figure than the area with the less fine-grained pattern. An example of this granularity effect was presented by Maurits Escher in his picture of ducks and fish shown in Figure 5.8. In the lower part of the picture, the fish are drawn in white with a fine-grained

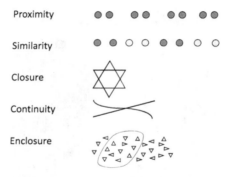

Figure 5.9   Overview of the Gestalt laws

pattern and seen as figures in front of a black background. In the upper part, the ducks are drawn in black with a fine-grained pattern and seen as figures in front of a white background. In between, the figure–ground distinction is ambiguous.

Gestalt Laws: Figures are coherent wholes consisting of elements. Their integrity can be described according to the Gestalt laws,[20] which specify how visual stimuli are grouped together to form larger units. The most important Gestalt laws are illustrated in Figure 5.9 and can briefly be described as follows.

Law of Proximity: Stimuli close to each other are perceived as belonging to a group.

Law of Similarity: Stimuli with similar visual features (e.g., similar form, color, orientation, texture, etc.) are perceived as belonging to a group.

Law of Closure: Stimuli are organized in the simplest possible way to create a closed concise figure. A Star of David, for example, is considered as consisting of two equilateral triangles rather than a hexagon with six attached triangles. By the same token, symmetric patterns are more likely to be considered as a unit than asymmetric patterns. The perception of a non-existing white triangle in Figure 5.6 can also be subsumed under the law of closure.

Law of Continuity: Intersecting lines remain distinguishable based on the implicit assumption that the lines proceed continuously.

Law of Enclosure: Stimuli that are enclosed by a boundary are perceived as belonging to a group.

---

[20] Wertheimer (1938).

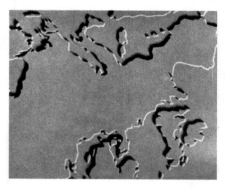

Figure 5.10   Example of a figure–ground distinction within a relief picture. Light comes
from the top left
(reproduced from Kanizsa, 1968, figure 27)

Grouping elements together into figures as larger units is an automatic, pre-attentive process. When a unit has been formed, visual attention is no longer subdivided between the single stimuli but focused on the unit as a whole.

An important part of figure–ground distinction is the perception of shape: its outline contours. Shapes that look like familiar objects can be recognized more easily than less familiar shapes. Because an object's shape depends on the viewer's perspective, perception of shape is part of viewer-centered perceptual representation according to Marr's theory of vision. It allows integration of local detailed information into an overall coherent whole. This is also supported by neurological data: Brain-injured patients who suffer from impaired object contour discrimination and impaired ability to analyze visual forms seem to be incapable of constructing viewer-centered representations. When copying drawings of objects, they pick up visual details, but they cannot correctly see the whole.[21]

Built-in Presuppositions: Pre-attentive perceptual processing implies that perception is governed by presuppositions the observer is not aware of. When you look at the picture in Figure 5.10, you see some elevated figures on a lower ground. When you look at the picture in Figure 5.11, you will see a very different set of elevated figures on a lower ground. However, the two pictures are identical, only one is turned by 180 degrees. The different perceptions result from the unconscious presupposition that light comes from above. This hidden assumption is plausible for ecological reasons

[21] Ellis and Young (1996).

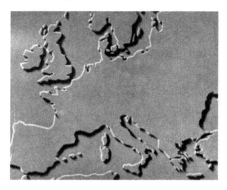

Figure 5.11   Example of a figure–ground distinction within a relief picture of Western
Europe. Light comes from the top left
(reproduced from Kanizsa, 1968, figure 27, upside down)

because it has been a constant condition of terrestrial life from day one. It
might, therefore, be hard-wired into our visual system without us being
consciously aware of it. This hidden assumption results in different figure–
ground distinctions. Most people hardly recognize anything familiar in
Figure 5.10, while people with basic geographical knowledge easily recognize a relief map of Europe in Figure 5.11.

Visual Vibrations: When different visual routines of pre-attentive
processing compete, it can result in visual vibrations. An example is shown
in Figure 5.12. As mentioned earlier in this section, specific visual neurons
react on specific stimuli such as lines with different spatial orientations. As
vertically oriented objects (trees, fellow humans, etc.) and horizontally
oriented objects (horizon, water, etc.) dominate in our environment
compared to other orientations, one can speculate that evolution has
preferred neurons that detect lines with a vertical and horizontal orientation compared to other neurons. When in doubt, vertical or horizontal
orientations are therefore more likely to be perceived than other orientations. In Figure 5.12, the dots can be visually organized into a vertical
($90°$) and horizontal ($0°$) orientation. However, the Gestalt law of proximity suggests that the dots are perceived as if they are arranged in
45 degree lines. This conflicts with the 90 and 0 degrees orientations,
which seems to make the dot pattern in Figure 5.12 look like it is visually
"vibrating."

Compare this to Figure 5.13, where the Gestalt law of proximity favors
the arrangement of the dots in 90 and 0 degrees lines and is, therefore, well
aligned with the vertical–horizontal preference. As a result, the dot pattern

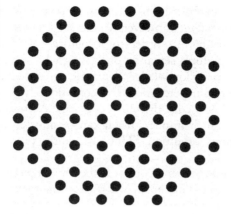

Figure 5.12   Visual vibrations resulting from competition between Gestalt laws and orientation preferences

Figure 5.13   Visual vibrations of Figure 5.12 removed

shown in Figure 5.13 looks more serene, because a stable perceptual pattern can be created. In fact, the dot patterns in Figures 5.12 and 5.13 are identical. One of them is just turned by 45 degrees.

5.4   Semantic Perceptual Processing

The sub-semantic perceptual processing described in Section 5.3 transforms complex visual raw data into perceptual representations consisting of only a few objects in front of an undifferentiated background. Based on such representations alone, observers would see objects without knowing what they were seeing. In order to recognize and categorize objects, observers have to perform semantic processing which includes the activation of conceptual prior knowledge. Semantic perceptual processing serves as an interface between perception and cognition. It is both data-driven (bottom-up) and knowledge-driven (top-down). Accordingly, it is cognitively penetrable, which implies that it can be affected by the observers' goals and conscious attention. Thus, semantic perceptual processing is attentive.

What and Where: When an object is shown in a picture, it is presented at a specific location. This enables a distinction between two kinds of information: what-information and where-information. The what-information is about the attributes of the depicted object, indicated by its visual appearance. The where-information is about the location of the object in space. The distinction is universally applicable, but it is particularly important for maps which try to convey information about what is located where in a geographical space. The what-information on maps is conveyed with the help of icons or symbols which allow the association of the graphical entity on the map with the real entity in the geographic space. The where-information is conveyed by the location of the corresponding signs on the map. When processing a map, observers draw on their visual abilities for the what-information and use their spatial abilities for the where-information. Neurological evidence suggests that both kinds of information are stored at different sites of the brain. Some brain-injured patients can visually recognize objects immediately, but do not know where these objects are located. Other patients cannot recognize an object in a specific place in their visual field but can specify this place with high precision.

Object Recognition: The what-information related to perceived objects (apart from unknown objects) is the information that allows objects to be recognized. Recognition requires activation of prior knowledge implemented as cognitive schemata in long-term memory. These object schemata include knowledge about an object's perceptual attributes: what it looks like, how it sounds, how it feels, how it smells, or how it tastes. They can also include knowledge about how the object is used, what it is made from, and to what category it belongs. Ellis and Young[22] call these object schemata, which connect perception to cognition, "object-recognition

---

[22] Ellis and Young (1996).

units." A perceived object is recognized when its visual representation has accessed its object-recognition unit and a match has been found between what the viewer is seeing and what he or she knows. When unknown objects are shown, corresponding units have to be created first and then stored in long-term memory.

If the connection between vision and knowledge about objects is impaired, which can happen in the case of brain injuries, the individual suffers from visual agnosia; he or she cannot recognize an object or its picture just from seeing it. Even if these patients have intact visual perception, as in they can copy drawings precisely, they cannot relate what they see to what they know about an object. However, if the connections between an object-recognition unit and other sensory modalities are still intact, they can easily identify the object via sound or touch.[23] Visual agnosia can even occur when an individual has perfect knowledge about an object's visual appearance. Some patients can copy drawings, but cannot reproduce them from memory, and they cannot recognize objects from seeing their pictures. However, when they are told the object's name, they can draw the object quite well. Thus, the connection between the mental lexicon and the intact object-recognition units is still working. However, the connection between the intact object-recognition units and intact visual perception is blocked.

Mental Lexicon: It should be noticed that object-recognition units do not include the names of objects. The objects' names are stored in a mental lexicon which is separated from the object-recognition schemata.[24] Thus, object recognition does not require that the individual is able to name an object. This is illustrated by the everyday experience of "having something on the tip of one's tongue," when we wish to express something specific and cannot find the appropriate word to do so. Patients with an optic aphasia caused by brain injuries can also show intact perception and intact knowledge about objects, but these are disconnected from language. Their visual perception allows them to recognize objects, as demonstrated by the pantomimic use of these objects, but the patients cannot name the objects. The reverse connection can also be impeded: When the object's name is presented, the patient has difficulties drawing it. Despite being closely connected, language and world knowledge are separated.

Event Recognition: Cognitive schemata cannot only represent objects in space, but also events which occur over time. At higher levels, such cognitive schemata are referred to as "scripts." At lower levels, such

[23] Ellis and Young (1996).   [24] Carroll (2008).

schemata represent our knowledge about movements. In everyday life, we are confronted with lots of repetitive behavior which allows us to extract spatially and temporally invariant patterns. These patterns are subsumed under cognitive schemata of events. We can readily distinguish between the different kinds of movement pattern of humans, dogs, cats, horses, fish, or birds. We can differentiate between different horse gaits, such as walking, trotting, and galloping. We can easily detect even a slight limp in a person's walk as a deviation from normal movement patterns and infer that the person has an injured leg. Our perceptual and cognitive system is able to extract typical repetitive spatially and temporally invariant patterns of movement and to represent them with perceptual and cognitive schemata. The corresponding schemata can be activated pictorially by observing animations.

A highly convincing demonstration of dynamic schemata was proposed by Marey.[25] If a person dressed in black and wearing lights on his or her shoulders, elbows, hands, hips, knees, and feet is standing still in front of a wall covered by black velvet, it is impossible to recognize that he or she is a human being. Rather, the observer sees only a seemingly arbitrary distribution of light spots. As soon as the person starts walking, however, the observer immediately recognizes the presence of a human figure. The invariant pattern of the movement of the lights is sufficient to activate the appropriate dynamic schema so that the dynamic display can be recognized as a person walking.

Perspectives: It is assumed that all three visual representations in Marr's theory – the initial representation, the viewer-centered representation, and the object-centered representation – have access to object- and event-recognition units. A viewer-centered representation is always related to a specific perspective. This could explain why objects presented from a familiar perspective are more easily recognized than objects presented from an unfamiliar perspective.

Objects belonging to a specific category are frequently shown from a specific perspective which can become the object category's "canonical perspective." For example, four-legged animals such as dogs, cows, or horses are usually shown from the side, and not from the back or from the top. This was already demonstrated in Figures 2.5 and 2.8, which presented a buffalo in a cave painting and a rhinoceros in Dürer's drawing, both from a lateral perspective. Similarly, maps are usually presented with a north-facing orientation as the canonical perspective. Turning a familiar

[25] Marey (1895).

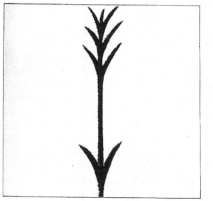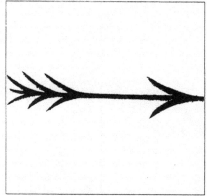

Figure 5.14   Example of a visual ambiguity solved by context

map of a geographic area (including its annotations) by 90 or 180 degrees can make a map difficult to recognize. Perspectives also frequently help to solve ambiguities. The graphical configuration presented in Figure 5.14, for example, can be perceived as a plant when shown upright and connected to the ground, but can also be perceived as a flying arrow when shown horizontally in free space.

Object recognition is enhanced if the object is presented from a familiar perspective because correspondence between what is seen and what is known can be noticed already at the level of viewer-centered visual representation. When objects are shown from an unusual perspective, the correspondence between what is seen and what is known can only be noticed at the level of the object-centered representation.

The role of prior knowledge in object recognition is not always immediately obvious because in most cases we easily recognize what is shown in a picture. However, unusual perspectives can make pictures unrecognizable, because the graphical configuration does not allow activation of the appropriate prior knowledge. An example is shown in Figure 5.15 (which is admittedly meant as a "droodle"[26]). Like most people, you will probably not be able to come up with a satisfactorily coherent interpretation of this graphical configuration without help. The configuration is too unfamiliar to enable activation of the corresponding object-recognition unit. The situation is equivalent to the text comprehension example used by

---

[26] A "droodle" is a pictorial riddle.

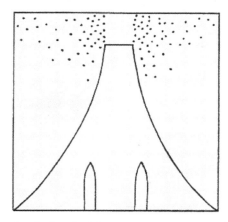

Figure 5.15   Example of a droodle: The picture cannot activate the prior knowledge required for interpretation. Comprehension needs an additional prompt (see the text)

Bransford and Johnson and presented in Chapter 4. The example remained incomprehensible as long as the relevant prior knowledge had not been activated by adding the headline "Washing clothes." In the present case, the graphical configuration makes no sense until the appropriate prior knowledge is activated by the headline "A ski jumper at the start."

Wholes and Parts: Complex objects may be decomposed into a hierarchy of parts and subparts. Such hierarchies are called "partonomies." A simple example is provided by the human body. It consists of a head, trunk, arms, and legs; the arms consist of an upper arm, lower arm, and hand; the hand consists of a palm and fingers, and so forth. A somewhat bizarre example, in which the whole object is composed of parts of another ontological category, is shown in Figure 5.16. The figure presents a work by late Renaissance painter Giuseppe Arcimboldo (1526–1593) who specialized in these kinds of pictures. The painting portrays the Holy Roman Emperor Rudolph II of Habsburg as "Vertumnus," the Roman god of seasons, change, and plant growth. In this picture, object recognition can take place at different levels of granularity. Macro-reading (which takes place at a level of low granularity) focuses on the human figure, while micro-reading (which takes place at a level of high granularity) focuses on the fruits, flowers, and vegetables.

The question as to whether macro-reading comes before micro-reading or vice versa corresponds to the question of what we perceive first: the parts or the whole? The answer is: It depends. At a distance, when the

Figure 5.16   Portrait of Emperor Rudolph II of Habsburg as "Vertumnus," the Roman
god of seasons, change, and plant growth, painted by Giuseppe Arcimboldo
(from Wikimedia Commons)

visual angle is small enough, the picture is seen as a whole unit and the
details do not receive separate attention. The picture thus appears to be
an ordinary portrait. However, when the observer approaches it, the
portrait is no longer within the manageable visual angle of the observer,
who realizes that the portrait is made up of fruits, flowers, and vegetables.
More generally, the order seems to be determined by the size of the
picture, the corresponding visual angle, and the informational density.
The partonomy level that takes precedence is characterized by a certain
amount of information within the visual angle. If there are too many
details within the visual angle, the observer is perceptually "drawn into"
the picture by a kind of "mental zooming," which gives precedence to
lower-level entities in order to keep the amount of information within the
visual angle near the optimum.[27] However, pictures are usually designed
and presented in a way that the size of the pictorial object and visual
angle encourage macro-reading before micro-reading. Thus, observers
typically first extract a global structure from a picture before they focus
on details.[28]

[27] Winn (1994).   [28] Liu and Jiang (2005); Oliva and Torralba (2006).

5.5   Conceptual Processing

When a match has been found between the perceptual representation of an object in a picture and the corresponding object schema, the schema are activated, making the conceptual object information available in working memory. The object is then recognized and categorized. However, picture comprehension requires more than recognition of the objects shown in the picture. As shown in the following examples, the observer also has to recognize relationships between objects and to construct complex conceptual structures about the content of a picture. In other words, based on its perceptual representation, a picture becomes the subject of schema-driven conceptual processing which draws on content-related prior knowledge.

Regardless of the kind of picture (realistic, map, or graph) and its content, conceptual processing of pictures has the following general characteristics. Processing takes place in working memory. It is conscious and attentive and includes bottom-up and top-down processing. Thus, it is heavily dependent on prior knowledge.[29] Due to the limited capacity of working memory, which allows an individual to grasp only four to seven elements simultaneously, conceptual processing of pictures takes place sequentially under conscious control. Observers search for specific objects or object configurations and read attributes or relations from their perceptual representations. The conceptual analysis of pictures is also co-determined by the observer's goals and tasks. Specific parts of the perceptual representation may be task-relevant and may, therefore, receive more emphasis during cognitive processing. Eventually, conceptual processing leads to the construction of coherent propositional representations of the depicted subject matter, which can include both entities shown in the picture and entities inferred by the observer.

As mentioned at the beginning of the chapter, there is no predetermined sequence of picture processing. Directive pictorial signs such as arrows, drawn pointers, "magnifying glasses," the framing of picture areas, or the exaggeration of visual contrast can affect the observer's attention. Ultimately, however, it is up to the observer as to whether and to what extent he or she follows such suggestions. Just as there is no specific order of conceptual processing, conceptual analysis has no pre-defined terminal point. Comprehension of pictures is an open-ended process which is not heavily constrained. The only constraints are: The resulting conceptual structure has to be supported by perceptual processing and the conceptual

---

[29] This corresponds to J. W. von Goethe's citation: "We only see what we know" (Goethe, 1833).

Figure 5.17   Sandro Botticelli. "Birth of the Venus"
(from Google Art Project)

structure must be coherent and free of contradiction, that is, consistent. Because the conceptual structure representing the content of a pictorial message is not heavily constrained, it is very possible that different observers come up with different interpretations depending on their prior knowledge.

Realistic Pictures: If the purpose of a realistic picture is only to inform people about the visual appearance of an unknown object, such as Dürer's drawing of a rhinoceros shown in Figure 2.8, very little conceptual analysis may be needed. Other pictures, however, need considerable conceptual processing which results in complex semantic structures allowing an observer to understand a picture. As an example, consider the famous painting by Sandro Botticelli entitled "Birth of Venus" which was created in around 1480, as shown in Figure 5.17. Perceptual object recognition would identify a naked woman standing on a shell at the shore, two male figures in the upper left of the picture, and another female figure standing at the shore who is receiving the naked woman. This is a correct perception, but far from understanding. Comprehending the picture requires knowledge about old Greek mythology, which would enable multiple inferences leading to the following interpretation: According to the Greeks' beliefs, Venus, who is painted as a naked woman, was born from the foam of sea waves and then blown by the winds Zephir and Chloris (the male figures on the left) in a shell, which serves as her boat, to the shore where she is received by the goddess Flora.

Figure 5.18   Pedro Berruguete: "The ordeal by fire"
(from Wikimedia Commons)

Even more complex conceptual structures have to be inferred in order to understand the picture shown in Figure 5.18. The picture was painted by Pedro Berruguete in 1503, a time when the Roman Catholic Church was struggling hard against emerging Protestantism. Perceptual object recognition would only recognize a fire in the middle of the painted scene surrounded by different groups of people with two men throwing books into the fire. This perception is entirely correct, but far from the intended message of the painting. The picture is meant to show the burning of heretical books under the supervision of a council of the Roman Catholic Church. Furthermore, while the heretic writings are being destroyed by the flames, a holy book containing a sacred text is miraculously spared from the flames and is floating upward by itself, as can be seen in the upper part of the picture.

Conceptual processing can draw on all kinds of prior knowledge stored in long-term memory, depending on the content of a picture. Because experts have deeper and broader knowledge about their domain, they can of course construct more elaborate conceptual structures than novices. Experts in the history of arts come up with much more extensive interpretations of Botticelli's or Berruguete's picture than the ones just given. The same is true for other kinds of pictures such as technical drawings, maps, and graphs. For example, for an individual to comprehend explanatory pictures of technical devices or natural processes, he or she has to identify causal relations based on sufficient prior knowledge about the domain and construct corresponding conceptual structures. Comprehension of Albrecht Dürer's explanatory drawing of Alberti's window theory of pictures, as shown in Figure 3.8, requires the observer to first infer the interrelations between a point on the painted object and its coordinate values from a fixed point of view, and second to transfer the coordinate values from one grid system to another one.

Maps: Like the just-mentioned realistic pictures, maps can also be the subject of intensive conceptual processing. Conceptual analysis of maps can deal with the relations between entities such as mountains, passes, rivers, lakes, cities, highways, railway lines, and so forth. Depending on the questions to be answered, processing can focus on which areas are separated by which rivers and which mountains, which mountains are the highest, which passes are the lowest, which cities are located on which rivers, which rivers flow into another river, which cities can be reached by which highways or by which railway lines, and so forth. Thematic maps enable observers to answer a large diversity of further questions. However, the observer has to keep in mind that there are well-defined structural correspondences between cartographic relations and geographical relations based on specific analogy relations. Conceptual analysis is constrained by the fact that only some features of the map have a representational function, while others do not. In other words, conceptual processing of maps has to be constrained by representational meta-knowledge about these maps.

Graphs: Graphs have no similarity with what they represent. They can even represent facts that cannot be observed at all, for example, the development of birth rates or the increase of imports. Thus, observers cannot rely on cognitive schemata used in their everyday life. Instead, conceptual processing of graphs requires special prior knowledge about this kind of presentation, so-called graphic schemata.[30] Without knowledge about the representation formats, the observer is unable to perform

---

[30] Pinker (1990).

appropriate conceptual analyses to create coherent propositional representations. The most frequent graph formats and their characteristics have already been shown in Figure 5.4. Observers need cognitive schemata for these formats in order to correctly comprehend the graphs. Although there are more possibilities of visualizing data, as demonstrated by William Playfair, one should keep in mind that alternative, "innovative" graph designs run into danger of being misinterpreted because the addressees lack the corresponding graphic schema. Comprehension of graphs is easier if an individual is familiar with the corresponding visualization format.

Conceptual processing of graphs involves associating graphical entities such as bars, lines, or circular sectors with real world entities. It also entails associating colors and textures with specific represented qualities. Conceptual processing includes further associating graphical features such as the axes of a Cartesian diagram, the heights or lengths of bars, the angles of sectors, and the heights of curves with real world variables. Accordingly, graphical measures correspond to real world values. Further, conceptual processing involves reading off certain single values, certain differences between values, or differences between differences of values. If one of the coordinate axes is time, conceptual graph processing allows the reading off of multiple changes in time and the acceleration or deceleration of these changes. Multiple line graphs with a time axis even allow myriads of comparisons between different rates of change over time.

Visual attributes of graph components are differently useful for representational purposes. Different hues of color and different textures, for example, can be used to designate different qualities. Colors and fonts can also be used to present the same kind of information in the same manner. However, color hue and texture are inappropriate for representing different quantities. Different degrees of saturation or lightness of color can only be used to coarsely represent quantitative differences at the level of an ordinal scale (in which one value is higher or lower than another value, regardless of the size of the difference). The obviously best (i.e., relatively unbiased) way to present quantities is to use the length of lines or bars (i.e., rectangles with the same breadth), because this kind of presentation is well suited to representing quantitative differences also at the level of interval and ratio scales. On the contrary, using the size of areas or volumes to display quantities is a no-go when designing graphs, because the perceived differences between areas are hopelessly underestimated by the human perceptual system. There is a strong bias when areas and – even worse – volumes are perceptually compared.

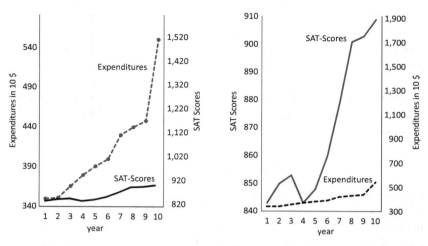

Figure 5.19   Double line graphs presenting SAT scores and funds for education (fictitious data) within a period of 10 years. The different scaling of variables creates fundamentally different visual messages
(adapted from Wainer, 1997)

Like for map processing, observers are in danger of miscomprehending maps and drawing unjustified conclusions if they ignore the processing constraints which should be part of their representational meta-knowledge. This can be illustrated with the two integrated line graphs shown in Figure 5.19.[31] They show how expenditures for students and SAT scores developed within a time period of 10 years. The left hand line graph in the figure seems to suggest that expenditure increased considerably during the time period but hardly resulted in better learning. This message could be summarized under the headline "More expenditures for students do not result in better learning." The right hand line graph in the figure, on the contrary, seems to suggest that, although expenditures hardly changed, SAT scores increased remarkably. The message could be summarized under the headline "Students show improved learning despite unchanged expenditures for education." In fact, both line graphs are based on the same data. Because the units of the two variables are arbitrary, both the expenditures and SAT scores can be rescaled ad libitum. This can lead to different graphs conveying seemingly different messages. Actually, none of the above conclusions is justified, because such double line graphs are

---

[31] The line graphs are modified versions of an example introduced by Wainer (1997).

misleading visualizations. They invite the observer to make comparisons where no comparisons can be made, because a basic prerequisite for such trend comparisons is not met: the use of a common scale for the developments that are being visualized. When observers lack the corresponding meta-knowledge about trend comparisons, they can easily be victims of visual lies and manipulations. Thus, it is important that conceptual processing of graphs is constrained by appropriate meta-knowledge in order to avoid incorrect inferences.

5.6   Mental Model Construction

On top of perceptual and conceptual processing, picture comprehension results in the construction of a mental model of the depicted subject matter. As mentioned in Chapter 4, mental models are hypothetical internal depictive representations which have structural analogies with the referents they represent. Thus, mental models can also be considered as hypothetical internal quasi-objects representing real or imaginary external referents by structural correspondence.

Mental model construction is an attentive conscious and goal-directed process which takes place in working memory. Accordingly, it proceeds through bottom-up and top-down processing, is heavily dependent on prior knowledge, and is affected by the observer's aims. More specifically, mental model construction takes place under the guidance of conceptual and perceptual processing. Like text comprehension, where a coherent conceptual structure – the propositional representation – guides mental model construction, picture comprehension entails constructing a mental model. This process is guided by the coherent propositional representation resulting from the picture's conceptual processing. Like text comprehension, the propositional representation acts as a conceptual framework for the construction of a mental model. Unlike text comprehension, however, mental model construction is also guided more directly by perceptual processing due to common representational principles such as depictive representations.

Pictures and mental models are closely related by analogy. In other words, the two representations have the same analogy-based relationship with the represented subject matter (the referent), which makes them both depictive representations. This follows consequentially from the transitivity of analogy relations. If an analogy relation holds between A and B, and the same analogy holds also between B and C, then the analogy necessarily also holds between A and C. This transitivity constitutes an overarching analogy relation between the represented content, the picture, and the mental model. The analogy relation between a picture and a mental model implies that picture comprehension is eventually a process of structure mapping. Graphic entities are mapped onto mental entities, and spatial relations are mapped onto analogy relations within the mental model which allow semantic interpretation.

The notion of structure mapping between pictures and mental models implies that pictures which visualize subject matter differently can lead to different mental models, even when the pictures are informationally equivalent. In a study of learning about the time differences and dates differences on the Earth, for example, students received texts either with a rectangular map of the Earth based on a Mercator projection or with a circular map of the Earth seen from the North Pole in order to learn about time and dates on the Earth. Both maps were informationally equivalent, as they included all the information required to answer specific questions about differences in time and dates on the Earth. However, the maps were not equivalent in terms of drawing new inferences. That is, they were not computationally equivalent.[32] After learning about time and date differences on the Earth with their text and map, the rectangular map learners, on the one hand, outperformed the circular map learners in the tasks requiring them to answer questions about daytime differences. On the other hand, the circular map learners outperformed the rectangular map learners on tasks requiring to answer questions about the change of the date when circumnavigating the globe.[33] Obviously, the structure of the picture is mapped onto the structure of the emerging mental model which, in turn, affects the model's computational efficiency for specific tasks.

It follows that picture comprehension is easier the better the perceived graphical configuration corresponds to the structure of the intended mental model. The individual is thus able to better recognize this correspondence by activating the appropriate cognitive schemata. Comprehension is difficult when the perceived graphical configuration does not correspond to the structure of the intended mental model because this requires perceptual reorganization in order to allow adequate interpretation. A mental model is goal-directed as long as the observer primarily selects task-relevant entities and constructs the mental model in a way that is most useful for the anticipated task.

Perceptual representations of pictures and mental models are both depictive representations, but they are qualitatively different. First, in terms of depth of processing, mental model construction involves a deeper level of

[32] Larkin and Simon (1987).   [33] Schnotz and Bannert (2003).

picture comprehension than creating only a perceptual representation of a picture. Second, perceptual representations are bound to a specific sensory modality; for picture processing this is usually the visual modality. Mental models, on the contrary, are not sensory specific. A mental model of a spatial configuration, for example, can be constructed by visual, auditory, or haptic perception. Because mental models are not bound to specific sensory modalities, they can be considered as more abstract than perceptual images. Third, mental models differ from visual images with regard to their information content. On the one hand, a task-oriented selection takes place in mental model construction. The process of structure mapping only includes those parts of the graphic configuration that seem to be relevant for present or anticipated tasks. In addition, the mental model has to be structured according to the task requirements. On the other hand, the mental model is elaborated through information from world knowledge and, thus, also contains information that is not included in the picture.

5.7 Communication Context and Meta-comprehension of Pictures

Verbal communication is governed by complex and sophisticated hidden cooperation principles, which are described by Grice,[34] among others, and mentioned in Chapter 4. This complexity possibly reflects the very long history of verbal communication. Pictorial communication, on the contrary, is less sophisticated in terms of its cooperation principles. Observers can expect realistic explanatory pictures to show an object from a usual canonical perspective. They can also expect maps to be drawn in accordance with the general conventions for using colors, icons, or symbols for the depicted entities. Furthermore, they can expect graphs to be drawn according to a standard format.

Observers of graphs, however, cannot expect that they were designed according to a maxim of communicating clearly and efficiently. If graphs are considered as containers for delivering information, one frequently comes across content-empty variations of containers which do not have an informative function. This includes, for example, various kinds of attention-catching bells and whistles or content-empty 3D-effects. Against this background, Edward Tufte suggested that graph design should focus on the data rather than the container and that graphs should include as much data information as possible.[35] This means that the data container should be well filled, maximizing data density (information per square

[34] Grice (1967).   [35] Tufte (1983).

inch). He proposed a so-called data–ink ratio, which is defined as the relation between the amount of ink used to display data variation and the total amount of ink used. According to Tufte, the data–ink ratio should be as high as possible. However, other graph designers do not share the idea of maximizing the data–ink ratio. They do not agree that graphs, as information containers, should carry as much information as possible. Instead, they see graphs as useful devices for conveying limited and well-selected sets of information as efficiently as possible. These designers also reject content-empty design variations, bells and whistles, or content-empty 3D effects, but they do not try to maximize the data–ink ratio.

When the conversational maxims for verbal communication described by Grice are transferred to pictorial communication, the basic rule is: "Be truthful!" Accordingly, information should be displayed in a non-manipulative way. Simply speaking, producers of pictorial messages should not lie. Like text communication, real-world pictorial communication does not always follow this rule. Not only do observers of a pictorial message have their own goals, the producers of pictorial messages also have their own goals. Sometimes, it is tempting to generate messages so that the observers' comprehension is manipulated in favor of the producer's intentions. Graphs are manipulatory when they depict non-existing real effects or when they hide existing real effects. Edward Tufte proposed computing a "lie factor" as a reality check for graphs. This lie factor relates visual effects to real effects, assuming that a truthful message would lead to a factor close to 1.0. Visual effects that overstate (exaggerate) the real effects would lead to a factor higher than 1.0, whereas visual effects that understate the real effects would lead to a factor lower than 1.0. Fraudulent graphs manipulate the data container, for example, by putting some information in the foreground or other information in the background. They also manipulate scales (e.g., by silently changing the size of units) in order to create visual effects that do not correspond to the real data.

Manipulation is also possible by inviting the observer to read and interpret visual effects that do not represent what they seem to. An example was presented in Figure 5.19. In two different line graphs based on the same data, but with different scales, one can visually read two different messages: Either that more expenditures for students did not result in essentially better learning or that students showed improved learning despite nearly unchanged expenditures for education. In fact, none of these conclusions was justified. The observer was invited to compare two developments, although a basic prerequisite for making a comparison was not met: a common scale for the two developments.

The example demonstrates that maximizing the data–ink ratio is not to be recommended under all conditions. The graph designer's fault was to use different y-axes for the two graphs. This meant that two different line graphs were combined into one. Such a combination increases data density and the data–ink ratio. However, it suggests comparing two developments without any rational basis, because the two developments cannot be compared directly. The graph format is, therefore, highly misleading.

It is important for the recipient of a pictorial message to understand such design tricks to avoid falling victim to truth manipulations. Recipients of a pictorial message have good reasons for reflecting about the communication goals of the producer of a message. Recipients can reflect about why a particular picture was chosen instead of another picture, why a specific perspective on an object was taken instead of another perspective, and what the specific communication aims behind these choices are. Similar to text comprehension, the recipient of a pictorial message can create a mental representation of the overall communication between the producer of a pictorial message and himself or herself as the recipient. Once again, this can be referred to as "meta-comprehension": that is, comprehension of the pictorial communication. This meta-comprehension is likely to affect recipients' willingness to integrate pictorial messages into their overall comprehension of a subject matter.

5.8   Takeaways

Pictures are two-dimensional depictive representations which simulate their referent instead of describing it. They present information more compactly and allow faster access to specific information than text. Static pictures can serve functions such as envisioning, explanation, organization, spatial orientation, and argumentation. They can display both static and dynamic content, just as animations do. However, animations allow changes to be perceived directly, whereas static pictures require the changes to be inferred. By manipulating speed, animations can transpose excessively slow or fast movements into the range of human perceptual sensitivity, thus enabling the movements to be recognized. Within that range, a high speed of presentation emphasizes slow macro-events whereas a low speed of presentation emphasizes fast micro-events.

Comprehension of pictures starts with sub-semantic processing, which is pre-attentive, primarily data-driven (bottom-up), and independent of the observer's prior knowledge and goals. This processing triggers the creation of different kinds of visual representations: initial representation, viewer-centered representation, and object-centered representation. Sub-semantic processing leads to pre-attentive segregation of the perceived world into figures and grounds, whereby figures are created according to the Gestalt laws. Processing is also influenced by unconscious presuppositions which are hard-wired into our visual system.

Sub-semantic processing by itself would allow observers to see something without knowing what they were seeing. In order to recognize and categorize seen objects or events, observers have to engage in semantic perceptual processing. This processing is data-driven (bottom-up) and knowledge-driven (top-down). It is cognitively penetrable, attentive, and can be influenced by the observer's goals.

When an object is seen somewhere, one can distinguish between what-information and where-information. What-information is about the attributes of the object, while where-information is about the location of the object in space. What-information serves object recognition. It activates cognitive object schemata (so-called object-recognition units) stored in long-term memory. These schemata include knowledge about an object's perceptual attributes, usage, material, and conceptual category. Similar to objects, individuals can recognize movement patterns occurring over time by subsuming them under event schemata.

Object- and event-recognition units can be accessed by all of the mentioned visual representations: the initial representation, the viewer-centered representation, and the object-centered representation. Recognition takes place when a match is found between what an observer sees and what he or she knows. Because viewer-centered representations are associated with specific perspectives, the correspondence between what is seen and what is known can be established more easily when objects or events are presented from a familiar perspective. Object-recognition units do not include the name of objects. The objects' names are stored in a mental lexicon which is separated from object-recognition schemata. Despite their close connection, language and world knowledge are separated.

Recognition of objects during semantic perceptual processing makes conceptual object information available in working memory. However, this does not yet result in picture comprehension. In order to understand a picture, an observer needs to engage in conceptual picture processing. He or she has to recognize further relationships and construct complex conceptual structures about the pictorial content in working memory. Once again, this processing is data-driven (bottom-up) and knowledge-driven (top-down). It is also affected by the aims of the observer. Conceptual processing results in a propositional conceptual representation. There is no specific order and no pre-defined terminal point for conceptual picture processing. The main criteria for successful comprehension are support by perceptual processing, coherence of the conceptual representation, and consistency with prior knowledge.

Comprehension of maps is frequently constrained by the fact that only some features of a map have a representational function, while others do not. This means that conceptual processing needs representational meta-knowledge about the corresponding map. Comprehension of graphs requires graphic schemata which include general knowledge about the different representation formats, the conventions governing the use of visual attributes such as lines, forms, colors, and textures for representational purposes, and the detection of unjustified, misleading visualizations.

Based on perceptual and conceptual processing, picture comprehension eventually results in the construction of a mental model of the depicted subject matter. Mental model construction is data-driven and knowledge-driven. As in text processing, the mental models employed to process pictures are constructed based on a conceptual structure, namely a propositional representation. Contrary to text processing, the construction of mental models for comprehending pictures is directly guided by perceptual processing. The latter involves structure mapping between the picture and the mental model: Graphic entities are mapped onto mental entities, and spatial relations are mapped onto semantic relations within the mental model. Perceptual representations and mental models are different kinds of depictive representations.

Recipients of pictorial messages can reflect about the communication situation, the goals of the message producer, and the motivations behind selecting and editing the picture at hand. This comprehension of the communication situation is a kind of meta-comprehension.

CHAPTER 6

Integrative Comprehension of Texts and Pictures

Abstract

Text comprehension and picture comprehension can be synthesized into a common conceptual framework which differentiates between external and internal descriptive and depictive representations. Combining this framework with the human cognitive architecture including sensory registers, working memory, and long-term memory leads to an integrated model of text and picture comprehension. The model consists of a descriptive branch and a depictive branch of processing. It includes multiple sensory modalities. Due to a flexible combination of sensory modalities and representational formats, the model covers listening comprehension, reading comprehension, visual picture comprehension, and sound comprehension. The model considers text comprehension and picture comprehension to be different routes for constructing mental models and propositional representations with the help of prior knowledge. It allows us to explain the effects of coherence, text modality, split attention, text–picture contiguity, redundancy, sequencing, and the effects of different types of visualization.

After the analysis of the basic forms of representations – text comprehension and picture comprehension – we are now in a position to combine the various theoretical building blocks into a coherent model of integrative comprehension.[1] As a first step, we will consider a theoretical framework for distinguishing between different representations in text and picture comprehension. In a second step, this will be followed by a closer look at

---

[1] It should be noted that text–picture relations have also been studied in other disciplines such as linguistics and art (McCloud, 1993). The cognitive framework for multimodal interactions, for example, analyzes the interplay of different modalities – phonological structure (spoken language), visual structure (pictures and written text), and bodily structure (gesture) – in comprehending sequential visual narratives such as comics from a linguistic perspective (Cohn, 2016).

memory systems within the human cognitive architecture. In a third step, we will discuss a model of integrative comprehension of texts and pictures which incorporates the representational framework and the human cognitive architecture. Finally, we will examine research findings that provide empirical evidence for the validity of the model.

6.1   Theoretical Framework of Representations

In Chapter 3 we considered two basic forms of representations: descriptive and depictive representations. As a reminder, their main characteristics will be briefly mentioned again. Descriptive representations consist of symbols, which are signs that have no similarity to their referent. The written word *bird*, for example, has no similarity to a real bird. It is a symbol, and its meaning is based on a convention. In texts, we use nouns (such as *bird* and *breeding*) as symbols for objects and events. We use verbs and prepositions (such as *feed* and *on*) as symbols for relations, and we use adjectives (such as *small* and *migrant*) as symbols for attributes. The use of symbols per se is *not* constitutive for descriptive representations. Maps also include symbols, although they are not descriptions. What makes a representation a description is the use of symbols for relations. In natural language, verbs and prepositions are such relational symbols which make natural language a tool for creating descriptive representations.

Depictive representations consist of icons. Icons are signs that are associated with their referent because they share a structural commonality, usually in the form of similarity. A realistic picture such as Dürer's drawing of a rhinoceros (as shown in Figure 2.8) or a map (as shown in Figure 2.11) are graphical objects that have some similarity to the corresponding referent (i.e., the real animal or Old China). Graphs have a more abstract structural commonality with their referent. The meaning of the bar graph shown in Figure 3.10, for example, is based on an analogy. The height of the bars corresponds to the number of marsh harriers observed in a habitat during the corresponding month, and the sequence of the bars corresponds to the sequence of months during the year.

Descriptive representations and depictive representations have different uses for different purposes. Descriptive representations are more powerful in expressing abstract knowledge, while depictive representations have the advantage of being informationally complete in terms of a certain kind of information. The latter characteristic makes them especially useful for drawing inferences, because new information can be read off directly from the representation.

The distinction between descriptive and depictive representations applies not only to external representations, such as texts and pictures, but also to internal, mental representations. A text surface representation and a propositional representation are descriptive representations, as they use symbols including symbols for relations to describe the subject matter. A perceptual representation (visual image) and a mental model, on the contrary, are depictive representations, as they are assumed to have an inherent structure that corresponds to the structure of the subject matter.[2] A perceptual visual image is sensory-specific because it is linked to the visual modality,[3] whereas a mental model is not sensory-specific because it is able to integrate information from different sensory modalities. It is possible, for example, to construct a mental model of a spatial configuration based on visual, auditory, and haptic information. This implies that a mental model is more abstract than a visual image. Mental models and visual images can also differ in terms of their information content. On the one hand, irrelevant details of a picture, which are included in the visual image, may be ignored in the mental model. On the other hand, the mental model can contain additional information inferred from prior knowledge which is not included in the visual image. A mental model of the European continent based on a geographical map about bird migration, for example, might include snowfall in northern areas during winter, although no snow is indicated in the presented map.

Based on the distinction between descriptive and depictive representations, Schnotz and Bannert[4] proposed a theoretical framework for different representations in text and picture comprehension. The framework, which is shown in Figure 6.1, includes a branch of descriptive representations (left side) and a branch of depictive representations (right side) with correspondingly different modes of information processing. The descriptive branch contains the external text, the mental text surface representation, and the mental propositional representation of the subject matter. Processing information from this branch implies sub-semantic and semantic analysis of symbol structures. The depictive branch consists of the external picture, the perceptual representation (visual image) of the picture, and the mental model of the subject matter. Processing this information requires analog structure mapping between the visual image and mental model based on perceptional and thematic selection. Within the branch of descriptive representations and the branch of depictive representations, a distinction is made between external representations

[2] Johnson-Laird (1983).   [3] Kosslyn (1994b).   [4] Schnotz and Bannert (2003).

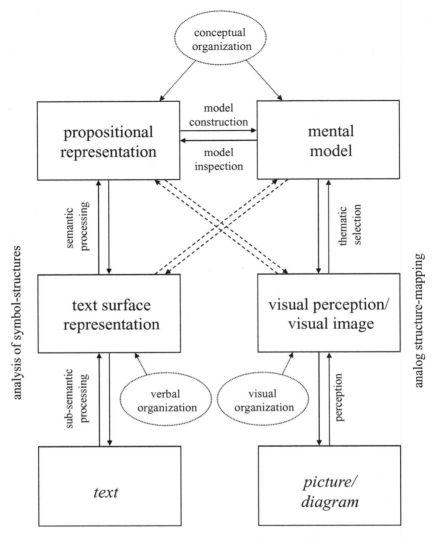

Figure 6.1   Theoretical framework for the distinction between different representations in text and picture comprehension proposed by Schnotz and Bannert (2003)

(text and picture) and internal, mental representations (text surface representations, propositional representations, visual images, mental models). Within internal representations, a distinction is made between surface structure representations (text surface representations and visual images) and semantic deep structure representations (propositional representations and mental models).[5]

6.2 Cognitive Architecture: Human Memory Systems

The representational framework described in Section 6.1 distinguishes between internal and external representations. However, it does not consider the constraints of the human memory system. As comprehension is a function of the cognitive system, integrative comprehension of texts and pictures is necessarily embedded in the human cognitive architecture and constrained by its memory system. I already outlined the characteristics of the human memory system in Chapter 1 and will further elaborate on them in the following.[6]

Sensory Registers: Information enters the cognitive system from the outside world through sensory organs, which convey information to working memory through sensory channels. It should be noted that there is no inherent relationship between the sensory modalities and the representational formats. For example, visual text is usually written language which is read with the eyes, but it can also be read with the fingers (e.g., in the case of blind people reading Braille). Similarly, pictures are usually seen with the eyes, but they can sometimes also be perceived by touch (e.g., maps for blind people). Spoken text is usually perceived by the ear, but deaf people can also read lips and touch the larynx while it is vibrating. Non-verbal sound patterns, such as the call of a bird, are also perceived by the ear. Although multiple sensory modalities can be involved in text and picture comprehension, for reasons of clarity and comprehensibility, we will consider only the visual and auditory modalities. Extensions to further modalities, such as touch, are possible if needed.

Visual information that meets the eye is stored very briefly (under one second) in a visual register. If attention is directed to information in the visual register, the information is transmitted to visual working memory. Auditory information that meets the ear is stored briefly (under three seconds) in an auditory register. If attention is directed to information in the auditory register, the information is transmitted to auditory working memory.

---

[5] The framework corresponds partially to the dual-coding concept of Paivio (1986), which assumes that there is both a verbal system and an image system in the human mind which have different forms of mental codes. However, contrary to the traditional dual-coding theory, the framework assumes that multiple representations are formed in text comprehension and picture comprehension.
[6] Atkinson and Shiffrin (1971).

Working Memory: Written or spoken text and visual or auditory pictures[7] are further processed in working memory, which has a highly limited capacity for storing and processing information, resulting in multiple mental representations. According to Baddeley,[8] working memory consists of a central executive and different subsystems for storing information. Two of these subsystems have received much attention in research: auditory working memory and visual working memory.

Auditory working memory is conceived as a phonological–articulatory loop. This subsystem specializes in verbal material presented in the auditory modality, but it can also deal with nonverbal sound. It has limited capacity, corresponding to what can be articulated within two seconds on average. Surprisingly, people with a highly reduced phonological–articulatory loop are still capable of normal language comprehension. Spoken text activates phonological lexical patterns, whereas non-verbal sounds activate acoustic patterns which lead to acoustic perceptual representations in auditory working memory.

Visual working memory is conceived as a visuo-spatial sketchpad. This subsystem specializes in spatial information presented in the visual modality. It has a limited capacity of about five units on average. Written text activates graphemic lexical patterns, whereas visual pictures activate visuo-spatial patterns, leading to visual perceptual representations in visual working memory. According to Marr's computational theory of seeing, this entails the creation of a viewer-centered representation, which includes a spatial arrangement of visible surfaces from the viewer's position as well as an object-centered representation which is independent of the viewer's position.

In text and picture comprehension, working memory processes both perceptual information and higher-order cognitive information, resulting in mental representations. Accordingly, one can assume that there is a subsystem for conceptual representations which is made up of propositions. These propositions result from descriptive processing of phonological or graphemic lexical patterns, which includes parsing of incoming words, access to the mental lexicon, and inferences from world knowledge. Due to capacity reasons, this subsystem can keep only a limited number of propositions in working memory simultaneously.[9]

Finally, one can assume a subsystem for constructing mental models in working memory. Mental model construction is strongly influenced by the

---

[7] We designate replicas of an original sound as "auditory pictures" in this context.
[8] Baddeley (1986).   [9] Kintsch and van Dijk (1978).

recognition of real or depicted objects and the activation of associated prior knowledge. The corresponding object schemata, which include what an object looks like, how it sounds, how it feels, how it can be used, what it is made of, and so forth, correspond to the object-recognition units[10] previously mentioned in Chapter 5. If the object's current perception matches an object-recognition unit stored in long-term memory, the object is recognized. Usually, both the viewer-centered and the object-centered visual representation have access to object-recognition units. In the case of viewer-centered representations, objects can be recognized faster and more easily when they are presented from a typical perspective than when they are presented from an unusual perspective.

Mental model construction seems to be based more on spatial processing than on visual processing. Information about objects' perceptual attributes and information about their location in space are stored at different neuronal sites. As mentioned in Chapter 5, some brain-injured patients can visually recognize objects immediately, but do not know where these objects are located. Other patients cannot recognize an object in a specific place in their visual field but can specify this place with high precision. Consistent with these findings, research indicates that visual imagery and spatial reasoning are based on different cognitive subsystems.[11] This suggests a distinction between visual working memory (or sketchpad) for visual images and spatial working memory for mental model construction. Accordingly, mental models result from depictive processing of visuospatial images or sound patterns through structure mapping.

Long-Term Memory: Text and picture comprehension is based not only on external sources of information (the text and the picture), but also on prior knowledge, as an internal source of information stored in long-term memory. Prior knowledge includes lexical knowledge as well as perceptual and cognitive world knowledge. Lexical knowledge is assumed to be stored in the mental lexicon, which encompasses the mental phonological lexicon and the mental graphemic lexicon. The two lexicons include knowledge about auditory and visual word forms. The phonological lexicon (also called the auditory lexicon) contains phonological lexical patterns, which represent knowledge about the sound of spoken words required for spoken word recognition. Listening to a text implies the activation of such phonological lexical patterns in working memory.

---

[10] Ellis and Young (1996).   [11] Knauff and Johnson-Laird (2002).

Individuals who suffer from word deafness (due to brain injuries) have a deficient phonological lexicon; they can hear sounds but cannot separate and identify words when listening to spoken language. Individuals who suffer from word meaning deafness can repeat spoken words without understanding them, although they can understand written words. These individuals possess a phonological lexicon, but this is unconnected to semantic (long-term) memory. The graphemic lexicon (also called the visual or orthographic lexicon) contains graphemic lexical patterns, which represent knowledge about the visual appearance of written words which is required for written word recognition. Reading a text implies the activation of such graphemic lexical patterns in working memory. Individuals who suffer from pure alexia (due to illiteracy or brain injuries) have a deficient graphemic lexicon; they can understand spoken words but cannot understand written words, although their vision is intact.[12]

Perceptual world knowledge stored in the form of object schemata refers to the appearance of objects. This knowledge is needed for the visual perception or imagination of objects, that is, for the creation of corresponding visuospatial patterns and for mental model construction in working memory.[13] The corresponding schemata (object-recognition units) help to match what one sees with what one knows. These units do not include the object's name but are usually connected to the mental lexicon. Thus, it is possible to recognize an object without remembering its name.

Conceptual world knowledge refers to relations between the entities of a domain – for example, how the breeding of birds is related to variations in meteorological conditions. It also includes knowledge about category membership, such as the relations of the marsh harrier to the family of migratory birds. Conceptual world knowledge is needed both for constructing a propositional representation and for constructing a mental model in working memory.

Prior knowledge can, to some extent, compensate for a lack of external information, for lower working memory capacity, and for deficits of the propositional representation. Thus, there seems to be a trade-off between the use of external and internal information sources. Accordingly, individuals analyze pictures more intensively if the content is difficult and their prior knowledge is low.

---

[12] Ellis and Young (1996).   [13] Rosch and Lloyd (1978); Johnson-Laird (1983); Kosslyn (1994b).

6.3   Integrated Comprehension

The idea of a representational framework differentiating between descriptive and depictive representations and the idea of a cognitive architecture including multiple memory systems are incorporated into the Integrated Model of Text and Picture Comprehension (ITPC model).[14] The model integrates Atkinson and Shiffrin's concepts of multiple memory systems which include working memory. It further integrates some aspects of Paivio's dual-coding theory, Marr's theory of computational vision, and the idea of multiple forms of mental representations in text comprehension and picture comprehension. In addition, it takes neuropsychological models of object recognition, word recognition, and reading into account. The model, which is schematically shown in Figure 6.2, aims at representing the conjoint comprehension of spoken text, written text, visual pictures, and auditory pictures (sound).[15] It is based on the following assumptions:

- Text and picture comprehension take place in a cognitive architecture which includes modality-specific sensory registers as information input systems, working memory with a limited capacity, and long-term memory.
- Verbal information (i.e., information from spoken or written texts) and pictorial information (i.e., information from visual pictures or from nonverbal sound[16]) are transmitted to working memory through visual channels and auditory channels. The channels have limited capacity to process and transmit information.
- Further semantic processing takes place in two different subsystems in working memory: in a descriptive subsystem and a depictive subsystem. Text (spoken or written) is first processed in the descriptive

---

[14] Schnotz (2014, 2022). The ITPC model is usually referred to as the "Integrated Model of Text and Picture Comprehension." However, it could also be referred to as the "Model of Integrative Text and Picture Comprehension." Both designations are semantically correct.

[15] The ITPC model has partial overlaps with the CTML (Cognitive Theory of Multimedia Learning) proposed by Mayer (2005, 2009, 2014). Both models are influenced by Paivio's Dual-Coding Theory and are based on the hypothesis that working memory has limited capacity. However, the CTML connects sensory modalities directly to representational principles by assuming an auditory–verbal channel and a visual–pictorial channel rather than separating the modality and the representation aspect. Furthermore, the CTML does not consider the difference between descriptive and depictive representations. It is based on the hypothesis that two mental models are created in text–picture comprehension, instead of one.

[16] The concept of pictorial information refers in this context not only to visual pictures, but also to replicas of sound as acoustic or auditory pictures.

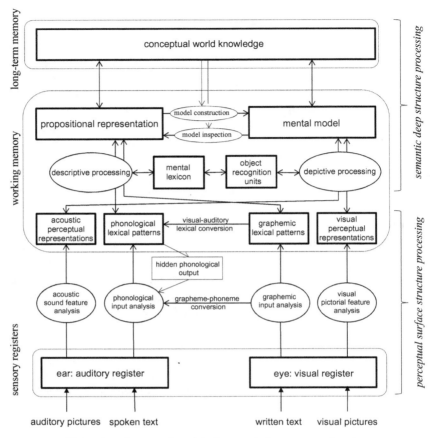

Figure 6.2   Integrated model of text and picture comprehension

subsystem through parsing and access to the mental lexicon. This is followed by processing in the depictive subsystem, leading to mental model construction. Visual pictures and auditory pictures (sounds) are first processed in the depictive subsystem until object recognition and structure mapping, followed by processing in the descriptive subsystem via model inspection, which results in propositional representations.

- Mental model construction in text comprehension is guided indirectly by the text-based propositional representation. Mental model construction in picture comprehension is guided not only indirectly by the picture-based propositional representation, but also more directly by the picture through structure mapping. Picture-based mental model construction therefore receives more direct guidance than text-based mental model construction.

- The ITPC model suggests a distinction between perceptual surface structure processing and semantic deep structure processing. Perceptual surface structure processing refers to the information transfer from the surface structure of texts, visual pictures, and sound to working memory. It is characterized by (verbal) phonological or graphemic analyses and (nonverbal) visual or acoustic feature analyses, leading to corresponding input patterns in auditory or visual working memory. Semantic deep structure processing refers to cognitive processing within working memory which results in propositional representations and mental models. It also involves information exchange between long-term and working memory.

- Text comprehension and picture comprehension are active processes of coherence formation. They require an active, flexible, and coordinated use of cognitive processes, including the selection of information, organization of information, activation of prior knowledge, and active coherence formation by integrating information from different sources. Individuals engage in building coherent knowledge structures from external information sources (texts and pictures) and internal information sources (prior knowledge).

- To comprehend written or spoken texts, the individual selects relevant verbal information from words, sentences, and paragraphs as external sources of information. He or she organizes the information, activates related prior knowledge as an internal source of information, and constructs both a coherent propositional representation and a coherent mental model. To comprehend visual pictures, the individual selects relevant pictorial information from a drawing, map, or graph as an external source of information, organizes the information, activates related prior knowledge as a further source of information, and constructs a coherent mental model complemented by a propositional representation. To comprehend auditory pictures (sound), the individual selects relevant acoustic information, organizes the information, activates related prior knowledge as an internal source of information, and constructs a coherent mental model complemented by a propositional representation.

Listening Comprehension: If a spoken text is understood, auditory verbal information enters the auditory register through the ear and then becomes the object of phonological input analysis, which identifies phonemes within the acoustic input, activating phonological lexical patterns. Further descriptive processing (including access to the mental lexicon, parsing of word sequences, and further semantic analysis) leads to a propositional representation, which finally triggers the construction or elaboration of a mental model. In the example of the text about bird migration, the phonological analysis of the spoken word "bird" activates (via the mental lexicon) the corresponding phonological pattern in auditory working memory. Further processing by the descriptive subsystem activates the concept BIRD, which is then included in the propositional representation. This representation finally triggers the construction of a mental model of bird migration.

Reading Comprehension: If a written text is understood, visually presented verbal information enters the visual register through the eye and is then subjected to graphemic input analysis, which identifies graphemes within the visual input. For a skilled reader, this analysis activates graphemic lexical patterns, which are further processed in the descriptive subsystem (including access to the mental lexicon, parsing, and semantic analysis). This processing results in the formation of a propositional representation, which in turn triggers the construction or elaboration of a mental model. In the text about bird migration, for example, graphemic analysis of the written word "bird" activates the corresponding graphemic lexical pattern in visual working memory. Access to the mental lexicon activates the concept BIRD, which is included in the propositional representation. This representation finally triggers the construction of a mental model of bird migration.

Beginners of reading initially have a poor graphemic mental lexicon which does not allow them to recognize written words as whole units. In order to read, they have to engage in tedious phonological recoding of the visual input by applying grapheme–phoneme conversion rules. This phonological recoding eventually allows them to understand what they have read when they hear the written words spoken out loud by themselves. The grapheme–phoneme conversion rules, which are neither lexical nor semantic, convert letter strings into phoneme strings.[17] When readers possess a comprehensive graphemic lexicon, on the contrary, texts can be understood via the activation of graphemic lexical patterns without the inclusion of any acoustic patterns. Nevertheless, even skilled readers engage in some graphemic–phonemic lexical conversion, operating at the whole-word (lexical) level instead of at the (sublexical) grapheme–phoneme level.

---

[17] Coltheart et al. (2001).

Lexical conversion per se is non-semantic because words can be recognized even when the meaning of the word is unknown.

When familiar written words are recognized, the activated graphemic lexical patterns usually activate phonological lexical output patterns which allow the reader to pronounce these words. Pronunciation does not imply that words are read aloud. It can also take the form of inner speech, as a hidden phonological output heard by the reader through his or her inner ear. Inner pronunciation feeds into the phonological input analysis and activates phonological lexical input patterns, which are further processed through the descriptive subsystem. As a result, read words can be processed via both graphemic and phonological lexical patterns. Lexical conversion from graphemic to phonological patterns seems to be especially important for triggering parsing procedures in syntactic analyses. Anomalies in the syntax of sentences are more easily detected when inner speech is possible than when it is suppressed. There is a direct route in reading from graphemic lexical patterns to further semantic analysis in the descriptive subsystem, but this route does not trigger syntactic analysis. Syntactic processes "appear to operate upon a speech-based code, so that written sentences which are to undergo syntactic analysis must first be converted into spoken form and then recycled back to auditory comprehension processes."[18] Once again, this syntactic analysis process can be seen against the backdrop of the extremely long history of oral language.

Visual Picture Comprehension: If a visual picture is understood, visual pictorial information enters the visual register through the eye and is then subjected to visual feature analysis, which leads to viewer-centered perceptual representations of the depicted content in working memory. Further processing by activating object-recognition units can add to perceptual representations which are independent of the viewer's position. Higher-order depictive processing includes mapping selected perceptual structures into the construction or elaboration of a corresponding mental model. This model can then be used by model inspection processes to read new information which is then added to the propositional representation in working memory. For example, when a map about bird migration in Europe is understood, a visual feature analysis of the visual patterns leads to a perceptual representation of the map in visual working memory. If the individual has sufficient knowledge about geography, the representation will also include the shapes of countries. Selected information is then further processed through structure mapping, which results in the

---

[18] Ellis and Young (1996, p. 221).

construction or elaboration of a mental model of bird migration in Europe. The individual can then read further information from the model, such as the fact that migrant birds fly from northern Europe to the Mediterranean area in the fall.

Sound Comprehension: If a sound (i.e., auditory picture) is understood, auditory information enters the auditory register through the ear and becomes the object of acoustic sound feature analysis, which results in acoustic perceptual representations in working memory. Further depictive processing through the activation of object-recognition units and the mapping of selected perceptual structures leads to the construction or elaboration of a corresponding mental model. This model can then be used by model inspection processes to read new information which is added to the propositional representation. For example, if the call of a marsh harrier (as a bird of prey) and the call of a small bird (as its possible prey) are heard, acoustic feature analysis leads to an acoustic perceptual representation in working memory. If an individual has sufficient knowledge about different birds, depictive processing of selected information through structure mapping leads to the construction or elaboration of the mental model of a predator–prey scenario. The individual can then read further information from the mental model, such as the fact that a small bird is in danger of falling prey to a marsh harrier.

In order to demonstrate its validity, the ITPC model should not only be able to predict under which conditions combinations of text and pictures are beneficial for comprehension. The model should also be able to predict under which conditions the combination of text and pictures has detrimental effects. In Section 6.4, the ITPC model is analyzed in terms of its ability to successfully predict positive and negative effects of integrative processing of texts and pictures instead of processing text alone or pictures alone.

6.4   Empirical Evidence: Positive Effects of Integrative Comprehension

Numerous studies have found that students learn better from words combined with pictures than from words alone.[19] Richard Mayer called this the "multimedia effect."[20] However, the effect is bound to specific conditions which are described here.

---

[19] Levie and Lentz (1982); Levin et al. (1987); Carney and Levin (2002).
[20] Levin and Mayer (1993); Mayer (1997).

Reading Skills and Prior Knowledge: The ITPC model considers text comprehension and picture comprehension to be different routes for constructing mental models and propositional representations with the help of prior knowledge as a third source of information. If one route does not work well or if one source provides little information, the other sources and routes become more important. When learners are poor readers, picture comprehension is more important. Thus, the ITPC model predicts that poor readers profit more from illustrations in written texts than good readers. This prediction is supported by various empirical findings.[21]

As text comprehension and picture comprehension are considered to be different routes for constructing mental representations, the ITPC model also implies that one route can be used more extensively at the expense of the other route. Pictures can be used more extensively at the expense of a text, and a text can be used more extensively at the expense of pictures. The model, therefore, predicts that if a picture is added to a text and if the mental effort invested by the learner is the same, the information provided by the text may become less important due to the additional information provided by the picture. The text is possibly processed less deeply, resulting in lower memory for text information than if the text had been processed without pictures. This prediction has been confirmed by various studies.[22]

When learners have low prior knowledge, constructing a mental model based only on written text can be excessively difficult. Adding a picture as another source of information can enhance comprehension, because it offers an additional route for mental model construction. Learners with high prior knowledge, on the contrary, are more able to construct a mental model without pictorial support. The integrated model, therefore, predicts that learners with low prior knowledge profit more from pictures in texts than learners with high prior knowledge. This corresponds to the results of various studies that found that pictures in texts are more beneficial for students with low prior knowledge than for those with high prior knowledge.[23]

Coherence and Contiguity: Students learn better from words and pictures than from words alone if the words and pictures are semantically related to each other (the coherence condition) and if they are presented closely together in space or in time (the contiguity condition). Text and pictures are assumed to contribute to the construction of a joint mental

---

[21] Cooney and Swanson (1987); Mastropieri and Scruggs (1989); Carney and Levin (2002).
[22] Mayer and Gallini (1990); Schnotz and Bannert (1999).   [23] Mayer (2009, 2011).

model only if they are semantically related and if the information in the text and the information in the picture are simultaneously available in working memory. Because information decays quickly within working memory, corresponding words and pictures should be presented as near to each other as possible. The integrated visual displays of verbal and pictorial information known as "infographics," which are frequently used to summarize information, employ this principle to the utmost.

The display of multimedia messages can (and frequently does) contain elements with little (if any) informational value. Such extraneous elements can be, for example, inappropriate headlines, needless pictorial elements, or unnecessary sound and music which attract the recipients' attention and distract concentration from the actual message. Computer-based multimedia messages are especially prone to including animated "fun elements" which serve as "eye-catchers" and claim to make multimedia communication "more fun." Such extraneous elements are called "seductive details."[24] They were shown to usually impair the cognitive processing of multimedia messages.[25] Multimedia designers should, therefore, resist the temptation to add such irrelevant bells and whistles into multimedia environments.

Modality: If a picture is combined with a written text, all information has to enter working memory through the visual modality. Different tasks loaded on the same sensory channel result necessarily in a split of attention. As the eye has to switch between pictures and words, only one kind of information can be processed at the same time. This split of visual attention implies that search processes switch from the picture to the text, and vice versa, and it affects the simultaneous availability of verbal and pictorial information in working memory.[26] When pictures and related written words are presented closely to each other (spatial contiguity), visual search processes are reduced. Spatial contiguity is a way of minimizing the loss of information caused by split attention and of allowing pictorial and verbal information to be approximately simultaneously available in working memory. In other words, spatial contiguity is a means of maximizing temporal contiguity in working memory under the condition where a written text is accompanied by pictures. Fully simultaneous availability can be ensured only when a picture is combined with auditory text, because pictorial and verbal information can then be processed at the same time (temporal contiguity) and be kept simultaneously in working memory. In this case, no split attention is required. Learners can devote their

---

[24] Harp and Mayer (1998).   [25] Schraw and Lehman (2001); Sanchez and Wiley (2006).
[26] Ayres and Sweller (2022).

full visual attention to the picture and their full auditory attention to the text. This has led to the assumption of a modality effect.[27]

According to the modality effect, students learn better from multimedia instructional messages when a text is spoken rather than written. Of course, it only makes sense to speak about the modality having an effect when individuals are literate. All humans grow into the oral language of their culture without effort, whereas considerable educational effort is required for them to acquire command of the written language. For this reason, an illiterate person would understand an auditory text accompanied by pictures but be unable to read the corresponding written text. This would result in a strong (and absolutely trivial) "modality effect."

The modality effect is a derivative of the multimedia effect insofar as it amplifies the latter. The rationale behind the modality effect is to take full advantage of text–picture combinations (i.e., of the multimedia effect) by maximizing the contiguity of verbal and pictorial information and by minimizing any obstacles to the simultaneous availability of verbal and pictorial information in working memory. The key to minimizing the obstacles and to maximizing contiguity is combining the auditory presentation of text and visual presentation of pictures. Because the modality effect acts as an amplifier of the multimedia effect, a modality effect is to be expected only if there is also a multimedia effect. If there is no multimedia effect, no modality effect is to be expected.

Currently, there is no straightforward answer to the question as to where exactly the modality effect comes from. The most popular explanation is that it is achieved by avoiding split attention, as already mentioned.[28] Split attention is a fundamental problem when written text is combined with animation. As soon as the learner reads some text, he or she is at risk of missing important pictorial information, a risk that can be avoided by using spoken text. Besides split attention, Moreno and Mayer[29] argue for an additional explanation of the modality effect. They presented text and pictures to learners consecutively and, thus, avoided split attention. Nevertheless, spoken text with pictures resulted in better learning than written text with pictures. The authors argue that parts of the modality effect result from the amount of working memory

---

[27] Castro-Alonso and Sweller (2022).
[28] Mousavi et al. (1995); Mayer and Moreno (1998); Leahy et al. (2003).
[29] Mayer and Moreno (1998); Moreno and Mayer (1999).

capacity required. Text comprehension and picture comprehension are enhanced if both visual and auditory working memory are involved, even if the two systems receive input in a consecutive manner. Although this explanation seems to be plausible, the ITPC model does not support this assumption because both the comprehension of spoken text and the comprehension of written text involve auditory working memory. Research findings suggest that even experienced readers engage in graphemic–phonemic lexical conversion and recode at least parts of visual information into auditory information.[30] Verbal information – either spoken or written – might generally be processed via the phonological loop rather than via the visuospatial sketchpad. Rummer and his colleagues[31] suggest that auditory recency explains the modality effect when text material consists of single sentences presented alternately with pictures. They argue that a sentence can be better maintained in working memory after it has been heard than after it has been read due to the longer duration of acoustic information in the auditory register than in the visual register.

It seems that the modality effect does not result from a unitary set of causal relationships. Instead, findings suggest that heterogeneous factors lead to similar outcomes due to rather different processing mechanisms. The ITPC model is in line with the split-attention explanation and the auditory–recency explanation of a modality effect, whereas it does not agree with an explanation based on increased working memory capacity. The ITPC model can also predict a reverse modality effect. Under specific conditions, written text with pictures can be better for learning than spoken text with pictures, because written text provides the individual with more control over cognitive processing. Readers can pause or slow down their reading or re-read difficult passages. In this way, they can adapt their perceptual processing to the needs of their cognitive processing. Thus, if a text is difficult to understand and if the accompanying picture is neither animated nor too complex and if learning time is not severely limited, the ITPC model predicts a reverse modality effect. That is, in this case, learning is better with pictures accompanied by written text than by spoken text. This is in line with recent research indicating that the modality effect occurs only under specific conditions.[32]

---

[30] Rieben and Perfetti (1991).   [31] Rummer et al. (2010).
[32] Leahy et al. (2003); Gyselinck et al. (2008); Stiller et al. (2009); Schnotz (2011); Schüler et al. (2011).

6.5 Empirical Evidence: Negative Effects of Integrative Comprehension

Text–Picture Redundancy: Contrary to the dual-coding theory, which assumes that adding pictures to text always leads to better learning, because two codes in memory are better than one, the ITPC model predicts that the combination of text and pictures can also have detrimental effects. This is because learners with high prior knowledge frequently do not need both text and pictures to construct a mental model. Under this condition, adding a picture to written text provides unneeded, redundant information.[33] Although one of the two information sources is not needed, the eye wanders between the two sources, splitting attention between them. Thus, the learner invests mental effort in processing redundant information and loses time, without a benefit for learning. This negative effect has been called the "redundancy effect." It implies that a combination of text and pictures, which has a positive effect on mental model construction when learners have low prior knowledge, may have a negative effect on learning when prior knowledge is high. Experts possibly perform better with only one information source (i.e., text or pictures) instead of two (i.e., text and pictures). This is supported by findings reported by Kalyuga, Chandler, and Sweller, who named it the expertise reversal effect.[34]

Text–Text Redundancy across Modalities: Multimedia designers frequently try to adapt to the needs of individual learners, who are assumed to prefer either spoken text or written text. They, therefore, present pictures simultaneously with both written text and spoken text. Learners are supposed to choose their preferred sensory modality; those who prefer to listen can focus on the spoken text, and those who prefer to read can focus on the written text. The ITPC model predicts that individuals do not learn better from pictures accompanied by both spoken and written text, but that they learn better from pictures combined with either only spoken or only written text. There are two reasons for this prediction. The first reason is that even if the same text is presented in an auditory manner, it is difficult for learners to ignore a simultaneously presented written text. Thus, the presentation of a picture combined with a written text will result in split visual attention. The second reason is a problem of synchronization between listening and reading. Skilled readers are often able to read a text

---

[33] Note that the word "redundant" is used in this context not in terms of semantic equivalence, but only in the sense of "unneeded extra information."

[34] Kalyuga et al. (2000).

faster than the auditory text is spoken. When they create inner speech (based on graphemic–phonemic lexical conversion) which they can hear with their inner ear, interference between external listening and reading (i.e., internal listening) is likely to occur. Various studies by Mayer and his co-workers have demonstrated that individuals who learn from pictures accompanied by spoken *and* written text, whereby the written text duplicates the spoken text, perform poorly compared to individuals who learn from pictures and only spoken text.[35] However, when pictures are presented with just two or three written key words from the text while the text is spoken, this "focused redundancy" is not harmful, but can even result in improved retention of the verbal material.[36]

Sequencing: If for any reason a picture has to be presented either before or after a text, research indicates that picture–text is better than text–picture.[37] The ITPC model explains this sequencing effect by the inherent ambiguity of text. A text never describes the subject matter in enough detail to fit just one picture or one mental model. Instead, it allows some degrees of freedom for pictures and for mental model construction. If a mental model is constructed only from a text, the model will therefore most likely differ from a picture presented to illustrate the subject matter, even if it fully corresponds to its verbal description. Thus, if the picture is presented after the text, the picture will most likely interfere with the previously constructed text-based mental model. Such interference is avoided when the picture is presented before the text even if the learner looks only briefly at the picture to benefit from its mental model scaffolding function. Even presenting a picture less than two seconds can have a scaffolding effect on mental model construction.[38] This might be due to the more direct access of pictures to mental models through depictive processing, whereas text comprehension has to make a detour through the descriptive subsystem.

Structure Mapping: The same subject matter can often be visualized in different ways. Contrary to the dual-coding theory, which assumes that conjoint verbal and pictorial coding is generally better for learning than single coding, the ITPC model considers the form of visualization to be an important predictor of a multimedia effect. Pictures are beneficial for learning only if task-appropriate forms of visualization are used, whereas they are harmful if task-inappropriate forms of visualization are used. This prediction derives from the assumption that pictures are processed in the

---

[35] Mayer (2009); Fiorella and Mayer (2022); Kalyuga and Sweller (2022).
[36] Mayer and Johnson (2008).   [37] Kulhavy et al. (1994).   [38] Eitel et al. (2013).

depictive subsystem through structure mapping which implies that the form of visualization is mapped onto the structure of the mental model. Accordingly, the ITPC model predicts that the efficiency of a mental model for a specific task corresponds to the picture's efficiency for this task. Various studies required participants to learn from texts with different kinds of pictures which were informationally equivalent but employed different forms of visualization. It was found that pictures enhanced comprehension only if the learning content was visualized in a way which emphasized the task-relevant content structure. If the visualization did not address the task-relevant structure, the pictures interfered with the construction of a task-appropriate mental model.[39]

Evidence from Neuropsychological Disorders: The assumptions of the ITPC model about the relation between visual perception, language, and object recognition can also be backed by analyzing processing disorders due to brain injuries, as described in Chapter 5. Patients with visual agnosia, who cannot recognize an object or its picture when they see it, show an impaired connection between object knowledge and vision. However, the knowledge still has intact connections to other sensory modalities when the patients are able to easily identify the object via sound. Other patients have intact visual perception and intact knowledge about objects but cannot relate what they see to what they know about the object's visual appearance. They can copy drawings but cannot reproduce them from memory and they cannot recognize objects from seeing their pictures. However, when they are told the object's name, they can draw the object quite well. Thus, the connection between the mental lexicon and the object-recognition units is still intact, but the connection between the intact object-recognition units and the intact visual perception is blocked. Patients with an optic aphasia show intact perception and intact knowledge about objects, but this knowledge is disconnected from language. Their visual perception can activate object-recognition units, as demonstrated by the pantomimic use of objects, but the patients cannot name the objects. The reverse also applies: When the object's name is presented, the patient has difficulties in drawing it.[40]

Cognitive Economy: The ITPC model finally provides a framework for considerations of cognitive economy related to the comprehension of multiple external representations, especially texts and pictures, and to learning from such representations. Multiple external representations support comprehension because they guide and constrain mental model

---

[39] Schnotz and Bannert (2003); Schnotz and Kürschner (2008).   [40] Ellis and Young (1996).

construction. However, understanding each representation also incurs cognitive costs. In the case of understanding multiple texts and pictures, the benefits and the costs of processing an information source depend on the ease or difficulty of using the corresponding sensory and representational channels. When more and more representations about one topic are processed, it is possible that the additional benefit for comprehension is not worth the additional cognitive costs that are incurred. If the benefits from processing an additional information source are lower than the required costs, a learner will follow the principle of cognitive economy and not engage in further cognitive processing. Instead, he or she will consider only some representations and ignore the rest. This could explain why individuals frequently ignore some information sources in self-directed learning. This finding has been reported repeatedly in research on learning from multiple representations. For media designers, the message could be: "Less can be more!"

6.6   Takeaways

Comprehension is a function of the cognitive system and should, therefore, be considered as embedded in the human cognitive architecture. Integrative text and picture comprehension means the conjoint construction of mental representations of a subject matter based on texts and pictures, as external sources of information, and on prior knowledge, as an internal source of information. This construction takes place in working memory, which has a limited capacity and receives its input from modality-specific sensory registers and from long-term memory.

The Integrated Model of Text and Picture Comprehension (ITPC model) presented in this chapter combines concepts from research on text processing and concepts from research on picture processing with concepts from memory research. It further includes concepts from semiotics and findings in neurology. The core of the ITPC model is a theoretical framework of representations. The framework makes a fundamental distinction between descriptive representations and depictive representations, which applies to external and internal (mental) representations. Descriptive representations are external texts, mental text surface representations, and propositional representations. Depictive representations are external pictures, perceptual visual images, and mental models. Text surface representations and visual images are mental surface structure representations, while propositional representations and mental models are semantic deep structure representations. Both visual images and mental models are depictive representations. However, visual images are sensory-specific, while mental models are not. Both types of representation can differ in terms of content details. Descriptions and depictions have different uses for different purposes. Descriptive representations are more powerful in expressing abstract knowledge, whereas depictive representations have the advantage of being informationally complete with regard to certain kinds of information, which makes them useful for drawing inferences.

The ITPC model includes sensory registers, long-term memory, and working memory. Sensory registers convey information from sensory organs, such as the eye or the ear, through sensory-specific channels to working memory. Verbal and pictorial information is transmitted to working memory through visual channels and auditory channels. For pragmatic reasons, the ITPC model considers only the visual and auditory channels – the two most important sensory modalities in multimedia comprehension. Further modalities such as touch can be added when needed. The different combinations of representational format and sensory modality allow a distinction between listening comprehension, reading comprehension, visual picture comprehension, and sound comprehension.

The individual's world knowledge is stored in long-term memory. It includes lexical knowledge as well as perceptual and cognitive world knowledge. Lexical knowledge is stored in the mental lexicon. The latter exists in the form of a phonological lexicon and a graphemic lexicon which include knowledge about auditory and visual word forms. The mental lexicon is connected to, but not included in perceptual and conceptual world knowledge. Perceptual world knowledge, which is stored in the form of object schemata, refers to the appearance of objects. Conceptual world knowledge refers to the conceptual relations within a content domain.

Information from sensory registers and from long-term memory is further processed in working memory, which has a limited capacity, resulting in multiple mental representations. The ITPC model suggests that a distinction should be made between perceptual surface structure processing and semantic deep structure processing. Auditory working memory specializes in spoken text, which activates phonological lexical patterns, and in acoustic non-verbal sound patterns as auditory perceptual surface structures. Visual working memory specializes in written text, which activates graphemic patterns, and visual pictures which activate visuo-spatial patterns as visual perceptual surface structures.

Semantic processing in working memory takes place in two different subsystems: the descriptive and depictive subsystems. The descriptive subsystem performs conceptual processing which leads to propositional mental representations. The depictive subsystem performs processing through structure mapping, which leads to the construction of an analog mental model. Verbal information is first processed in the descriptive subsystem and then processed in the depictive subsystem, which leads via propositional representations to the construction of a mental model. Pictorial information and sound information are first processed in the depictive subsystem until object recognition and structure mapping onto a mental model are complete. This is followed by processing in the descriptive subsystem which again results in a propositional representation. In text comprehension, mental model construction is guided by a text-based propositional representation. In picture comprehension, mental model construction is guided not only by a picture-based propositional representation, but also by the picture's perceptual representation through analog structure mapping. Thus, picture-based mental model construction receives more guidance than text-based mental model construction.

The ITPC model considers the integrated comprehension of texts and pictures as a process of active sensemaking. It has been shown to successfully predict various effects of integrated processing as well as their moderation by processing conditions such as prior knowledge, coherence, contiguity, split attention, sensory modality, redundancy, sequencing, and visualization formats.

CHAPTER 7

Quasi-symbiotic Relations between Text and Picture Comprehension

Abstract

Text and pictures serve different purposes in multimedia comprehension. Conceptual processing of texts and pictures results in propositions, whereby text-based propositions and picture-based propositions specialize in different kinds of information. These propositions are merged into an overarching conceptual semantic network guiding mental model construction. The construction process receives descriptive guidance by text-based and picture-based propositional representations as well as depictive guidance by perceptual representation of pictures through structure mapping. Because texts are more constrained in terms of processing order, they can provide more conceptual guidance through a subject matter than pictures. A distinction can be made between initial model construction and adaptive model specification. Initial model construction aims at general coherence formation; adaptive model specification aims at selective processing of task-relevant information. Initial mental model construction is more likely to be text-driven than adaptive mental model specification, while adaptive mental model specification is more likely to be picture-driven than initial mental model construction.

In Chapter 3, we made a fundamental distinction between two kinds of representations – descriptions and depictions – which operate according to different representational principles and which are differently useful for different purposes. In Chapter 6, this distinction was specified in the Integrative Model of Text and Picture Comprehension (ITPC model) by assuming that working memory has corresponding descriptive and depictive subsystems which are responsible for cognitive processing in the course of conjoint comprehension of texts and pictures. This chapter aims at further elaborating the differences between the two kinds of representations, highlighting further asymmetries between texts and pictures. It will be pointed out that texts and pictures have different, yet complementary functions in multimedia comprehension which causes them to play different roles during different phases of cognitive processing.

7.1 Inter-representational Coherence Formation

7.1.1 Cohesion

We have already pointed out that texts are coherent (see Chapter 4). This means that successive sentences are semantically related and that there is also an overarching thematic connection between all sentences. Semantic connections usually manifest themselves at the text surface in terms of cohesive devices. Cohesion can, therefore, be seen as the precipitation of semantic coherence at the text surface. Cohesive devices are markers at the text surface which signal relationships between words and phrases. Such cohesive devices include, for example, recurrence (i.e., repetition of previously used words), pronouns (substitutes of nouns), connectives, deictic words, correspondence of temporal forms, and others.

The principle of using markers in the surface structure of representations to signal connections can also be applied to combinations of texts and pictures. However, while cohesive devices in texts refer to intra-representational cohesion, cohesive devices in text–picture combinations refer to inter-representational cohesion. They include markers at the text surface and picture surface which signal connections between verbal entities (words and phrases) and pictorial entities. These markers play an important role for cognitive processing because the individual has to identify which pictorial entities correspond to which verbal concepts. Depending on how pictorial entities are mapped onto verbal entities, one can distinguish between color cohesion, symbol cohesion, and verbal cohesion.

Color cohesion usually uses the same color for a word or phrase in the text and the corresponding pictorial entity in order to link them to each other. Alternatively, a key can be used which specifies what the different colors stand for. Color cohesion can also be used to connect different pictures. An example is shown in Figure 7.1, which presents a text–picture combination about the European viper from a schoolbook on biology for seventh graders reproduced in grey shades.[1] The text deals with the structure of the viper's head skeleton,

---

the reproduction, which is in shades of grey, the names of colors have been added instead of the colors in the original.

The European viper is a venomous snake (Fig. A: closed mouth). The poison is formed in the poison glands (1) of the venom apparatus (Fig. C). The viper follows silently the smell of its prey. During the bite, the poison enters the victim's body through the lower opening of the poison channel (3) in the poison fang (2). Due to the mobility of the bones of the head skeleton, the viper can devour prey animals that are much larger than their own head. When the bones between the skull (4) and the lower jaw (5) rise, the gullet is greatly widened so that the prey fits through (Fig. B: open mouth).

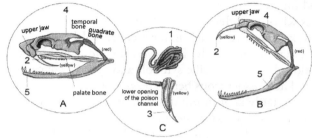

Figure 7.1   Example of a text–picture combination about the European viper

its venom apparatus, and the manner in which it devours prey. It is combined with three schematized pictures, A, B, and C, which illustrate these topics. The pictures are connected by color cohesion, as one and the same entity is always shown in the same color – the poison fang in yellow, the quadrate bone in red, and so forth.

Because color cohesion between a text and picture operates on perceptual mapping processes only, the correspondences between verbal and pictorial entities can be seen directly. As the capacity of the human perceptual system for discriminating different colors is limited, the number of graphical elements involved in color mapping should be limited to five or six. In addition, the colors need to be sufficiently distinct. If a key is used, the use of color cohesion becomes more difficult; the individual has to learn associations between specific colors and specific concepts. These associations between colors and their meaning have to be kept in mind temporarily, which imposes additional cognitive load on working memory.[2] Sometimes, color cohesion is also used to indicate thematic cohesion within a picture, for example, in a schematic drawing of blood circulation, when arteries are represented in red and veins are represented in blue.

Symbol cohesion uses symbols such as letters or numbers or any other arbitrary signs to designate pictorial entities. Symbols can be inserted

---

[2] Sweller et al. (2011).

into texts and into pictures. In Figure 7.1, this kind of symbol cohesion has been extensively used to map verbal entities onto pictorial entities. Letters refer to the different pictures, and numbers refer to individual entities of the snake's head. Symbols can also be inserted only into the picture and combined with a key which specifies what the different symbols stand for. Symbol mapping with a key is cognitively demanding for recipients. Usually, the symbols can be discriminated easily. However, the individual has to learn associations between specific symbols and specific concepts in a local context. These associations between symbols and their meaning have to be temporarily kept in mind which once again imposes additional cognitive load on working memory.

Verbal cohesion involves the use of verbal labels from the text – usually the names of concepts. They are inserted into the picture in order to designate the pictorial entities. Verbal mapping has low cognitive demands for recipients; the verbal labels do not require them to learn temporary associations, because they use previously learned word meanings which can easily be retrieved from long-term memory. In Figure 7.1, there are no verbal cohesion devices between the text and pictures. The pictorial entities have been labeled, but these labels are not used in the text. There is only one common label ("upper jaw") connecting pictures A and B.

The use of color, symbols, or verbal labels as cohesive devices in text–picture combinations gives rise to different perceptual, cognitive, and spatial constraints.[3] Color cohesion is simple, as it requires only perceptual capacities. However, it is limited to five to six easily distinguishable colors, which also reduces the number of different kinds of entities to five or six. Color cohesion should not be used to discriminate single entities from each other because this would lead to gaudy and spotted pictures which compromise the holistic quality of a visualization. Verbal cohesion poses low demands on readers in terms of cognitive processing. It requires no learning of temporary associations, because the verbal labels in the picture can directly address concepts that are stored in the reader's long-term memory. However, verbal cohesion has an important disadvantage; verbal labels need space, and space in a graph is limited. This can lead to competition between different kinds of mapping devices used to enhance text–picture cohesion. When a high number of entities have been mapped

[3] Kosslyn (1994b).

between the text and the picture, the use of verbal labels in the picture can result in space problems. These problems can be resolved by using symbols, because symbols require less space than verbal labels. However, symbols as cohesive devices save space only at the expense of being cognitively more demanding for the recipient, because associations between symbols and their meaning have to be learned and maintained in working memory during text–picture integration.

7.1.2   Conceptual Coherence

A text and picture are semantically related when some of the entities that are mentioned in a text are visualized in the picture. Usually, this does not apply to all entities, because there are also entities that are referred to in the text which are not visualized, and there are visualized entities that are not mentioned in the text. Thus, there are entities that are only mentioned in the text, entities that are only visualized in the picture, and entities that are mentioned in the text and visualized in the picture. Accordingly, text-mentioned entities can be categorized into those that are visualized and those that are not visualized. Similarly, visualized entities can be split into two categories: those that are mentioned and those that are not mentioned in the text. As elucidated in Chapters 4 and 5, both texts and pictures can convey propositions to a reader (or observer) through conceptual processing.

Figure 7.2 illustrates schematically the different categories, which are based on a distinction between text information (lower level) and picture information (upper level). The text–picture combination about the European viper shown in Figure 7.1 displays examples of these categories. "Viper" and "prey" are entities mentioned in the text but not visualized in the picture. (Note that there is no picture of the whole snake.) As the text

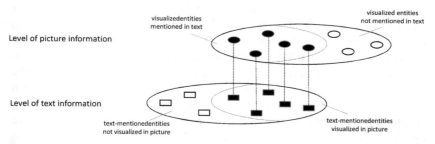

Figure 7.2   Categorization schema for visualized versus not visualized text-mentioned entities and text-mentioned versus not text-mentioned visualized entities

informs the reader that the viper follows the smell of its prey, the reader can create a corresponding (text-based) proposition. Readers with sufficient prior knowledge might also infer that the snake is likely to feed from small animals such as mice and lizards. This allows them to create another corresponding (knowledge-based) proposition regarding the snake's prey. On the contrary, if an unknown word, such as "ophiotoxine" (which refers to the main chemical component of the snake's poison), were used, it would not be likely to activate any prior knowledge and would not trigger the generation of a proposition.

The entities "upper jaw," "temporal bone," "quadrate bone," and "palate bone" are visualized in the picture, but not mentioned in the text. Observers can extract extensive information from the pictures regarding the shape of the bones or the physical and spatial relations between the bones. Based on this visual information, readers can create a multitude of (picture-based) propositions. However, this is just an option; it does not imply that readers really do create a large number of propositions.

The entities "poison glands," "poison fang," "poison channel," and "lower opening of the poison channel" are entities that are mentioned in the text *and* visualized in the picture. The reader and observer can extract verbal and pictorial information in order to generate propositions, for example, a proposition describing how the poison flows from the glands through the channel and then from the channel's lower opening into the body of the prey.

Propositions extracted from pictures and propositions extracted from texts *can* be informationally equivalent.[4] In this case, the text and picture are redundant. However, such semantic equivalence between the text and picture is an exception rather than the rule, because texts and pictures specialize in different aspects of content. Texts specialize in information about causal, temporal, and functional relations. They frequently convey information that is difficult to present in a picture. Pictures, on the contrary, specialize in information about shape or visual attributes and can easily convey spatial information – information that is more difficult to present in a text. Thus, text-based propositions and picture-based propositions are usually different, because the predications originating from the text differ from the predications originating from the picture, even when they deal with the same entities. In other words, while there is often considerable overlap between texts and pictures in terms of common entities, there is usually little overlap between text-based propositions

---

[4] Larkin and Simon (1987).

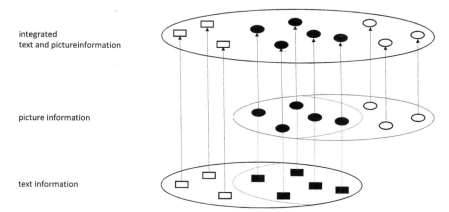

integrated
text and pictureinformation

picture information

text information

Figure 7.3   Schema for the integration of text-based and picture-based propositions into a
coherent semantic network

and picture-based propositions because texts and pictures generally convey
complementary rather than equivalent information. Accordingly, there is
usually little redundancy between a text and a picture, if any. It follows
that, in most cases, texts and pictures cannot replace each other, because
they serve different functions for different purposes.

Inter-representational coherence formation during conjoint text and picture comprehension results in an overarching conceptual structure covering
both text and picture information. This conceptual structure results from
text-based propositions and picture-based propositions merging into one
coherent semantic network. This is illustrated schematically in Figure 7.3,
which extends Figure 7.2. For the example of the European viper, an
overarching conceptual semantic network including both text-based and
picture-based propositions is shown in Figure 7.4. Nodes representing
text-mentioned entities and text-based propositions are depicted with
solid-line white rectangles. Nodes representing visualized entities and
picture-based propositions are depicted with dot-dashed white ellipses.
Nodes representing entities mentioned in the text and visualized in the
picture and their associated propositions are drawn as shaded grey ellipses.
The nodes of text-mentioned entities are labeled with numbers. These
numbers reflect the order of the corresponding propositions and their entities
within the text. There is no such order for only picture-based propositions.

In the example of the European viper shown in Figure 7.4, there seems
to be a relatively balanced relation between the support provided by the
text to the overall conceptual network and the support provided by the

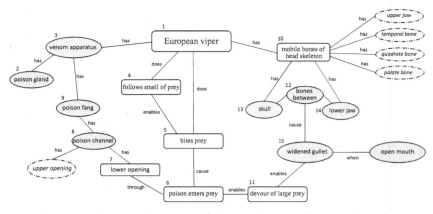

Figure 7.4   Conceptual structure of the text–picture combination about the
European viper

*In autumn, the hedgehog is looking for a suitable winter quarter in piles of leaves or deadwood. Previously, it
eats a fat pad as a food reserve, from which it eats through the winter. When its body temperature (red curve),
which is normally 35°C, drops to 6°C, it falls into a deep hibernation. During this time, all processes such as the
breathing of the hedgehog are reduced. If the average outside temperature (blue curve) decreases too much,
the hedgehog is in danger to freeze. In this case, it wakes up so that its breathing, cardiac activity and body
temperature return to normal levels for a short time to search food. If the outside temperature rises
permanently again, the body temperature of the hedgehog rises also again to 35°C, and the hedgehog slowly
awakes from its hibernation.*

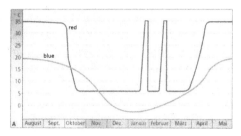

Figure 7.5   Example of a text–picture combination about hedgehog hibernation

picture. However, there is no need for a balanced relationship, because
pictorial support can vary to a large extent. Figure 7.5 presents an example
of a text–picture combination taken from a sixth-grade biology schoolbook. The example deals with the hibernation of the hedgehog[5] and is

---

[5] In the reproduction of the line graph, which is shaded in grey, the names of colors have been inserted
instead of showing the two curves in their original colors.

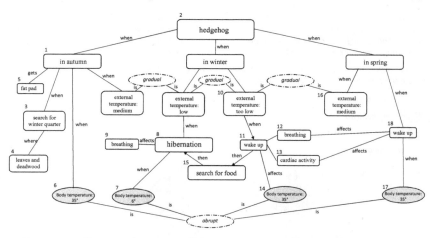

Figure 7.6   Conceptual structure of the text–picture combination about hedgehog hibernation

predominantly based on text. The text–picture combination depicts the hedgehog's strategy for surviving in winter, which includes preparation of hibernation and an emergency program against freezing. Hibernation is triggered by lower outside temperatures and is characterized by a sharp drop of the body temperature, with reduced breathing and heartbeat. The emergency program means that the hedgehog interrupts its hibernation in order to avoid freezing if the outside temperatures become too low. Hibernation is terminated when the outside temperature drops below a certain level.

The corresponding conceptual structure is presented in Figure 7.6. As can be seen, this conceptual structure is mainly supported by the text, which conveys the central concepts and causal relationships. There are only two references (in the original, via color cohesion) to the accompanying line graph, which shows the profile of the outside temperatures and the animal's body temperature during the course of the year. Because the text presents the central concepts and explains the causal relationships, it is possible to understand the hedgehog's hibernation without the picture. The graph specifies only that the outside temperature changes relatively smoothly, whereas the hedgehog's body temperature changes rather abruptly at the beginning and at the end of hibernation or when hibernation is interrupted. This difference is not made explicit in the text. Note that the graph alone allows an abundance of other interpretations. One could read from the graph that the hedgehog wakes up exactly two times

Animals exhibit very different behaviors. The behavior of the animals among themselves is of particular interest. Behavior to other animals of the same species ranges from peaceful coexistence to quarreling and struggles. The following two graphs show selected behaviors in monkeys. They show how many hours the animals are engaged in the respective behaviors per day.

Figure A refers to the groups of monkeys that do not have a pack leader.
Figure B refers to the monkey groups with a pack leader.

☐ *food behavior*   *(beige)*

▨ *resting behavior*   *(pink)*

■ *fighting and threatening*   *(blue)*

▨ *grooming*   *(green)*

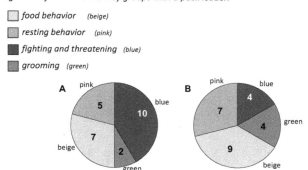

Figure 7.7   Example of a text–picture combination about the social behavior of monkeys

within one hibernation, that the outside temperature in December is exactly minus 3° Celsius, or that the outside temperature in August is plus 19° Celsius. Such interpretations are of course unintended. What helps to block them is the conceptual structure conveyed by the text, which focuses only on the general conditions of the hedgehog's hibernation.

A very different example of a text–picture combination is shown in Figure 7.7. In this case, the pictures convey all of the specific information while the text provides only a general framework to incorporate specific data. The example is taken from a schoolbook of biology for eighth graders and is reproduced here in grey shades. It deals with the social behavior of monkeys. The text conveys the conceptual distinctions between packs of monkeys with and without leaders, the distinction between activities, and the quantitative variable "hours per day" for the different activities. The types of activities are mentioned in a key which connects the text and pictures through symbol cohesion (for pictures) and color cohesion[6] (for activities). The hours-per-day spent doing different activities are specified in the pictures.

The corresponding conceptual structure is presented in Figure 7.8. In this figure, there are no entities mentioned in the text and visualized in the

---

[6] Once again, the names of colors have been added instead of the real colors in the original.

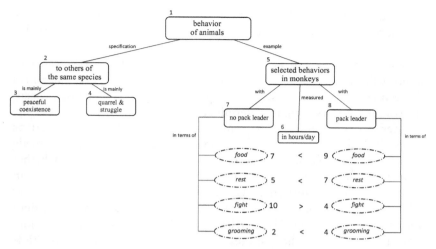

Figure 7.8   Conceptual structure of the text–picture combination about the social
behavior of monkeys

picture. The general framework is provided only by the text, and the
pictures deliver the data required to fill the framework. Without the text,
the pictures are meaningless. Without the pictures, nothing can be determined about the monkeys' behavior. The conceptual structure might lead
to the inference (although it is not explicitly stated) that monkeys with a
pack leader have more time for eating food, resting, and grooming than
monkeys without a pack leader.

7.1.3   Ambiguities and Disambiguation

As mentioned in Chapter 3, texts and pictures are differently useful for
different purposes. Texts, on the one hand, have higher representational
power but they are selective and, therefore, usually incomplete. Thus, texts
are ambiguous insofar as various options exist for implementing a description
into an image or a model. Thus, pictures can disambiguate texts because they
constrain text interpretation by specifying aspects that were left open by the
text. Pictures, on the other hand, have lower representational power, but are
informationally complete regarding a certain class of information (e.g.,
shape, size, spatial orientation, etc.). However, pictures are ambiguous
insofar as they usually allow an abundance of possible interpretations. In
order to find the intended interpretation, the recipient has to select specific
conceptual structures out of many possibilities. These structures are usually

delivered by the text. Thus, texts can disambiguate pictures because they constrain their interpretation by reducing the number of possible interpretations.[7]

While both texts and pictures can convey propositions to a reader or observer through conceptual processing, there are fundamental differences between text-based and picture-based propositions. The semantic conceptual content of texts is highly determined as texts explicitly present specific, well-defined propositions. The semantic conceptual content of pictures (especially realistic ones) is less determined because an observer can usually extract an abundance of propositions from them without knowing whether these propositions are relevant or not. For example, the pictures in Figure 7.1 allow the inference that the poison fang of the European viper points to the back of the viper's mouth when it is closed but is upright when the viper is biting. This is relevant for the functioning of the venom apparatus. However, the pictures also allow the creation of multiple propositions comparing the size of the different bones in the animal's skull, which are not relevant for understanding the viper's behavior. Accordingly, pictures are conceptually more ambiguous as they allow more varied conceptual interpretations than texts.

In order to reduce the ambiguity of pictures, texts frequently include paragraphs that describe how the content is visualized in the picture. While the other paragraphs describe the content, the topic of these specific paragraphs is not the content, but the picture. Consider, as an example, the text–picture combination about plate tectonics shown in Figure 7.9. The content-related text paragraph describes plate tectonics in general words, before moving on to a specific tectonic process: subduction. It then explains that subduction leads to the creation of new magma which rises to the Earth's surface. All of this is described without referring to the picture. The picture visualizes information about the subduction process, specifying what is described in the content-related text. The picture-related paragraph describes the picture and how it visualizes the content. It guides the reader through where to look and what to notice, making what can be seen in the picture explicit. In this way, it suppresses the abundance of possible interpretations. Such picture-related paragraphs are also frequently used when the reader cannot be expected to process the picture with sufficient depth based only on content-related text information.

Because picture-related text paragraphs require the reader to look more directly at the picture, as written texts they are more likely to suffer from

[7] Ainsworth (1999).

[Content related text:] *Plate tectonics is a scientific theory that describes slow large-scale motions in the Earth crust usually measured in centimeters per year. Among these motions, one type - called 'subduction' - frequently leads to the formation of volcanoes. Subduction means that one tectonic plate moves under another tectonic plate. As the plates converge, the lower plate sinks into the Earth mantle, where it partially melts due to high temperatures. The resulting magma rises toward the surface, where it forms volcanoes ...*

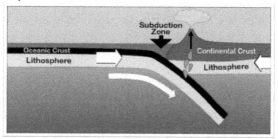

[Picture related text:] *The picture above shows as a cross-section through the earth's mantle which processes occur when one tectonic plate, visualized by the left dark band (Oceanic Crust), slides under another tectonic plate, visualized by the right thick dark band (Continental Crust). The bubbles above the dark band sliding downwards (Oceanic Crust) show areas of partial melting turning into magma. The upwards arrow indicates the rise of the magma towards the earth surface ...*

Figure 7.9   Example of a text–picture combination about plate tectonics including content-related text and picture-related text

split attention between the text and picture than content-related paragraphs. Thus, picture-related paragraphs should be presented as auditory texts if possible, rather than visual texts in order to avoid splitting visual attention. Experimental findings have confirmed these effects.[8]

7.2   Mental Model Construction

7.2.1   Constraints on Mental Model Construction

We know from text comprehension, as described in Chapter 4, that propositional mental representations can serve as a basis for the construction of mental models with the help of prior knowledge. By the same token, propositional mental representations that include text-based and picture-based propositions can also be used for constructing mental models. Beyond mental model construction based on propositional mental representations, mental models can also be created on the basis of pictorial data through structure mapping, as described in Chapter 5. Accordingly, there can be descriptive and depictive constraints on mental model construction.

[8] Lowe and Boucheix (2011); Schnotz et al. (2014).

Descriptive Constraints: As described in Section 7.1.2, coherence formation during integrated comprehension of texts and pictures results in comprehensive propositional representations which include information from both texts and pictures. For inter-representational coherence formation, text-based propositions and picture-based propositions are merged into coherent semantic networks, as illustrated in the examples shown in Figures 7.1, 7.5, and 7.7. The resulting overarching propositional representation provides a broader conceptual basis for mental model construction than a text-based or picture-based proposition alone.

The construction of mental models through conjoint propositional representations is usually guided more by text-based propositions than by picture-based propositions, because text-based propositions are more clearly defined, whereas pictures are often conceptually vague. Pictures allow an observer to read off multiple conceptual relations without clarification as to which of these conceptual structures the picture aims to convey. This conceptual ambiguity of pictures is constrained by the text. However, mental model construction under the guidance of only descriptive representations also suffers from ambiguity. There are usually different possibilities as to how entities can be arranged, whereby all arrangements still correspond perfectly to the description. Admittedly, prior knowledge can point toward typical arrangements, if those exist. In many cases, however, there are various degrees of freedom and additional constraints are, therefore, required to disambiguate the text.

Depictive Constraints: Pictures illustrating a text add information which constrains the degrees of freedom, thus disambiguating the text. Mental model construction based on depictive representations is performed through structure mapping based on analogy relations which are mediated by prior knowledge. Depictive constraints can be coarse or detailed. When readers of a text look only briefly at the outline of a visualization in a picture, they only receive depictive guidance in the form of a rough scaffold for constructing their mental model. On the contrary, an elaborate and detailed structure mapping based on a thorough analysis of the picture provides fine-grained, detailed depictive guidance for mental model construction.

According to the Integrated Model of Text and Picture Comprehension (ITPC model) described in Chapter 6, we can assume that mental model construction is guided by descriptive *and* depictive constraints. Accordingly, mental models constructed during the integrated comprehension of a text and picture are anchored both in a propositional (descriptive) representation and a perceptual (depictive) representation through structure mapping. In text comprehension, on the other hand,

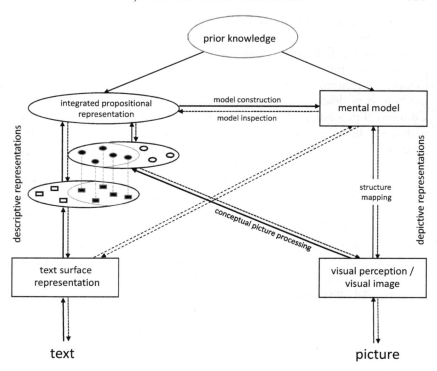

Figure 7.10   Theoretical framework for combining descriptive guidance (through text-based and picture-based propositions) and depictive guidance (through structure mapping) for mental model construction

mental models are anchored only in a propositional representation. In other words, the conjoint comprehension of texts and pictures combines two ways of constructing mental models by anchoring the models both in descriptive and depictive representations. Picture comprehension enables more direct access to mental model construction than text comprehension, because pictures are immediately processed by the depictive subsystem through structure mapping, whereas texts have to be processed first by the descriptive subsystem. Thus, the depictive guidance of mental model construction provided by pictures is more direct than the descriptive guidance provided by texts. This is because the latter requires a switch from the descriptive branch to the depictive branch of cognitive processing.

   The interplay between the descriptive guidance of mental model construction through propositions and the depictive guidance of mental model construction through structure mapping is visualized in Figure 7.10. The figure is an extension of the conceptual framework for integrated text and picture comprehension presented in Figure 6.1. Contrary to the latter figure, Figure 7.10 also incorporates a distinction between text-based propositions (referring to visualized or not visualized entities) and picture-based propositions (referring to text-mentioned or not text-mentioned entities) as described in Section 7.1.2. Text processing within the branch of descriptive representations leads to text-based propositions. Conceptual processing of pictures – triggered by visual images of pictures within the branch of depictive representations – results in picture-based propositions in the descriptive branch. Text-based and picture-based propositions are merged into an integrated propositional representation.

In integrative text and picture comprehension, mental model construction takes place on a descriptive basis and a depictive basis. The propositional representation is merged from text-based and picture-based propositions and serves as the descriptive basis for mental model construction. The visual perception or visual image of a picture and the process of structure mapping within the branch of depictive representations serve as the depictive basis for mental model construction, reducing the degrees of freedom left open by the propositional representation.

7.2.2   Sequential Processing

Due to the limited capacity of working memory, coherence formation and mental model construction cannot take place at the same time. Instead, they occur in a sequential manner. Due to the inherent linear structure of texts, the processing order of texts is highly constrained. Texts are expected to be read word by word and, therefore, provide more guidance for sequential processing than pictures. They convey clearly defined propositions in a specific order which are expected to be processed in this order. Thus, texts are well suited for providing conceptual guidance for the process of comprehension.

By comparison, the comprehension of pictures is less constrained. Although pictorial entities can differ in their visual salience, which makes them more or less likely to be perceived, and despite the possibility of pictorial signaling, there is no pre-determined order of processing for pictures. Furthermore, their propositional semantic content is often ambiguous, as it can lead to an abundance of possible interpretations. As picture processing is optional as compared with text processing, readers have more freedom to choose the extent to which they elaborate their mental model with pictorial information than they have with text information. In brief, while text-based propositions have well-defined semantic content, are presented in a specific order, and are expected to be processed in that order, there is no such order in picture-based propositions, which are also less clearly defined. During integrated comprehension, texts are therefore more likely to guide the recipient conceptually through the subject matter than pictures.

Due to the need for sequential processing and the difference between texts and pictures in terms of sequential processing and conceptual guidance, integrative processing of texts and pictures takes place as a conjoint flow of consciousness. This process consists of the stepwise construction of topic-specific mental models based on the information provided by the text and the picture under the guidance of the text. After taking a brief initial look at the outline of the picture in order to scaffold mental model construction, readers process the text sentence by sentence. When the text and picture have been processed with great care, readers check sentence by sentence whether the entities described in the text are also shown in the picture. They focus on the corresponding pictorial entities, add information about the shape and visual appearance of these entities, or extract further information not included in the text. For example, they extract relations to other entities and integrate them into their mental model. Readers then turn to the next sentence, process it in the same way, and so forth.

Accordingly, the integrated processing of a text and picture takes place step by step, proceeding from coherence formation to construction of topic-specific mental models, and is primarily guided by the text. During processing, increasingly complex conceptual structures and mental models are carried from sentence to sentence, constituting a flow of consciousness. The picture per se does not usually provide clear conceptual guidance through its content. Thus, conceptual guidance is imported from the text if there is not sufficient prior knowledge stored in long-term memory which can be retrieved. Conjoint processing of a text–picture combination can, therefore, be seen as a guided tour through the conceptual structure led by the text. As this manifests itself in a trajectory characterized by attentive processing of the corresponding pictorial entities, conjoint processing can also be seen as a guided tour through the picture. Similar to single text comprehension, a continuous flow of consciousness without unneeded topic changes is advantageous for the conjoint processing of text–picture combinations.

7.2.3 Initial Construction and Adaptive Specification of Mental Models

Text processing can be directed toward certain reading goals. Such goals can be introduced by instructing learners to prepare for specific tasks. The corresponding goal-directed processing puts special emphasis on task-relevant information. The same has been demonstrated for picture processing. When constructing a mental model, individuals can direct their attention specifically toward task-relevant information. Accordingly, multimedia comprehension can be seen as a goal-directed activity in which individuals follow certain strategies in order to process the presented information according to their aims. The comprehension goals of an individual can vary on a continuum ranging from general to specific. A general goal is to simply understand what is explained in the text and shown in the pictures, which means constructing a coherent mental representation without a specific reason. A specific goal is to solve certain problems or answer certain questions which require specific information. Thus, a distinction can be made between general coherence-oriented processing and specific task-oriented processing, which in turn leads to a distinction between initial mental model construction and adaptive mental model elaboration.

Initial Mental Model Construction: If learners study text with pictures without a specific task in mind, they engage in general coherence-oriented processing as a default strategy, resulting in a general orientation about the subject matter which can be further elaborated if required. This processing corresponds to coherence formation with text and pictures, as described in Section 7.1.2. It aims at overall understanding of the content and can be called "initial mental model construction."

As mentioned in Section 7.2.2, texts are better suited for providing conceptual guidance for mental model construction than pictures. This is because processing of texts is more constrained due to their linear structure, and the conceptual semantic content of texts is more clearly and explicitly defined than that of pictures. It follows that initial mental model construction tends (*ceteris paribus*) to be text-driven rather than picture-driven – apart from brief glances at the picture to disambiguate the text and to quickly acquire an advance organizer (a scaffold) for mental model construction. Because pictures do not possess an inherent linear structure, their processing order is less constrained in terms of processing order. Furthermore, as their propositional content is usually less clearly defined, pictures provide poorer conceptual guidance for initial mental model construction than texts.

Adaptive Mental Model Specification: If learners study a text with pictures in order to complete a specific task, they engage in goal-directed selective processing at some point in order to update and elaborate their mental model accordingly, placing special emphasis on task-relevant information. This processing, which requires searches for specific information, can be called "adaptive mental model specification." Texts are less favorable for this kind of processing as their linear structure makes them less suitable for searching for a specific piece of information, and search paths can be relatively long. Readers can, admittedly, speed up their search by scanning the text, but this entails the risk of overlooking relevant information. Contrary to texts, pictures have a two-dimensional structure instead of a linear structure. This allows easier access to specific information due to considerably shorter search paths. In brief, while texts provide better conceptual guidance than pictures, pictures allow easier access to specific information than texts. It follows that adaptive mental model specification tends (*ceteris paribus*) to be picture-driven rather than text-driven. This is even more the case as the text has already been read during the preceding initial mental model construction phase.

In brief, text and pictures play fundamentally different roles and serve different purposes in multimedia comprehension. Initial mental model construction is more likely to be text-driven than adaptive mental model specification, while adaptive mental model specification is more likely to be picture-driven than initial mental model construction.

Evidence from Eye Tracking Data: Eye tracking data analyses have shown that students allocate more cognitive resources to text processing during initial mental model construction than during adaptive model specification. Conversely, they allocate more resources to picture processing during adaptive mental model specification than during initial mental model construction.[9] In a series of experiments, Fang Zhao and her colleagues[10] presented text–picture combinations from geography and biology textbooks to secondary school students from Grades 5 to 8. In one condition, students were just asked to read and understand the text–picture combinations without answering any questions. Under this condition, students were assumed to engage in globally understanding the subject matter, that is, in general coherence formation and initial mental model construction without considering specific tasks.

Figure 7.11 shows the average accumulated eye fixation times on the text and the picture across the course of processing under this condition. As can be seen from the figure, the text received a lot more attention than the picture, especially at the beginning, which supports the assumption that initial mental model construction is primarily text-based. It can also be seen from the figure that text usage within the first segment of the comprehension process was slightly lower, while picture usage was slightly

[9] Hochpöchler et al. (2013); Schnotz and Wagner (2018).   [10] Zhao et al. (2020).

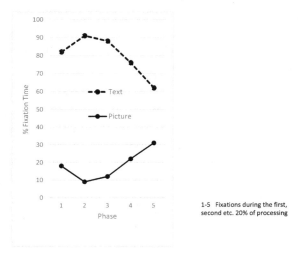

Figure 7.11   Accumulated eye fixation times of secondary school students on texts and
pictures in the course of initial mental model construction

higher in the second and third segments. This seems to mirror the
scaffolding function of pictures during initial mental model construction.
Individuals receiving a text with an accompanying picture look briefly at
the outline of the picture to acquire a coarse scaffolding for their mental
model construction before reading the text in detail.

After participants had read the text–picture combinations with the aim
of generally understanding the subject matter, they were presented the
same combinations again, but this time each with a specific question they
had to answer based on the corresponding text–picture combination.
Under this condition, students were assumed to engage in adaptive mental
model specification. The average accumulated eye fixation times on the
text, on the picture, and on the question across the course of processing are
presented in Figure 7.12. Not surprisingly, the question – which was new
information – received the most attention at the beginning of processing.
The students wanted to know what they were expected to find out. Most
importantly, however, the relation between the text and picture changed
fundamentally. While the text dominated initial mental model construction when no question was asked, it was now of secondary importance
during the question-answering phase. Because the text had been read
before, only minor re-reading of the text was required for adaptive mental
model specification. The picture received much more attention during

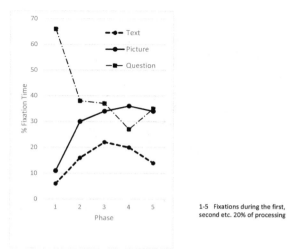

Figure 7.12   Accumulated eye fixation times of secondary school students on texts, pictures, and questions in the course of adaptive mental model specification

task-oriented processing than the text. This difference between the usage of the text and of the picture increased over the course of processing. All in all, the pattern supports the assumption that adaptive mental model elaboration is primarily picture-based, because pictures allow easier access to specific information than texts.

One could assume that learners engage in adaptive mental model specification as soon as they know which tasks or questions they have to solve or to answer. However, this does not seem to be the case. In one of their experimental conditions, Zhao et al.[11] presented text–picture combinations together with specific questions right from the beginning. Because the participants were informed about their task from the outset, one might expect them to immediately read the question in order to adapt their processing to the task.

They did not. The average accumulated eye fixation times on the text, on the picture, and on the question across the course of processing under this condition are presented in Figure 7.13. The question received surprisingly little attention during the first segments of processing. Instead, during the first segments, processing was predominantly text-driven.

[11]   Zhao et al. (2020).

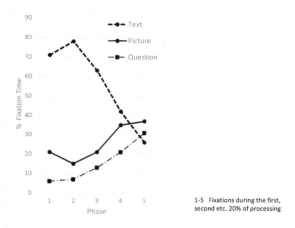

Figure 7.13   Accumulated eye fixation times of secondary school students on texts, pictures, and questions in the course of processing where the students knew the questions they had to answer from the beginning. Thus, initial mental model construction and adaptive mental model specification were not separated

The trajectory of eye fixations on the text and the trajectory of eye fixations on the picture resembled the trajectories of the conditions where no questions were asked at all. Also under this condition, text usage was slightly lower and picture usage slightly higher in the first than in the second segment, probably due to the scaffolding function of pictures at the beginning of mental model construction.

Although participants knew the question right from the beginning, processing started with primarily text-driven initial mental model construction. It seems that learners want to have at least some minimal knowledge about a subject matter before answering questions about it. Once again, this finding is in line with the assumption that learners engage in general coherence formation and initial mental model construction at the beginning before their processing becomes more task-oriented. Figure 7.13 shows that the text and picture switch roles in terms of which dominates processing after the question has received more attention. There are inherent sequential constraints between initial mental model construction and adaptive mental model specification. The latter is assumed to take place on top of the former because a mental model must exist before it can be adapted to specific purposes. This also justifies referring to it as *initial* mental model construction.

7.3 Takeaways

Texts and pictures serve different, yet complementary functions in multimedia comprehension. The asymmetry between them leads to different roles during coherence formation and mental model construction within different phases of comprehension.

Coherence formation during the conjoint comprehension of texts and pictures is supported by inter-representational cohesive devices at the text and the picture surface, such as color cohesion, symbol cohesion, and verbal cohesion. These devices help the recipient to identify which pictorial entities correspond to which verbal concepts and vice versa. The text and picture are semantically coherent when entities mentioned in the text are also visualized in the picture.

Although there is frequently an overlap between texts and pictures in terms of common entities, there is usually little overlap between the propositions resulting from them. A text-based proposition and a picture-based proposition are informationally equivalent only when they provide exactly the same information about the same entity. In this case, the two propositions are redundant. However, such equivalence is the exception rather than the rule, because texts and pictures specialize in different kinds of information even when dealing with the same entities. Furthermore, text-based propositions explicitly convey clear and well-defined semantic content, whereas picture-based propositions are less clearly defined because pictures allow more varied conceptual interpretations. Accordingly, it is rare that there is complete redundancy between texts and pictures.

Texts are ambiguous insofar as there are usually different ways in which a description can be implemented in external reality or in an internal mental model. Pictures can disambiguate texts because they constrain their interpretation. Pictures are ambiguous insofar as they usually allow an abundance of possible interpretations. Texts can disambiguate pictures because they constrain the scope of the possible interpretations of pictures. This disambiguation also applies to paragraphs that describe how content is visualized in a picture. The topic of such paragraphs is the picture and not the content.

Inter-representational coherence formation during the conjoint processing of a text and picture results in overarching conceptual structures which merge text-based propositions and picture-based propositions into a coherent semantic network. Mental model construction in multimedia comprehension is guided by descriptive and depictive constraints. On the one hand, model construction is anchored in text- and picture-based propositional representations, which provides descriptive guidance. On the other hand, it is anchored in the perceptual representation of pictures which constrain mental model construction through structure mapping, providing depictive guidance. Picture comprehension enables more direct access to mental model construction than text comprehension, because pictures are immediately processed by the depictive subsystem through structure mapping, whereas texts have to be processed first by the descriptive subsystem.

Integrated processing of a text and picture takes place initially as step-by-step coherence formation and construction of topic-specific mental models, which is primarily guided by the text. Due to their inherent linear structure, texts provide more conceptual guidance for sequential processing than pictures. While text-based propositions have well-defined semantic content, which is presented in a specific order, there is no such order among picture-based propositions. During initial integrated comprehension, texts are, therefore, more likely to provide conceptual guidance through the subject matter than pictures. Pictures per se do not usually provide clear conceptual guidance through content, which is why conceptual guidance is imported from the text. This "import" enables a "guided tour" through the conceptual structure and visualization of the content. In brief, initial integrative processing of texts and pictures takes place as a conjoint flow of consciousness which consists of a stepwise construction of increasingly complex topic-specific mental models based on information from the text and the picture under guidance of the text.

Texts and pictures accomplish different functions during different phases of multimedia comprehension. Initial mental model construction is oriented toward global understanding without a specific task in mind. It is inclined to be (*ceteris paribus*) text-driven, probably due to the explicit conceptual guidance provided by texts. Conversely, adaptive mental model specification takes place when readers have a specific task in mind. It is inclined to be (*ceteris paribus*) picture-driven, because the nonlinear structure of pictures provides faster and more flexible access to specific information. As a result, initial mental model construction is more likely to be text-driven than adaptive mental model specification, while adaptive mental model specification is more likely to be picture-driven than initial mental model construction. There are inherent sequential constraints between the different phases of mental model construction. Initial mental model construction precedes adaptive mental model specification.

As texts and pictures serve different functions, they cannot replace each other. We frequently find examples in nature of one agent (i.e., an organism) which can only attain its aims with a certain contribution from another agent and vice versa. Such relationships, in which weaknesses are mutually compensated, are usually called "symbiotic." One could, thus, view the interaction between text processing and picture processing in multimedia comprehension as a kind of symbiotic relation, in which both sides are fundamentally different, but well aligned in order to attain their common goal of comprehension.

CHAPTER 8

Beyond Comprehension
Multimedia in Thinking and Problem-Solving

Abstract

Comprehension can be the starting point for further cognitive activities such as thinking and problem-solving. Productive thinking requires a specific interaction between descriptive and depictive representations combining representational power and inferential power. The interaction takes place through processes of mental model construction and model inspection. Descriptive representations are combined and coordinated with the corresponding depictive representations, whereby each representation constrains the construction and usage of the other representation. Model inspection requires systematic and exhaustive interrogation of depictive representations in order to read off relevant information. Depictive representations have to grasp task-relevant structures and facilitate performance of the required procedures. Required operations should not be difficult to perform and the sequences of operations should be relatively short. Inappropriate perceptual structures of visualizations can obscure relevant structural attributes, preventing the application of correct procedures and stimulating the application of incorrect procedures.

The most important thing to do when dealing with a complex subject matter is to comprehend it as far as possible. Comprehension allows prediction of events, reflection about the consequences of further activities, comparison of different alternatives, estimation of expected results, and decision-making about what should be done next. If such activities are not simply done by trial and error, they are usually referred to as thinking or (if there is no algorithm available) as problem-solving. The individual tries to gain further information by operating on his or her mental representations which are created by comprehension. In brief, comprehension is not a terminal cognitive activity, but rather the starting point for further cognitive activities such as thinking[1] or problem-solving.

The previous chapters were all about comprehension. We characterized comprehension as the construction of mental representations of a subject matter (i.e., facts and circumstances in the real world or an imaginary world) by an individual in working memory based on the available information. Multimedia comprehension was characterized as the construction of mental representations based on multiple external representations such as texts and pictures. We are now in a position to explore how mental representations constructed during multimedia comprehension enable further cognitive processing, such as productive thinking or cognitive problem-solving.

Thinking can be viewed as operating on a mental representation and as transforming a mental representation in order to estimate the consequences that follow from a certain situation or from possible activities in a given situation. The kind of representation determines which kinds of cognitive activities can operate on the representation and which kinds of transformations can be executed. As multimedia comprehension leads to multiple mental representations which interact, it follows that productive thinking and problem-solving require that cognitive operations on these representations are coordinated. Thus, this chapter will investigate how multiple mental representations, notably descriptions and depictions, can be used together in order to enhance productive thinking and problem-solving.

8.1 Views on Thinking and Problem-Solving

Research on thinking and problem-solving has been strongly influenced by two theoretical schools: Gestalt psychology and the psychology of information processing. Gestalt psychology saw the main requirement of problem-solving as finding the right representation of a problem, while the psychology of information processing saw the main requirement of problem-solving as finding the right way through a kind of complex maze, the so-called problem space.

---

[1] The term "thinking" applies both to productive reasoning and to logical (syllogistic) reasoning. Syllogistic reasoning refers to the generation of true conclusions from true premises according to the rules of formal logic. Productive reasoning refers to finding new solutions to cognitive problems without knowledge of specific rules. In this chapter, we will skip syllogistic reasoning and focus only on productive thinking (see Duncker, 1935; Johnson-Laird, 1983; Johnson-Laird and Byrne, 1991).

Structural Issues: Finding the Right Representation: One of the main research areas of Gestalt psychology was visual perception. Against this background it seems consequential that Gestalt psychology considered problem-solving mainly as a matter of perception.[2] We know that perception is often constrained by experience. For example, the repeated experience of perceiving an object in one way, such as a pair of tongs as a tool, may hinder the individual from perceiving it in another way, such as seeing it simply as a possible ballast for a ballistic pendulum. Gestalt psychologists coined the term "functional fixedness" for this phenomenon. According to their view, problem-solving takes place when the perception of a situation is suddenly reorganized. The new, reorganized perception (if it is the right one) makes the solution immediately obvious. In other words, the solution can be immediately read off from the new perception. Accordingly, Gestalt psychology considered problem-solving as the result of a sudden insight.

Karl Duncker, a leading proponent of Gestalt psychology, illustrated reorganization and sudden insight in problem-solving in his work about productive thinking[3] with an autobiographic experience. When he and his friends hiked to a mountain hut one day and returned back to the valley on the next day (on the same path and at about the same time of day), they were puzzled by the question as to whether there was a point on their way down where they were at the same time of day as when they were hiking uphill the day before. Duncker reported that they were puzzled by this question and could only find a clear answer by restructuring the problem situation. Instead of the same person going up on one day and going down on another day, they considered a situation with two persons, one going up and the other going down. The idea of merging the representations of two separate days (each including one person) into the representation of a single day (including two persons) is presented in Figure 8.1 with the help of path-time curves. In the merged representation, the two curves intersect at the point where the two persons are in the same place at the same time. So, the answer is "yes." However, this solution only became obvious when the problem was perceived differently, which led to a new representation.

Procedural Issues: Finding the Right Way: In the psychology of information processing, the main requirement of problem-solving was seen as finding a way through a kind of maze, the problem space. The problem space includes the given state of a situation as well as all other possible states into which the given state can be transformed by applying certain operations. A classic example is the so-called Tower-of-Hanoi

[2] Köhler (1969); Montgomery (1984).   [3] Duncker (1935).

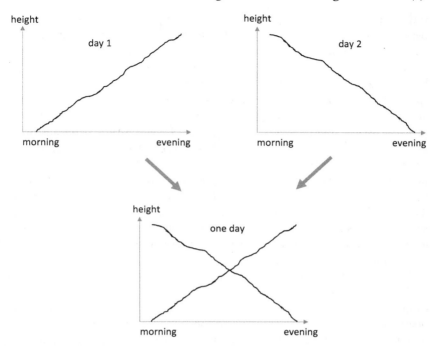

Figure 8.1   Visualization of Duncker's hiking problem

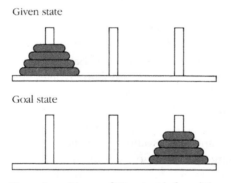

Figure 8.2   Tower-of-Hanoi with four disks

(see Figure 8.2). A number of differently sized disks (there are four disks in the present figure) are stacked on one rod, which is part of a set of three rods. This stack of disks on the initial rod constitutes the given state. The stack of disks has to be transferred from the initial rod to a specific other rod. The stack of disks on this other rod constitutes the goal state. In between the given state and the goal state, there are multiple intermediate states; for example, the smallest disk could be slid onto the middle rod, etcetera. The initial state, the goal state, and all the other possible states in between constitute the problem space. For moving through the problem space, the following operation rules apply. Only one disk can be moved at any time; a larger disk can never be put onto a smaller disk. Thus, problem-solving requires finding a sequence of operations which transform a given initial state into a goal state via intermediate states by applying certain operations. In other words, the problem-solver has to find his or her way from a given initial state to a goal state through the problem space, whereby short paths are better than long ones. The problem space of a Tower-of-Hanoi problem with few disks is rather simple, but the problem space increases as more disks are introduced, and the transformation of the given state into the goal state becomes a non-trivial task, which certainly qualifies as problem-solving.

There are numerous problems that require finding a way through a problem space. One example is the problem of how to convey three cannibals and three missionaries across a river with a boat (without a boatman!) which can carry only two persons, where the number of cannibals on either of the riverbanks must never exceed the number of missionaries (because the cannibals would immediately start preparing their meal). Another example is how to transport a wolf, a sheep, and a cabbage head across a river, when the boat enables only one object to be transferred per crossing. In this case, the constraints are that the wolf and the sheep must never be left alone because the wolf would kill the sheep, and the sheep and the cabbage head must never be left alone because the sheep would eat the cabbage. In both of these cases, the problem involves finding a path through a more or less complex problem space.

Combining Structure and Process: Do Gestalt psychology, which focuses on finding the right representation and on restructuring the problem situation, and the psychology of information processing, which focuses on searching for a path from an initial state to a goal state through a problem space, contradict each other? No, they merely focus on two different aspects of problem-solving which are equally important: structure and process. The two concepts can be synthesized, as suggested by Stellan Ohlsson in his Representational Change Theory.[4] According to this theory, problem-solvers must have a representation of the initial state and a

[4] Ohlsson (1992).

rather concrete idea about the goal state. They must be able to set up a space which includes paths leading from the initial state to the goal state. Further, they need to have operators at their disposal which can be applied to the initial state in order to transform it stepwise into intermediate states until the goal state is reached.

How the initial state of a problem is represented in an individual's mind is of crucial importance for successful problem-solving, because mental representations serve as memory probes which activate operators in long-term memory. An appropriate representation of the initial state activates operators that are relevant for solving the problem, whereas an inappropriate representation activates operators that lead to an impasse. In the latter case, the problem-solver has to find an alternative, more appropriate representation of the initial state. Representations can be changed by adding new information to the current representation or by relaxing constraints, which allows new aspects to unfold.

So, problem-solving requires representations with an adequate structure and processes that operate on this structure. Gestalt psychology focused primarily on structures, whereas the psychology of information processing focused primarily on processes. Whereas Gestalt psychology did not sufficiently take into account the fact that insight problems also have a problem space and require operations within this space, the psychology of information processing did not sufficiently take into account the fact that problem-solving can require the transformation of a given problem space into another problem space, because restructuring the problem representation enables easier sequences of operations. In short, problem-solving is about finding the best representation (i.e., structure) which allows the easiest and shortest sequence of procedures (i.e., process) operating on this structure to transform a given state into a goal state.

Duncker's above-mentioned mountain-hiking problem nicely demonstrates how an inappropriate initial problem representation can be restructured as well as the interplay between different representation formats. The hiking problem is set out in a descriptive format, with natural language. Based on this description, the problem-solver creates a depictive representation, which can be a perceptual image of hiking uphill and another image of hiking downhill, or more abstract representations with path-time curves, as shown in the upper half of Figure 8.1. Operating with these representations, however, leads to deadlock because coordinating the two representations is difficult. Thus, the problem is restructured and re-described. The two-different-days condition is omitted. The condition that only one person is involved is also omitted. With this new description,

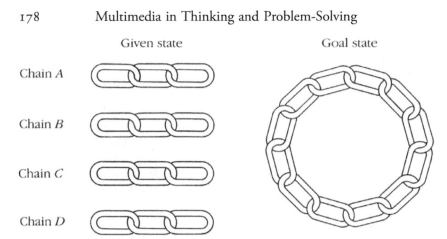

Figure 8.3   The necklace problem (original)

a new depictive representation can be constructed which allows the problem-solver to directly read off the point where the two persons meet, that is, the point where they are in the same place at the same time. In short, the new description leads to a new depictive representation which allows the required information to be read off.

Simplifying Operational Sequences: The relaxation of constraints in a descriptive representation can also serve to simplify the required problem-solving procedures. A corresponding example of the restructuring of an inappropriate representation is the so-called necklace problem described by Silveira.[5] Participants are presented with four separate chains (A–D). Each chain consists of three connected links, as shown in Figure 8.3. The four chains form the initial state of the problem. The participants' task is to create a necklace consisting of 12 interconnected links as the goal state, as shown in the figure.

When the problem is presented in this way without further constraints, the solution is very easy. The participants connect the four separate chains to each other one by one. Each connection requires one link to be opened, attached to the neighboring chain, and then closed again. So, one would open Link number 3 of Chain A, connect it with Link number 1 of Chain B, and close the link. Then, one would open Link number 3 of Chain B, connect it with Link number 1 of Chain C, close the link, and so forth. Because four chains have four contact points, connecting all chains requires four openings and closures. This view of the problem is visualized in Figure 8.4.

[5] Silveira (1971).

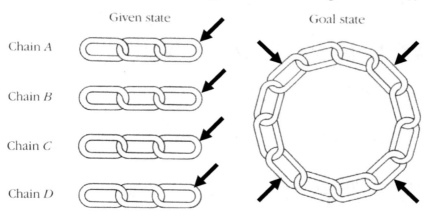

Figure 8.4   The necklace problem: Four links solution

The goal state can be described as "Four connections between four chains, each with three connected links, resulting in a 12-link necklace" or simply described with the multiplication "4 × 3 = 12." Accordingly, the path from the initial state to the goal state involves opening and closing four links. The problem becomes more difficult, however, when it is presented in the following way:

> "You are given four separate pieces of chain which each have a length of three links. It costs 20¢ to open a link and 30¢ to close a link. All links are closed at the beginning of the problem. Your goal is to join all 12 chain links to create a single circle at a cost of no more than $1.50."

This means that the problem cannot be solved by four openings and closures as described above, because the total cost would exceed $1.50. In order to find a solution, the initial state of the problem has to be re-described. Instead of four chains, only three chains need to be connected, which requires only three connections to be made. The fourth chain is no longer considered as a permanently linked chain, but as a collection of three single links used to connect the three chains, as visualized in Figure 8.5. The goal state can now be described as "Three connections between three chains, each consisting of three links, with the help of three further links, resulting in a 12-link necklace" or simply described with the multiplication "3 × (3 + 1) = 12." Now, the path from the initial state to the goal state involves opening and closing only three links, which satisfies the financial constraints.

The key to solving this problem is the relaxation of unnecessary constraints. The initial assumption that the four chains have to be maintained

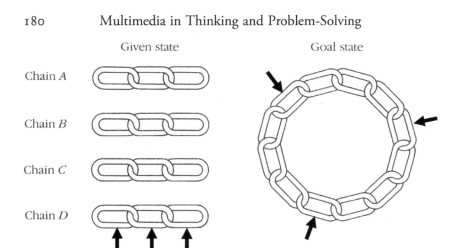

Figure 8.5   The necklace problem: Three links solution

as separate entities, which impedes problem-solving, has to be abandoned. The resulting re-description of the initial state activates other knowledge from long-term memory and allows alternative solution paths to be detected. When the unnecessary constraint is omitted from the descriptive representation, the problem is seen from a new perspective and the solution becomes straightforward.

Interplay of Descriptive and Depictive Representations: The previous examples illustrate how descriptive and depictive representations interact and thus combine representational power and inferential power in thinking and problem-solving. This interaction takes place through processes of model construction and model inspection, as described in Chapter 6 with regard to the ITPC model. For problem-solving, this means that a propositional representation of the problem serves as a basis for constructing a corresponding mental model of the problem situation. The propositional representation guides mental model construction by imposing constraints on the mental model. When the model allows the required information to be read off through model inspection, the problem can be solved directly. In the case of the hiking problem, for example, this occurs when the problem-solver notices that the path-time curves of the two hikers intersect. This implies that they meet, which means that they are in the same place at the same time. This result is read off from the mental model and encoded in a descriptive, propositional format.

The examples also illustrate that flexible, productive thinking requires a specific interplay between mental structures and mental procedures. First, the mental structures need to grasp the structures of a subject matter correctly. Second, they have to facilitate performance of the required procedures. Easy performance of procedures means that the required operations are not difficult and that the sequences of operations are relatively short.

Descriptions usually allow construction of different depictive representations. These depictive representations may all comply with the description, but nevertheless allow different operations to be applied to them. These operations can differ in terms of difficulty. Depictive representations that allow fewer or easier operations than others are advantageous for solving a problem. Accordingly, higher-order cognitive processing largely involves searching for the best depictive representation based on the initially given descriptive representation.

When the mental model of a problem does not allow the required information to be read off even after the model has been operated on, the representation of the problem needs restructuring. Restructuring of descriptive propositional representations includes relaxing constraints by omitting irrelevant details (such as the condition of two separate days in the hiker problem), adding new elements (such as a second person), or re-encoding some aspects (such as adding the concept "meet"). Restructuring of the depictive representation occurs by transforming the previous mental model into a new model with a new structure, for example, by merging two previously separated models into one integrated model, as visualized in Figure 8.1.

8.2 Implications for Mathematics Education

Experts in mathematics education have repeatedly pointed out that students in primary school receive much training in operating with numbers, but very little training in thinking mathematically and in solving problems with mathematics (if any). The spontaneous strategies applied by young children when solving mathematical tasks that are problems for them, because they do not know the corresponding algorithms yet, provide interesting insights into their usage of representations. In this section, we will consider the strategies of elementary school children who solved tasks expected to enhance mathematical thinking. The tasks were taken from a selection of early mathematical problem-solving tasks published by Renate Rasch.[6]

---

[6] Rasch (2003).

There are 4 children. Each child
shakes hands with 3 children.
4 × 3 = 12. Twelve handshakes.

Mary   Christine   Kevin   Paul

Figure 8.6   Handshake task: John's solution

The Handshake Task

"When Mary, Christine, Kevin, and Paul meet on their way to school in the morning, they shake hands. How many handshakes take place among them?"

This task was given to students in the fourth grade. In order to solve the task, many students stated that there are four children and declared correctly that each child shakes hands with three other children. So, they inferred that the total number of handshakes must be 4 times 3, which equals 12. Accordingly, they answered that 12 handshakes take place. Of course, this answer ignored the fact that a handshake is a bi-directional activity; when A shakes hands with B, B also shakes hands with A.

Note that the above solution was essentially based on a descriptive representation. The students read the description and transformed their verbal description into a mathematical description. The resulting term "4 × 3" was then operated on according to numerical rules.

John: The shortcomings of students' mathematical thinking on a purely descriptive basis can often be overcome by adding a depictive representation. This is why teachers frequently advise students to imagine the described situation and to create a picture of it. One student, John, followed this advice and created the picture shown in Figure 8.6. However, this picture only portrayed the irrelevant outer appearance of the four children. It did not grasp the mathematical structure of the described situation in terms of handshakes. John's picture was useless for answering the question. He came up with the same incorrect result of 12 handshakes. Like other students who had not drawn a picture, John operated only on a descriptive representation by mechanically performing numeric operations (i.e., symbol processing) triggered by this representation.

Sarah: Another student, Sarah, created another picture of the handshake task, as shown in Figure 8.7. This picture is very different from

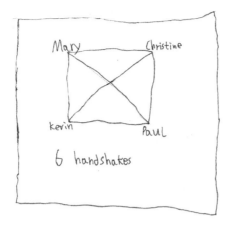

Figure 8.7   Handshake task: Sarah's solution

John's picture. It is more abstract and does not include irrelevant visual attributes of the children. Instead, it visualizes the mathematical structure of the described situation in terms of the interaction between the children. Handshakes are represented by lines, each line representing one handshake. In other words, Sarah created a mindful depictive representation which triggered the adequate inspection processes. In this case, model inspection required her to only count the connections. There were six lines, representing six handshakes, which was the correct response.

The results of model-inspection processes operating on depictive representations can be stored in a propositional format as additional parts of the descriptive representation. Adequate depictive representations can provide guidance for symbol processing, such as numerical computations operating on descriptive representations, and they can block inappropriate numerical operations or other incorrect inferences. Further, they should allow easy performance of task-relevant operations. Sarah's drawing fulfilled this requirement, whereas John's drawing did not.

The example of the handshake task demonstrates that successful problem-solving can be enhanced by depictive representations such as visualization and mental model construction. However, depictive representations do not per se support problem-solving. They only do so if they emphasize the task-relevant mathematical structure of the problem at hand. A depictive representation that does not grasp the underlying mathematical structure can give rise to flawed descriptions and lead to erroneous results.

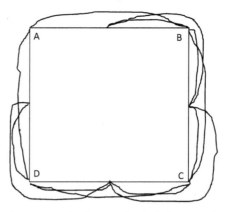

Figure 8.8   Little ant task: Cathy's approach

The Little Ant Task

> "A square has a side length of 200 meters. A little ant walks along the sides of the square. In the daytime, the ant travels exactly 200 meters. At night, however, a strong wind blows the ant back half of the distance that it has traveled during the day. The ant starts on Monday morning. It starts from A moving to B, C, and D, and then back to A. When will the ant arrive at A?"

This task was given to students in the fourth grade together with a drawing of a square illustrating the described situation. The students implemented very different strategies to answer the question depending on the kind of representation they were operating on.

Cathy: The strategy used by Cathy was to reproduce the ant's path. She used the drawing of the square and elaborated it, as shown in Figure 8.8. Cathy explained her strategy as follows:

> "I went from A to B, and then I went 100 meters back. I continued along this path until I reached A again. I found that the ant arrives at A after 7 days. So, it should arrive at A on Sunday."

Cathy's strategy was totally depictive. She operated exclusively on a pictorial representation, trying to reconstruct the ant's path step by step on the square. In order to find the solution, she counted the days required to follow this path back to A. Although this strategy led to the correct answer in her case, it is generally prone to error, because one can easily miss a step or miscount the performed steps.

David: Another student, David, concluded that the ant needed eight days for its journey and would arrive next Monday. He explained his thinking as follows:

> "The square has four sides. Each side has a length of 200 meters. So, the ant has to travel 800 meters. The ant travels 200 meters in the daytime but is blown back 100 meters at night. Altogether, it moves forward only 100 meters per day. Therefore, the ant needs 8 days, because 800 divided by 100 equals 8. So, it should arrive at A on Monday."

David's strategy was mainly descriptive. The pictorial representation was used, if at all, to verify that a square has four sides of equal length. All the rest was done by numerical symbol processing based on the task description:

$$4 \times 200 \text{ m} = 800 \text{ m}$$
$$200 \text{ m} - 100 \text{ m} = 100 \text{ m}$$
$$800 \text{ m} / 100 \text{ m} = 8.$$

David used the descriptive symbolic representation in a mechanical way with no reference to the depictive representation as a means for checking and constraining his computations. Due to this lack of interaction between the descriptive and depictive representations, he failed to recognize that the ant is more advanced in the evening than it is the next morning. The ant arrives at point A already by the end of the seventh day. If David had mapped the descriptive symbolic representation on the depictive representation, he could have recognized the evening–morning difference. This might have helped him to find the correct solution.

Rahel: A further student, Rahel, used a strategy whereby her depictive representation closely interacted with her descriptive representation. She placed distance tags on the square (100, 200, 300, ... 800) which allowed one-to-one mapping of the graphical entities onto the descriptive terms. Rahel's solution is shown in Figure 8.9. She created a table which described the beginning and the end of the distance traveled by the ant for each day: 000–200 for Day 1, 100–300 for Day 2, 200–400 for Day 3, and so forth. In this way, she created a set of separate descriptions, one for each day, which served as a kind of "log file" of the ant's journey around the square. The data in the table can be interpreted as the results of her inspecting the model. The stepwise elaboration of the table finally led to the entry "600–800 for Day 7," which allowed her to answer the question correctly: The ant needs seven days. Rahel's strategy avoided the weaknesses of the approaches used by Cathy and David by conjointly utilizing

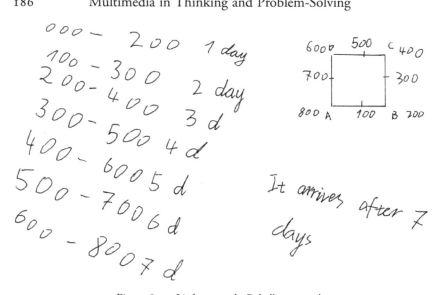

Figure 8.9   Little ant task: Rahel's approach

two kinds of representations and by systematically applying inspection processes to the depictive representations.

Thus, the example illustrates that the interaction between a depictive and a descriptive representation can provide a better basis for successful problem-solving than the usage of only one kind of representation, because one kind of representation constrains the construction and usage of the other one.

Fraction Numbers

After having been educated about how to operate with integer numbers in elementary school, most students learn in Grades 5 and 6 how to operate with fraction numbers. They usually have no difficulty to understand that a whole (symbolized by "1") can be divided into equal parts. Mostly, teachers introduce the fraction concept together with area models. A whole can be visualized by a circle, and its parts by circular sectors. Students can easily see that a division into 2, 3, 4, 5 (and so forth) equally sized parts results in halves, thirds, quarters, fifths (and so forth). They can also see that one-half is bigger than one-third, one-third bigger than one-quarter, one-quarter bigger than one-fifth (and so forth). Area models also make it easy to understand why only fractions of the same kind (i.e., with the same denominator) can be added or subtracted by adding or subtracting the numerators while retaining the denominator. Fractions with the same denominator represent the same kind of entity, which is a prerequisite for addition and subtraction.

Multiplication of fractions is conceptually more demanding than addition and subtraction, because the status of the whole changes during the course of the operation. In a multiplication such as "$1/2 \times 1/3$" ("one half of one third"), a whole of size 1 is first subdivided into three equal parts, each $1/3$ in size. In the next step, one of the parts of the size $1/3$ becomes a new whole. This new, subordinated whole is then subdivided into two equal sub-parts. The result is, therefore, a part of a part of the whole (which is of course necessarily also a part of the whole by itself). In brief, the multiplication of fractions is about determining the size of parts of parts of a whole.

The abovementioned operations – addition, subtraction, and multiplication – with fraction numbers and their underlying concepts, are usually explained with the help of area models. That is, the descriptive representations of fractions are combined and coordinated with the corresponding depictive representations. Surprisingly, this is frequently not the case when it comes to learning about the division of fractions. Instead, the division of fractions is learned only with a purely syntactic rule for symbol processing, which can be applied mechanically without deeper understanding:

"Multiply the dividend with the reciprocal value of the divisor."

Accordingly, the division of fractions is practiced in a mechanical, purely syntactic way by following algorithms without further consideration of what these operations really mean. As a result, students and even teachers are often unaware of the semantics behind these algorithms.

A telling example was reported by Orrill and her colleagues.[7] In their study, teachers (who taught both mathematics and other subjects) were asked to solve fraction tasks such as "$(3/4) / (1/8)$" ("three-quarters divided by one-eighth"). Nearly all of them came up with the correct result, which is 6 in this case. In the final step of each task, the teachers were asked to choose the adequate visualization of the result among different alternatives. For the division task "$(3/4) / (1/8)$," for example, they had to choose between the two visualizations shown in Figure 8.10. Surprisingly, the majority of the teachers opted for the incorrect visualization (a) instead of the correct visualization (b).

---

[7] Orrill et al. (2008).

3/4 : 1/8

Choose the right visualization!

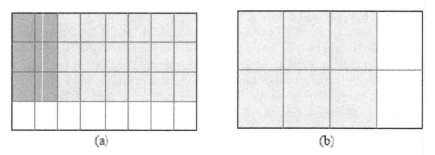

(a)   (b)

Figure 8.10   Division of fractions with depictive area models

Why did this happen? Teachers who chose the incorrect model obviously performed the computations using routine arithmetic symbol processing, which led them to the correct result of 6. Then, they looked for a graphical entity that appeared six times and found it in the left panel of the figure. In other words, they used the depictive representations only as a means of illustrating the solution which they had found by other means. They did not use the depictive representation as a cognitive tool for finding the solution, which was demonstrated by their limited understanding of the numerical symbol processing based on descriptive representations.

In the present case, the depictive representation could be used as a cognitive tool as follows. We know that a division answers the question as to how often the divisor fits into the dividend. For example, the term "12 / 3 = 4" means that 3 fits 4 times into 12. By the same token, the division of fractions simply identifies how often one part of the whole fits into another part of the whole. In other words, the divisor part is used as the unit for measuring the size of the dividend part. This idea is visualized in image (b) in Figure 8.10. One part of the whole is the shaded area which is "3/4" in size. The whole was also divided into eight equal parts, as shown by the eight rectangles in image (b). Thus, the division described by the term "(3/4) / (1/8)" answers the question as to how often these rectangles of size "1/8" fit into the shaded area. Thus, the correct answer 6 is shown by visualization (b), not by visualization (a).

It goes without saying that operating with area models should not replace operating with numbers when computing fractions. However, these depictive representations can be used as tools that help students to understand what the arithmetic operations of computing fractions are about. The numeric symbol processing operations can be mapped on to equivalent operations based on depictive representations. This should contribute to understanding the semantics of arithmetic operations, which could finally lead to deeper comprehension of the mathematical content. The use of depictive representations is not just about visually elaborating mathematical content; it is not about adding pictures of the initial state and goal state of a problem or about embedding mathematical content in everyday contexts. It is about flexibly using multiple representations, which can be called "representational flexibility." Students need to learn how to map different representations systematically onto each other and use depictive representations as cognitive tools for their operations.

Mathematical Proofs

A famous mathematical problem which was pointed out by Greek philosopher Plutarch is the following:

> "For which rectangles of whole-number side lengths (of any unit) are the perimeter and area numerically the same? Can one be sure that there are no further rectangles that satisfy this condition?"

Students in upper-secondary schools are usually able to answer the first question without serious difficulties. They identify "4×4" and "3×6" as possible solutions by trial and error. However, it is difficult for them to answer the second question, which requires proof that these are the only possible solutions. In fact, there are multiple possible proofs which operate on different kinds of representations.[8] We will consider two of them: the factorization proof and the tiles proof.

Factorization Proof: This proof starts with the Osiris equation

$$a \times b = 2a + 2b.$$

This statement of equivalence can be transformed into further equivalence statements within the descriptive problem space, such as

---

[8] Greer et al. (2009).

$$a \times b - 2b = 2a; \quad b \times (a - 2) = 2a; \quad b = 2a/(a - 2).$$

The latter can be further transformed into $b = (2a - 4 + 4) / (a - 2)$. This can be transformed into $b = (2 \times (a - 2) + 4) / (a - 2)$, which in turn leads to

$$b = 2 + 4/(a - 2).$$

Because a and b are whole numbers, the term "$4 / (a - 2)$" must also represent a whole number. This requires that $(a - 2)$ is a factor of 4, which means that 4 is a multiple of $(a - 2)$. Thus, only the following possibilities remain: $(a - 2) = 1$, $(a - 2) = 2$, and $(a - 2) = 4$. From this, one can conclude that a is either 3, 4, or 6. Because $b = 2 + 4 / (a - 2)$, b is either 6, 4, or 3. Thus, one can conclude that only the following rectangles satisfy the Osiris equation:

$$3 \times 6, \quad 4 \times 4, \quad \text{and} \quad 6 \times 3.$$

Because 3×6 and 6×3 are equivalent descriptions of the same rectangle, in fact only two rectangles are possible solutions of the Osiris problem. Note that the factorization proof is purely descriptive. Proceeding from an initial description of the subject matter, the problem-solver generates new descriptions by manipulating symbols which eventually narrow down the range of possible solutions to two options.

Tiling Proof: This proof is based on the fact that a rectangle with whole-number side lengths can be constructed with tiles of 1×1 size. If one adds tiles within a rectangle only along the perimeter of the rectangle, the number of tiles equals the perimeter minus 4, because the four corners of the rectangle are not tiled twice. After tiles have been laid along the perimeter, which is referred to as the outer area of the rectangle, there remains an inner area without tiles. Figure 8.11 demonstrates the concept of a rectangle's outer and inner areas as a result of laying tiles along the perimeter. The outer area and inner area together form the total area of the rectangle. This implies:

Total Area = Perimeter minus 4 plus Inner Area.

The Osiris criterion requires the total area and the perimeter to be numerically the same. This is only true when the inner area is of size 4. An inner area of size 4 is only possible when the inner area measures 2×2, 1×4, or 4×1 (whereby the latter two are equivalent). Because the side lengths of the total rectangle are longer than the side lengths of the inner rectangle by +2, it follows that only two rectangles are possible solutions of the Osiris problem – 4×4 and 3×6 – as shown in Figure 8.11. Note that this proof operates primarily on depictive representations, whereby the

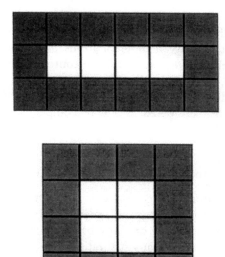

Figure 8.11   Tiling proof of the Osiris problem

representation's attributes are read off via inspection processes and recorded in a descriptive format in terms of equations.

In a study about the opinions of future teachers of mathematics, Greer and his colleagues[9] found a higher preference for the factorization proof, while the tiling proof was considered as relatively "unmathematical." This raises the question as to whether there is a culture of teaching mathematics with a disposition to using descriptive algebraic representations that are relatively unrelated to depictive representations. If this supposition is correct, pictures possibly serve only for an initial visualization of basic concepts, but then play only a minor role in "real mathematics." The main emphasis in mathematics teaching would then be on the virtuosic, efficient (mechanical) manipulation of symbols according to algebraic routines without semantic reference to depictive representations and, thus, without attainment of a deeper understanding. This kind of teaching would aim at developing routine expertise (i.e., the ability to find quick and exact solutions to mathematical tasks by manipulating symbols, even without semantic understanding) instead of adaptive expertise (i.e., the ability to flexibly adapt procedures in a mindful and creative way).[10]

[9] Greer et al. (2009).   [10] Hatano and Inagaki (1986).

Cognitive flexibility in solving mathematical problems requires more than quick and effective manipulation of algebraic terms. It also requires the ability to switch between different forms of representations, understand their interrelationships, translate the content of one representation into one another, and apply the relevant operations. Representational flexibility – including flexible use of both descriptive and depictive representations – can be considered as a core competence of mathematical creativity.

8.3   Implications for Science Education

Pictures such as sectional images or schematic drawings are used everywhere in science and technology. In order to communicate knowledge, these pictures need to be read carefully based on sufficient prior knowledge. It goes without saying that visualizations also play an important role in science education. The broad range of scientific subjects and phenomena are mirrored in a vast abundance of pictures, maps, graphs, and other kinds of visualizations, as demonstrated by the work of Edward Tufte[11] and Harry Robin,[12] for example. These visualizations need to be carefully designed so that they grasp and emphasize the basic structure of a subject matter. The importance of this has already been pointed out. A depictive representation that does not grasp the underlying structure of a subject matter can give rise to flawed descriptions and lead to erroneous results. However, even after adequate model construction and correct visualization, model inspection can lead to incorrect results when operations are not applied systematically to depictive representations with sufficient care. This will be demonstrated through some examples.

An Example from Learning about Geometrical Optics
Students of geometrical optics who were learning about the course of light rays in case of reflection received the following task:

> "Imagine two large mirrors M1 and M2 positioned in a room so that their configuration is approximately rectangular, as shown in Figure 8.12. There is a burning candle in the room and an observer. How many times does the observer see the candle? Demonstrate where the candles seem to be for the observer."

---

[11] Tufte (1990, 1997).   [12] Robin (1992).

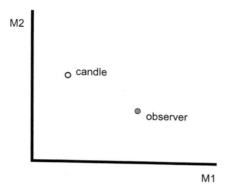

Figure 8.12   A candle observed in a room with two mirrors, M1 and M2

Note that the question does not refer solely to the candle's reflections. The observer can see the candle both by reflection and directly, which students sometimes forget to take into account. The others usually answer that the observer sees the candle three times: once directly and two times in the two mirrors M1 and M2. These students' drawing of the assumed course of the light rays is shown in Figure 8.13. Their usual explanation is that a light ray emitted by the candle is reflected at R1 and then meets the eye of the observer, who sees the candle (as Candle 1) at the corresponding location. Another light ray emitted by the candle is reflected at R2 before it meets the eye of the observer, who sees the candle (as Candle 2) at the corresponding location.

These answers are not fully correct, because the observer sees the candle four times: once directly, once reflected by mirror M1, once reflected by mirror M2, and once reflected by mirrors M1 and M2. In the latter case, a light ray emitted by the candle is reflected at R3' and then at R3", before it meets the eye of the observer who sees the candle (as Candle 3) at the corresponding location. The correct drawing is shown in Figure 8.14.

Model inspection processes aim at reading off task-relevant attributes from a depictive representation. In the case of the initial depictive representation shown in Figure 8.12, model inspection can be compared to an interrogation. Two things are essential for this interrogation. First, the student has to ask the right questions in order to obtain the right answers from the depictive representation. Second, the set of questions should be exhaustive with regard to the task at hand. Otherwise, the result is likely to be incorrect. In the above example, the students asked the right questions:

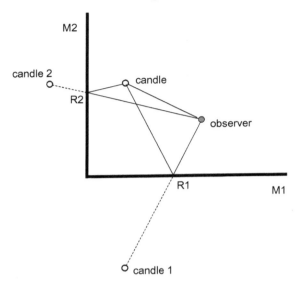

Figure 8.13   Candle–mirror solution: "Candle appears three times"

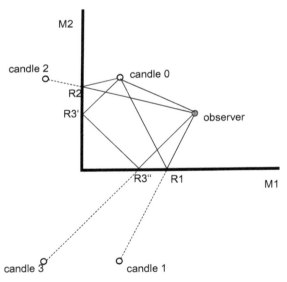

Figure 8.14   Candle–mirror solution: "Candle appears four times"

- How do the light rays emitted by the candle meet the observer's eyes directly?
- How are the light rays emitted by the candle reflected by mirror M1 before they meet the observer's eyes?
- How are the light rays emitted by the candle reflected by mirror M2 before they meet the observer's eyes?

However, these questions were incomplete because they lacked a further possible question:

- How are the light rays emitted by the candle reflected by mirror M1 and by mirror M2 before they meet the observer's eyes?

In brief, the example demonstrates that model inspection requires systematic and exhaustive interrogation of depictive representations in order to read off relevant information. The results are not "just there." Investigating the depictive representation may need a well-planned task-oriented sequence of processes which involve reading off the required relevant information in order to make sure that interrogation of the depictive representation is really complete.

An Example from Learning about Electricity
Erroneous model inspection can also result from semantic inconsistencies within the inspection process or from incorrect inferences drawn from the inspection results. This is demonstrated by the following example from learning about electricity. Students learning about electricity are frequently required to analyze pictures of complex electric wirings and answer specific questions about these wirings. Complex electric wirings can be segmented into sub-structures, which in turn can be replaced by simple elements in such a way that the functioning of the whole system remains the same. For example, a complex circuit of ohmic resistors can be replaced by a single ohmic resistor without changing the functioning of the whole electric system. So, the single resistor functions as a substitute for the circuit of ohmic resistors. Students learning about electricity are usually expected to know how to determine the substitute ohmic resistance for a given wiring of ohmic resistors.

An example of this kind of task which was presented to secondary-school students is shown in Figure 8.15. The figure shows a wiring of three Ohm's electric resistors accompanied by a verbal description of the wiring. Students were asked to determine which ohmic resistance would be a substitute for the combination of resistors shown in the figure.

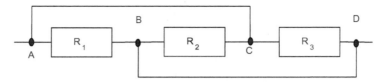

Point A is connected via resistor R_1 to point B. Point B is connected via resistor R_2 to point C.

Point C is connected via resistor R_3 to point D. Point A is connected with no resistance to C, and

point B is connected with no resistance to D. All resistors R1, R2 and R3 have the same

amount R.

What is the substitute resistance of the whole circuit?

Figure 8.15   Structure of an electric resistance problem

Depending on their inspection processes, students came up with different answers. One of the students, Michael, gave the following answer:

> "Direct connections between two points in an electric circuit have an extremely small resistance which can be ignored. Therefore, the connections between A and C and between B and D are not important for computing the substitute resistance. Accordingly, the structure corresponds to a simple serial combination, and the substitute resistance is 3 R."

Another student, Peter, answered as follows:

> "At Point A, the electric current divides into two partial currents: I1 and I2. The current searches for the lowest resistance. Thus, it flows on the one hand from A to C and from there via R3 to D and, on the other hand, from A via R1 to B and from there to D. Accordingly, there is a parallel combination of resistances R1 and R3, and no current flows through R2. Thus, the substitute resistance for the combination above is R/2."

A third answer given by another student, Gretchen, was:

> "The structure is a parallel combination of three equal resistances. Therefore, the substitute resistance for the above combination is R/3."

What was the correct answer and what had gone wrong when students came up with an incorrect one? Michael's view of a simple linear combination of resistors might be triggered by the linear appearance of the wiring, as shown in Figure 8.15. He assumed that the connections between A and C and between B and D could be ignored. This was not correct. The resistance of these connections could be ignored, but the connections themselves could not. Thus, Michael falsely replaced "ignoring the resistance of connections" with "ignoring the connections." This semantic lapse led him to fundamentally misread the depictive representation and give a false response.

Peter's description of the current's flow was largely correct. The electric current flows indeed from C to D via R3 and from A to B via R1, insofar as R1 and R3 are in fact combined in parallel. However, Peter incorrectly assumed that no current flows through R2. This might again have been triggered by the depiction in Figure 8.15, in which the total current flows from A to D, that is, from left to right. The picture suggests that the current can "bypass" R2, on the one hand via the connection A–C and, on the other hand, via the connection B–D. This misreading of the depictive representation also resulted in a false response.

Why is it so difficult to find the right answer in this example? Remember that, according to Ohlsson's Representational Change Theory, the initial state of a problem represented in the individual's mind serves as a memory probe which activates operators in long-term memory. An inappropriate representation of the initial problem state activates inadequate operators which lead to an impasse. In the present case, the difficulty might originate from the visual appearance of the depictive representation shown in Figure 8.15, which seems to show a serial circuit of resistors due to its visual similarity to serial combinations. This similarity obviously dominates model inspection and activates inappropriate schemata which then trigger unsuitable operations leading to misinterpretations of the depictive representation. Likewise, the visual structure of the depictive representation does not activate the appropriate schemata and, thus, blocks appropriate inspection processes. The task is much easier when the depictive representation shown in Figure 8.15 undergoes a topologically invariant transformation, as shown in Figure 8.16. The transformation follows a simple rule: "If two points are directly connected, they can be merged into one point." The result of the transformation has the same topological structure as the previous depictive representation. After the transformation, it can easily be seen that the overall structure of the wiring is indeed a parallel circuit of three resistors. Thus, Gretchen's solution was the correct one. The transformed depictive representation triggers the appropriate inspection processes and blocks the inappropriate ones.

As the example demonstrates, it is not sufficient to construct a depictive representation of a specific task. Instead, it is also important that the depictive representation allows the relevant features to be read easily.

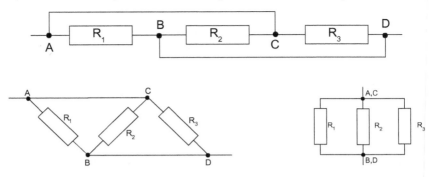

Figure 8.16   Structure of an electric resistance problem: Transformed

The specific perceptual structure can obscure the relevant structural attributes, preventing the application of correct procedures and stimulating the application of incorrect procedures. Beyond that, all the examples considered here demonstrate that thinking and problem-solving profit not only from combining descriptive and depictive representations but also from ongoing close and mindful interaction between these representations. This interaction influences the construction processes (which create and constrain depictive representations based on descriptive representations) and the inspection processes (which elaborate descriptive representations based on the systematic and careful analysis of depictive representations).

8.4   Exploratory Thinking

Searching for the Causes of an Epidemic: Depictive representations can also help to collect data in a way that enables them to serve a heuristic function for problem-solving. Figure 8.17 shows an early historic example where a picture is used to explore the causes of a phenomenon. The figure shows a map of Central London drawn by Dr. John Snow during a cholera epidemic in 1854. Snow depicted every death with a small dot. He hypothesized that the outbreak of cholera was in some way related to the water supply. Thus, he depicted every well in the area with a cross (×) on the map. He noticed that most people who died lived close to the well in Broad Street in the middle of the map, perhaps because they took their water from there. Further investigation revealed that some people who lived further outside had also taken water from this well, because it was on their way home from work. Dr. Snow had the handle removed from the well, which put an end to the disease.

Figure 8.17   Dr. Snow's map of Central London with dots for cholera deaths and crosses
for water pumps
(from Tufte, 1983)

It should be noticed that the map alone could not solve the problem. Snow also needed a hypothesis, namely the hypothesis that the disease was caused by drinking contaminated water. This led him to note the location of water wells. With another hypothesis, he might have noted very different things. But Snow was lucky and his hypothesis was confirmed. A further (albeit trivial) hypothesis was that most people avoid walking long distances and instead fetch their water from the closest well. The few exceptions of people living and dying further away from the Broad Street well could be explained by the fact that these people took their water from

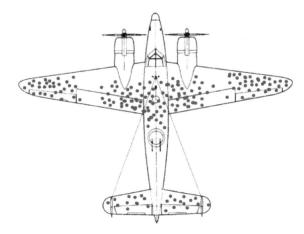

Figure 8.18   Abraham Wald's depictive solution of the airplane armoring problem in
World War II
(from Researchgate.net)

this well on their way home, as revealed in interviews with their neighbors. In short, the data were collected and visualized in a depictive representation which was implicitly guided by a specific hypothesis. This resulted in a thematic map with two themes: deaths and the water supply.

Protection of War Planes: Another famous example of the heuristic usage of pictures stems from the Hungarian mathematician Abraham Wald. In 1943, when American bombers suffered losses due to Nazi Germany's air defense, the military searched for advice to reduce these losses. Wald started to map each bullet hole on the planes that returned from a combat mission onto an outline of the bomber, as shown in Figure 8.18. The resulting visualizations showed that most bullet holes were located on the wings and the tail of the planes, but less on the cockpit, the engines, and the rudder. While military officers concluded that the heavily damaged areas should receive more armor, Wald suggested the opposite:

> "Do not arm the damaged areas of the returning planes! They came back. They obviously could sustain damage and bring their pilots home despite the damage. Thus, reinforce the areas that were not damaged!"

Wald's reasoning was that the enemy's bullets were being randomly fired, because accurately targeting specific parts of the bomber was not possible at great distances. Thus, he assumed that there must have been bombers with bullet holes in the areas that appeared to be undamaged. However, these bombers were not included in the sample of the returned planes because they could not come back. In other words, these areas on the surviving planes were only undamaged because they were lucky not to be hit. Those planes that were hit in these areas were no longer able to fly and could not return from their missions. Once again, the visualization alone did not do the job of problem-solving. Wald had to combine the data in the visualization with hypotheses from mathematical probability theory and biased sampling in order to draw his ingenious conclusion which saved numerous lives.

8.5 Takeaways

Comprehension can be (and usually is) the starting point for further cognitive activities such as thinking and problem-solving. These activities operate on the mental representations created by comprehension, which include conceptual propositional (descriptive) representations and mental models (depictive representations). Descriptive representations and depictive representations interact via model construction and model inspection processes, whereby each representation constrains the construction and usage of the other representation.

Thinking can be viewed as operating on mental representations in order to obtain new information about a subject matter. Thinking takes the form of cognitive problem-solving when the individual has to transform an initial state of a subject matter representation into a desired goal state of the subject matter representation without knowing an algorithm for performing this transformation. The latter qualifies cognitive problem-solving as productive thinking. Problem-solving implies that the individual tries to find the shortest and easiest sequence of procedures to transform the initial state into the goal state.

Model inspection includes reading off task-relevant attributes by "interrogating" the model. When the mental model allows the required information to be directly read off from its current state (i.e., when it is in the goal state), problem-solving is successful. If the representation does not allow such a state to be created and the required information to be extracted, another approach is required and the problem representation needs to be restructured. Descriptive propositional representations are restructured by adding new information or by relaxing constraints. Depictive representations are restructured by transforming the previous mental model into a new model with a new structure.

Thinking and problem-solving require adequately structured representations and appropriate processes which operate on these structures. Thus,
they require a specific interplay between mental structures and mental
procedures. The mental representations need to grasp the structures of a
subject matter correctly and allow easy performance of the required procedures. Mental representations serve as memory probes which activate
operators in long-term memory. If the mental representation activates
inappropriate operations, the problem cannot be solved. Accordingly,
depictive representations such as graphics need to be designed with great
care, because their perceptual representation can obscure task-relevant
structural attributes. In such cases, model inspection can be dominated
by inappropriate cognitive schemata which prevent activation of the
required correct operations and lead to misinterpretation of problems.

Pictures should not only serve to illustrate an initial state or a goal state
of a problem and visually elaborate a subject matter within the context of
everyday experiences. They can also serve as cognitive tools, when they
emphasize the task-relevant structure of a problem and support understanding of the semantics of descriptive symbol processing routines.

Productive thinking and cognitive problem-solving require the ability to
switch between different forms of representations, understand their interrelationships, and translate representations and their associated operations
into each other. In education, students need to learn how to systematically
map different representations onto other representations. Such flexible use
of multiple representations constitutes representational flexibility. Based
on specific a-priori hypotheses, depictive representations can serve as useful
tools for collecting data for heuristic purposes.

CHAPTER 9

Practical Implications

Abstract

Multimedia communication design is a form of complex problem-solving. It requires heuristics which take into account addressees' cognitive abilities and prior knowledge, the complexity of the subject matter, processing conditions, time limits, and other factors. Multimedia designers have to be aware of the asymmetry between texts and pictures in terms of representational principles and communication functions, including the fact that texts and pictures compensate for their inherent ambiguities by reciprocal disambiguation. Designers have to be further aware that multimedia comprehension starts with initial mental model construction primarily guided by the text, which is then followed by adaptive mental model specification primarily guided by the picture for specific task requirements. Text design should enable smooth continuous coherence formation within the right text modality. Picture design should enable scaffolding for mental model construction and visualize the essential structure of a subject matter with regard to future tasks. Above all, multimedia design needs to adequately synchronize the different comprehension processes.

What are the implications of the previous analysis for the design of multimedia messages? Answering this question requires the consideration of numerous aspects which have to be weighted and balanced against each other according to the specific context. It goes without saying that such complex design tasks cannot be approached solely with lists of simple rules of thumb. In fact, multimedia communication is complex problem-solving based on heuristics. These heuristics can act as orientation guides, helping designers to focus on the relevant aspects and to weight these aspects in terms of their relative importance. In this way, such guides help designers to find well-balanced solutions for the communication problem at hand. Such orientation guides need to be derived from sufficient theoretical background knowledge about human perception and cognition based on empirical research. The following chapter presents a sketch of such orientation guides for the design of multimedia messages derived from the previous analysis.

9.1 Use or Non-use of Multimedia?

When should we use multimedia to convey messages and when should we not use them? A combination of text with semantically related pictures is recommended if addressees have sufficient cognitive abilities to process both texts and pictures and relate them semantically to each other, but find it too difficult to construct a mental model of the subject matter based only on a text or only on a picture. The difficulties may result from a lack of prior knowledge, the high complexity of the subject matter, or limited processing time. If addressees have sufficient prior knowledge to construct a mental model only from a text or only from a picture and there are no serious time constraints, there is no reason to use multimedia to convey messages. Using multimedia in this case would waste time and cognitive resources. Thus, the following recommendation can be made:

> Use text combined with content-related pictures when recipients have low prior knowledge but sufficient cognitive abilities to process both the text and the pictures. Do not combine text and pictures if recipients have sufficient prior knowledge and cognitive abilities to construct a mental model from one source of information only.

This recommendation does not require an all-or-nothing decision for the whole message. Instead, the decision as to whether text paragraphs should be supplemented with pictures or not has to be made in an iterative manner during the design process, resulting in a higher or lower share of multimedia.

9.2 Complementary Functions of Texts and Pictures

Texts and pictures use different representational principles and have different representational and inferential characteristics. Accordingly, they are tools for different purposes. Multimedia designers should be aware of this asymmetry between texts and pictures.

Texts and pictures can also enhance the process of multimedia comprehension through reciprocal disambiguation. Descriptions of a subject matter by a text are usually not completely specific but allow some degrees of freedom when the subject matter has to be imagined or drawn (with varying images or drawings all matching the same text description). This inherent ambiguity of text can be reduced by a picture that provides the specificity that was lacking in the text. Conversely, pictures usually allow multiple interpretations and an accompanying text can make it clear which interpretation is meant. Thus, texts and pictures can compensate for each other's inherent ambiguities through mutual disambiguation, as explained in Chapter 6. As a result, the following recommendation can be made:

> Present a pictorial sketch of the subject matter without unnecessary details as an external scaffold for the addressee's initial mental model construction.

9.3 Phases of Multimedia Comprehension

Before recipients of multimedia messages go into the detail of messages in order to deal with specific problems, they typically want to acquire a general understanding of what the message is about first. Their processing is directed at forming general coherence and constructing an initial mental model before they begin further elaborating and adapting their model according to the requirements of specific tasks. In brief, the initial phase of general coherence formation and initial mental model construction are oriented toward global understanding. After attainment of an initial general understanding, the phase of adaptive mental model specification follows, which involves updating the model to meet specific task requirements.

Do texts and pictures play different roles in these phases? Due to the asymmetry between texts and pictures, the two forms of representation do indeed play different roles during different phases of multimedia comprehension, as explained in Chapter 7. Initial mental model construction is primarily directed by the text which provides explicit conceptual guidance for the process of comprehension in addition to minor initial pictorial scaffolding of mental model construction through a coarse pictorial sketch of the subject matter. Adaptive mental model specification receives its primary information input from pictures, because pictures provide highly flexible access to manifold pieces of specific information in order to update the mental models for specific task requirements. When text information is presented and processed conjointly with picture information, the two kinds of representation should result in mutually constrained interpretations, excluding ambiguities as far as possible. Further, designers of multimedia messages should take into account the different functions of texts and pictures as complementary tools for comprehension during initial mental model construction and adaptive mental model specification.

9.4   Text Design

How should texts for multimedia messages be designed? Texts play a central role in initial mental model construction by providing explicit guidance for a recipient's conceptual analysis of a subject matter and its visualization. The words and phrases in the surface structure of a text can be considered as triggers which activate cognitive procedures, leading to the construction of mental representations. The author (or speaker) contributes to comprehension by continuously supplying information and providing aids for coherence formation, allowing a mental model to be constructed as smoothly as possible. However, the author (or speaker) is not the only one to contribute to comprehension. The reader (or listener) also adds his or her own inferences to enhance coherence formation. As already mentioned in Chapter 4, communication is a cooperative process. Accordingly, text design is about finding a reasonable balance between providing external guidance to the recipient and the recipient's own autonomous processing.

9.4.1   Text Modality

When texts about a subject matter are combined with pictures, the texts can be presented in different modalities. They can be presented as spoken texts in the auditory modality, as written texts in the visual modality, or as spoken and written texts in both modalities.

Which sensory modality should be used to present a text about a subject matter? The answer to this question depends on the kind of picture, the difficulty of the text, and temporal constraints, as explained in Chapter 6. If a picture is animated, written text leads to split visual attention between the text and picture, which inevitably results in a loss of some information due to the fluent nature of animation. Spoken text helps to avoid splitting visual attention. If a picture is static and presented for an unlimited period of time, the split of visual attention is less important, and the use of the auditory modality is less advantageous. In this case, one should balance the advantage of auditory text (i.e., avoiding split attention), against the possible advantage of written text (i.e., higher control of cognitive processing by the reader). Control of cognitive processing is especially important when the text is difficult to understand.

Which sensory modality should be used to present a text when the text is not about the subject matter, but about its visualization in a picture? In this case, written texts explaining a picture require readers to look at the picture while reading the text explaining the picture. Such conditions inevitably split the reader's visual attention between the text and the picture. This can be avoided by using the auditory modality.

Could the best approach be to combine pictures with spoken and written text? Multimedia designers frequently try to adapt to the needs of individual recipients. Because some recipients are assumed to prefer spoken text and others are assumed to prefer written text, designers sometimes present pictures simultaneously with both written and spoken text. In this way, recipients can choose their preferred sensory modality. Recipients who prefer listening can focus on the spoken text, and those who prefer reading can focus on the written text. In fact, however, individuals do not learn better from pictures accompanied by spoken and written text. There are two reasons for this. The first reason is that it is difficult to ignore a written text, even if it is also presented in an auditory manner. Thus, the written text results in split visual attention anyway. The second reason stems from the challenge of synchronizing listening and reading. Skilled readers are often able to read a text faster than the auditory text is spoken. When they create inner speech, which they can hear with their inner ear (based on visual–auditory lexical conversion), they are likely to experience interference between external listening and internal listening (triggered by reading).

For texts about the visualization of a subject matter in a picture, the following recommendation can be made:

- When text paragraphs are about pictures in multimedia messages, use spoken text rather than written text to avoid splitting visual attention.

For texts about a subject matter (rather than its visualization), the following recommendations can be made:

- When animated pictures are combined with text, use spoken text instead of written text due to the fluent nature of animations in order to avoid splitting visual attention.
- When static pictures are combined with easy texts and presented for a limited length of time, use spoken text in order to avoid splitting visual attention.
- When static pictures are combined with difficult texts and presented for an unlimited length of time, use written text to allow better control of cognitive processing by the reader.
- Do not add written text that duplicates spoken text combined with pictures.

9.4.2   Text Organization

How should texts in multimedia messages be organized? Texts provide conceptual guidance due to their inherent linear organization. Therefore, the sequencing of their content is of central importance for multimedia comprehension. Sequencing is dependent on various constraints. First, there are inherent comprehension requirements within the content, which are usually based on semantic inclusion. If a higher-order, more complex propositional meaning unit can only be understood after having understood another, simpler unit, the latter has to be presented first as it is a prerequisite for comprehending the higher-order unit. The higher-order meaning unit has to be presented afterward. Second, text organization should allow a text to be smoothly processed in an integrated manner. This takes the form of a step-by-step process of coherence formation and construction of topic-specific mental models, as explained in Chapter 4.

Smooth continuous coherence formation and initial mental model construction under the conceptual guidance of a text requires text organization that is characterized by various forms of continuity. These include continuity of granularity, continuity of topics, and continuity of semantic relations.

- *Continuity of granularity* means that the level of detail in a description should vary as little as possible. Text descriptions should start with a coarse overview followed by stepwise more detailed descriptions of the content. Authors (or speakers) should avoid volatile levels of granularity following one another.
- *Continuity of topics* means that a topic introduced by a text should be treated without unnecessary interruptions in order to allow mental models to be constructed as completely as possible. Otherwise, a topic-specific mental model would be abandoned and then be reactivated when the author (or speaker) returns to the topic. This reactivation of previously abandoned topics causes unnecessary cognitive load.[1] Furthermore, the reactivated mental model is frequently incomplete, because the reader or listener forgets some pieces of information.
- *Continuity of semantic relations* means that the kind of semantic relations used to connect consecutive topics should be maintained and used to connect the following topics whenever possible. This applies to all kinds of relations, such as causal, spatial, temporal, functional, purposeful,

---

[1] Sweller et al. (2011).

intentional, and other relations. For example, if an author describes Content A as the cause of the following Content B, and if B is in turn the cause of Content C, sequencing the content according to A–B–C would benefit from the fact that A–B has already activated the schema for causal relations. Thus, the reader can use the causality schema again to connect B and C, which makes cognitive processing easier. On the contrary, if the sequencing principle changes in a haphazard way, the expectations of the reader regarding the following information are repeatedly confounded, undermining the flow of consciousness.

To enhance the transparency of written text organization, boundaries between consecutive text segments should be signaled by visual markers such as different fonts, paragraphs, indentions, shadowing, boxes, and headlines. Because information is presented in a linear manner, the flow of consciousness in multimedia comprehension is admittedly guided primarily by the text during initial mental model construction. Texts convey propositions in a well-defined specific order, whereas no such sequential order exists in propositions conveyed by pictures. The flow of consciousness also includes pictorial content, but this flow still takes place with guidance by the text. When a text paragraph is not about the content, but about a picture, and when the text provides an instruction about how to conceptually process the picture, the flow of consciousness directed by the text is a kind of "guided tour" through the picture.

Texts should be designed according to the requirements of initial mental model construction. In order to enhance smooth coherence formation and continuous initial mental model construction (i.e., a continuous flow of consciousness), the following approach is recommended:

- Avoid changes in representational granularity between idea units so that the same level of detail is maintained as far as possible.
- After starting to treat a topic, continue to treat this topic as far as possible.
- The kind of semantic relation used to connect the previous topic with the current topic should also be used to connect the current topic with the following topic whenever possible.

Of course, these recommendations do not imply that there should be no changes in the level of granularity, no topic changes, or no changes in the semantic relations between successive topics at all. They only suggest that there should be as few of these changes as possible in order to enable a smooth flow of consciousness.

9.4.3   *Directing the Flow of Consciousness*

When designing texts, authors (or speakers) include aids for coherence formation in the text surface in the form of cohesive devices, as described in Chapter 4. These cohesive devices include signals to direct the reader's (or listener's) flow of consciousness. The signals enable the reader (or listener) to track the sequence of topics presented by the author (or speaker). As described in Section 4.5 about directing the flow of consciousness, the author (or speaker) continuously conveys hints on what he or she is writing or talking about. These hints are given by the topic information of the respective sentences or text segments. In case of a topic change, the new topic information is used by the reader (or listener) as a search profile to identify the new topic.

The topic information can range from a single pronoun like "she" or "it" to complex sentences or even paragraphs explaining what the following text segments are about. Whenever new topic information does not fit to the previous topic, a mental search process is triggered in the previously constructed mental model and in prior knowledge. The topic information tells the reader (or listener) what to search for and where to search for it, including how "far" the new topic is away from the previous one. The use of pronouns signals an already introduced referent, which can be identified with only a few search parameters. On the other hand, the use of nouns and noun phrases signals a referent that needs a more elaborate description to be identified. Topic sentences and topic paragraphs provide even more elaborate search profiles which signal even more demanding topic changes.

As explained in Chapter 4, topic information can receive more or less emphasis through topic marking, which signals to the reader (or listener) how far the new topic is away from the previous one. So, topic markedness signals the size of the required topic shift. Low topic markedness signals a small topic shift, whereas high topic markedness signals a large topic shift. In order to decide what kind of topic information to include, authors (or speakers) can consider the following recommendations:

> Think about what is in the reader's (or listener's) current focus of attention, which prior knowledge is currently activated, and how big the size of the required topic shift is (i.e., how "far" the new topic is from the previous one). Then decide how to adequately word the topic information and decide about its markedness in order to ensure that the reader (or listener) can identify the new topic easily.

As mentioned in Section 4.4, thematically continuous text organization requires less cognitive capacity for focus tracking, because fewer shifts in the focus of attention are required.

9.5 Picture Design

How should pictures for multimedia messages be designed, and what kind of pictures should be presented and when? Depending on where pictures are located in multimedia messages, they serve different functions. An important distinction can be made between the scaffolding function of pictures during initial mental model construction and their function for the elaboration of knowledge in adaptive mental model specification.

9.5.1 Pictorial Scaffolding for Mental Model Construction

Although initial mental model construction is primarily guided by the text, pictures can play an auxiliary role in this phase of processing. Due to the relatively direct relationship between pictures and mental models based on analog structure mapping, a brief pictorial sketch of a subject matter without unnecessary details can serve as a scaffold for initial mental model construction. This pictorial sketch should not include details because they could distract the recipient from reading the text. The pictorial sketch should be presented as early as possible to avoid interfering with mental model construction. If a picture is presented after a text, it is likely to interfere with the previously constructed text-based mental model. Such interference can be avoided when a picture is presented before the text, even if the learner looks only briefly at the picture to benefit from its mental scaffolding function, as explained in Chapter 6. Thus, the following recommendation can be made:

> Include a pictorial sketch of the subject matter with no unnecessary details as a pictorial advance organizer for initial mental model construction as early as possible.

9.5.2 Elaborative Pictures

After initial mental model construction guided by the text, adaptive mental model specification is performed to fulfil task requirements; it is strongly influenced by pictorial information. How should these pictures for adaptive mental model specification be designed? How should a subject matter be presented?

Mental model construction is strongly influenced by perceptual processing of pictures. Accordingly, one has to make sure that the basic structure of the subject matter as described in the text can be easily perceived in the picture. Comprehension is easier, the better the perceived graphical configuration corresponds to the basic structure of the content and the better the recipient is able to recognize this correspondence by activating appropriate cognitive schemata for structure mapping. For a mental model to help solve specific tasks, the structure of the visualization should also reflect these tasks, because the form of visualization is mapped onto the structure of the mental model. In other words, the visualization used in the picture should be optimally suited for solving expected future tasks, as explained in Chapter 6. Pictures with inappropriate forms of visualization can undermine adaptive mental model specification. Thus, the design of elaborative pictures is not only about visualization per se. The pictures have to grasp and visualize the essential structure of a subject matter with regard to the task or problems to be solved later.

Of course, pictorial design has to follow the laws of visual perception. Graphical entities must be perceivable, discriminable, and identifiable. Semantically-related entities should be spontaneously grouped together according to the Gestalt laws and form complex higher-order perceptual units. Visual features must be semantically appropriate for the intended representational function. Color can be used (within limits) to designate qualities. Saturation and lightness can be used within limits to express coarse quantitative differences. Lengths are appropriate for representing quantities and quantitative differences, whereas the size of areas or volumes should never be used to express quantities because this would result in systematically biased misjudgments, as explained in Chapter 5.

Pictorial design should avoid depicting thematically irrelevant features in a perceptually salient manner. Such irrelevant visual surface features can mislead perceptual and conceptual picture processing, hide underlying relevant structures, and undermine successful comprehension. Multimedia designers should also resist the temptation to add irrelevant "bells and whistles" to multimedia environments. Visual effects that do not contribute to the message should be abandoned. Less can be more.

Further, the information density of a picture should not be increased as far as possible, because pictorial design for multimedia environments is about conveying messages, not about maximizing the amount of stored information. Pictorial design should be parsimonious and include only graphical entities representing relevant content which can be interpreted semantically. The following recommendations can be made for designing and selecting elaborative pictures:

- Make sure that the structure of the subject matter is made perceptually salient. More specifically, make sure that the subject matter is visualized from a perspective that makes its structure as transparent as possible.
- Make sure that the perceptual structure does not obscure relevant structural attributes or guide the recipient to read and interpret attributes or relations from the picture that are visually salient but have no representing function.
- If the subject matter can be visualized by different pictures in different ways, although these pictures are informationally equivalent, use the picture with the form of visualization that is the most appropriate for solving future tasks.

9.5.3 Graph Formats

Which formats should be used when graphs are presented? When relations between qualitative and quantitative variables are to be visualized, one can use established forms of graphs. These "ready-made" forms benefit from the fact that recipients have prior knowledge about their underlying representational principles. The recipients usually possess the appropriate graphic schemata. That is, the form of visualization is familiar to them.

For example, pie graphs should be used to visualize the quantitative break-up of a whole into parts. Bar graphs should be used to visualize the size of qualitatively different entities. Line graphs should be used to visualize single or multiple developments. Scatterplots should be used to visualize stochastic relationships, as explained in Chapter 5. Authors should not deviate from these schemata without good reason, because recipients' familiarity with them enhances their comprehension. When an author creates new, unusual forms of visualizations, readers are not familiar with them, which can impede comprehension. Accordingly, the following recommendations can be made:

> When relations between qualitative and quantitative variables are to be visualized with the help of graphs, refrain from creating new, "innovative" formats which readers have not seen before. Use standard graphic formats instead.

9.6   Text–Picture Coordination

How should texts and pictures be sequenced and coordinated in multimedia messages? As texts provide explicit conceptual guidance for constructing initial mental models, the need to achieve coherence between the texts and pictures dictates that the sequencing of pictures follows the order of the text. This implies:

> Sequence multiple pictures according to the description of the subject matter in the text.

Due to the difference between initial mental model construction and subsequent adaptive mental model specification, designers of multimedia messages should take care that recipients can first concentrate on the text, as it provides conceptual guidance for initial mental model construction. There should be a clear, visually salient "entry point" into the text which leads naturally to systematic text reading. During this phase, readers should not be distracted by complex pictures with exaggerated detail. Instead, a coarse visual sketch of the content, which provides only the outline of the subject matter without unnecessary details, might be sufficient as a pictorial scaffold or advance organizer for initial mental model construction. After the phase of initial mental model construction, when recipients are sufficiently prepared and have conceptual guidance for studying pictures, elaborated and detailed pictures can be presented for the purpose of adaptive mental model specification. During this kind of processing, the pictures serve as easily accessible external tools for task-driven selective information processing in order to update the mental model according to the requirements of specific tasks, as explained in Chapter 7. This leads to the following recommendation:

> Include highly detailed and elaborated pictures only after a pictorial sketch of the subject matter has been presented as a visual scaffold for constructing mental models. Include such detailed and elaborated pictures toward the end of initial mental model construction.

9.6.1   Text–Picture Contiguity

Regardless of whether spoken text or written text is combined with a picture, multimedia designers should take care that closely related verbal information and pictorial information are simultaneously in working memory in order to allow conjoint processing for coherence formation and mental model construction. This means that the design should be guided by spatial and temporal contiguity. If pictures are combined with spoken text, text information and pictorial information about the visualized content should be presented in close temporal proximity. If pictures are combined with written text, the text information and pictorial information about the visualized content should be presented in close spatial proximity, up to the point that text information is spatially integrated into the picture.[2] In order to avoid interference between spontaneous model construction and model construction under pictorial guidance, paragraphs that are semantically related to a picture should not be presented before the picture is perceivable, as explained in Chapter 6. This leads to the following recommendations:

> Make sure that text and pictures are presented temporally or spatially as closely as possible. If written text is used, present it in close spatial proximity to the picture. If spoken text is used, present it in close temporal proximity to the picture. Do not present a text that is semantically related to a picture before the picture can be observed by the recipient.

9.6.2 Text–Picture Cohesion

Can designers of multimedia messages enhance coherence formation by signaling semantic relations between a text and pictures? Multimedia messages are coherent when texts and pictures are semantically related. These relations can be signaled to the recipient with the help of cohesive devices in the form of color cohesion, symbol cohesion, and verbal cohesion, as explained in Chapter 7. Graphical entities in the picture have to be clearly related to the corresponding verbal entities in the text (usually expressed by noun phrases). Relevant relations between graphical entities have to be made explicit in the text (usually expressed by relational word concepts such as verb phrases or prepositional phrases). To enhance text–picture coherence, the relevant graphical entities and the corresponding visuo-spatial relations between them must be easily noticeable. Pictures that are not clearly semantically related to the text should not be included in multimedia messages.

As already mentioned in the preceding chapters, successful multimedia comprehension does not depend only on multimedia being appropriately designed, but also on the recipients' knowledge and cognitive skills and on their willingness to engage in the required cognitive processing. Multimedia

---

[2] Chandler and Sweller (1992); Bobis et al. (1993).

comprehension does not require a recipient to merely combine descriptive and depictive representations somehow. It requires ongoing mindful inter-action between these representations in terms of mental model construction and inspection processes. Accordingly, multimedia message design should invite recipients to integrate the different representations. The integrated use of representations requires the ability to recognize the abovementioned semantic relations between different representations, switch flexibly between them, and map results from one to the other. As has been shown in Chapter 8, flexibly combining descriptive and depictive representations is not only at the core of successful comprehension, but also of thinking and problem-solving, as explained in Chapter 8. This leads to the following recommendations:

> Make sure that mappings between texts and pictures are as clear as possible. More specifically, make sure that entities mentioned in the text (usually in the form of noun phrases) can be perceived easily as graphical entities in the picture. Make sure that the relations mentioned in the text (usually with verb or preposition phrases) can be perceived easily in the picture.

The transfer of multimedia comprehension research into the practice of multimedia-message design cannot follow a recipe or an algorithm because the inherent complexity of design tasks requires problem-solving. Dealing with the complexity of design tasks has similarities to solving crossword puzzles where filling one word into a box constrains the possibilities for filling in the other boxes. Similarly, solutions for partial design problems constrain each other, which often requires a re-designing process made up of iterative steps until a final consistent solution has been found for the whole design task. The recommendations mentioned in the present chapter are, therefore, to be considered as orientation guides for dealing with the complexity of design tasks. They are meant to have a heuristic function for solving design problems. Orientation guides must be practically manageable. They should be used in a flexible way to allow a comprehensive and differentiated analysis with the goal of finding appropriate practical solutions.

Orientation guides should prompt their users to take up multiple per-spectives. Their most important function is to help users ask the relevant questions. As is well known, asking the right questions is a prerequisite for finding good solutions. In brief, there is no simple recipe for solving multimedia design tasks. The design of multimedia messages requires adequate heuristics, prior knowledge, experience, and creativity.

Concluding Remarks

In future, an increasing number of people will need to learn continuously in order to orient themselves in the quickly changing world around them. Multimedia communication and multimedia comprehension will be key elements of their learning. Accordingly, it is very important to have a sufficiently deep understanding of the psychological processes behind multimedia comprehension. This understanding should be rooted in theory-driven empirical research about the cognitive processing of multiple representations, particularly of texts and pictures. It should also allow practice-oriented basic recommendations to be derived for the design and usage of multimedia. These recommendations should go beyond everyday knowledge, practical experience, intuition, and the use of seemingly professional surface features. Design of multimedia communication has to be based on sufficiently deep knowledge about the psychological processes involved in comprehension and knowledge construction. Practitioners need to receive scientific support for them to better understand the laws of perception and cognitive processing underlying comprehension and knowledge acquisition.

The present book covers only parts of this kind of knowledge, as its analysis is conducted only from a cognitive perspective. It focuses on the structural characteristics of multimedia messages and the effect of these characteristics on conjoint cognitive processing. Various issues have not been taken into consideration and need further research. These include, for example, motivational and emotional aspects of multimedia comprehension which can be expected to interact with the conjoint cognitive processing of multiple external representations. We also need developmental studies about how children and adolescents use different kinds of representations for different kinds of tasks at different ages. In order to broaden the perspectives of analyses, an interdisciplinary cooperation between psychology, cognitive linguistics, education, and art seems highly recommendable.

References

Ainsworth, S. (1999). The functions of multiple representations. *Computers & Education, 33*, 131–152.

Atkinson, C., & Shiffrin, R. M. (1971). The control of short-term memory. *Scientific American, 225*, 82–90.

Ayres, P., & Sweller, J. (2022). The split attention principle in multimedia learning. In R. E. Mayer, & L. Fiorella (eds.), *The Cambridge handbook of multimedia learning* (pp. 199–211). Cambridge: Cambridge University Press.

Baddeley, A. D. (1986). *Working memory.* Oxford: Clarendon Press.

Berendt, B., Barkowsky, T., Freksa, C., & Kelter, S. (1998). Spatial representation with aspect maps. In C. Freksa, C. Habel, & K. F. Wender (Eds.), *Spatial cognition – An interdisciplinary approach to representing and processing spatial knowledge* (pp. 313–336). Berlin: Springer.

Bertin, J. (1967). *Sémiologie Graphique. Les diagrammes, les réseaux, les cartes.* Paris: Gauthier-Villars. (Translated 1983. *Semiology of Graphics*, by W. J. Berg.)

Bobis, J., Sweller, J., & Cooper, M. (1993). Cognitive load effects in a primary-school geometry task. *Learning and Instruction, 3*, 1–21.

Bransford, J. D., & Johnson, M. K. (1972). Conceptual prerequisites for understanding: Some investigations of comprehension and recall. *Journal of Verbal Learning and Verbal Behavior, 11*, 717–726.

Bühler, K. (1934). *Sprachtheorie.* Jena: Fischer.

Bull, P. (1990). What does gesture add to the spoken word? In H. Barlow, C. Blakemore, & M. Weston-Smith (Eds.), *Images and understanding* (pp. 108–121). Cambridge: Cambridge University Press.

Carey, S. (2009). *The origin of concepts.* New York: Oxford University Press.

Carney, R. N., & Levin, J. R. (2002). Pictorial illustrations still improve students' learning from text. *Educational Psychology Review, 14*(1), 5–26.

Carroll, D. W. (2008). *Psychology of language.* Belmont, CA: Thomson Wadworth.

Castro-Alonso, J. C., & Sweller, J. (2022). The modality principle in multimedia learning. In R. E. Mayer, & L. Fiorella (Eds.), *The Cambridge handbook of multimedia learning* (pp. 261–267). Cambridge: Cambridge University Press.

Cavalli-Sforza, L. L. (1996). *Gènes, peoples et langues*. Paris: Odile Jacob.

Cavalli-Sforza, L. L., Piazza, A., Menozzi, P., & Mountain, J. (1988). Reconstruction of human evolution: Bringing together genetic, archeological, and linguistic data. *Proceedings of the National Academy of Sciences, 86*, 6002–6006.

Cermak, L. S., & Craik, F. I. M. (Eds.) (1979). *Levels of processing in human memory*. Hillsdale, NJ: Lawrence Erlbaum.

Chafe, W. L. (1970). *Meaning and the structure of language*. Chicago: University of Chicago Press.

 (1979). The flow of thought and the flow of language. In T. Givón (Ed.), *Syntax and semantics, Vol. 12: Discourse and syntax* (pp. 159–181). New York: Academic Press.

Chandler, P., & Sweller, J. (1992). The split-attention effect as a factor in the design of instruction. *British Journal of Educational Psychology, 62*, 233–246.

Chomsky, N. (2007). Approaching UG from below. In U. Sauerland, & H.-M. Gärtner (Eds.), *Interfaces + recursion = language? Chomsky's minimalism and the view from syntax-semantics* (pp. 1–29). Berlin: De Gruyter.

Clark, H. H. (1996). *Using language*. Cambridge: Cambridge University Press.

Cohn, N. (2016). A multimodal parallel architecture: A cognitive framework for multimodal interactions. *Cognition, 146*, 304–323.

Coltheart, M., Rastle, K., Perry, C., Langdon, R., & Ziegler, J. (2001). DRC: A dual route cascaded model of visual word recognition and reading aloud. *Psychological Review, 108*(1), 204–256.

Comenius, J. A. (1999). *Orbis sensualium pictus* [Facsimile of the 1887 edition]. Whitefish, MT: Kessinger.

Cooney, J. B., & Swanson, H. L. (1987). Memory and learning disabilities: An overview. In H. L. Swanson (Ed.), *Memory and learning disabilities: Advances in learning and behavioral disabilities* (pp. 1–40). Greenwich, CT: JAI.

Corkin, S., Amaral, D. G., González, R. G., Johnson, K. A., & Hyman, B. T. (1997). H. M.'s medial temporal lobe lesion: Findings from magnetic resonance imaging. *The Journal of Neuroscience, 17*(10), 3964–3979.

Crowder, R. G. (1993). Auditory memory. In S. McAdams, & E. Bigand (Eds.), *Thinking in sound: The cognitive psychology of human audition* (pp. 113–145). New York: Oxford University Press.

Dahl, C. D., & Adachi, I. (2013). Conceptual metaphorical mapping in chimpanzees (Pan troglodytes). *eLife*. Published online October 22, 2013. Available at: www.researchgate.net/publication/326065433_Conceptual_metaphorical_mapping_in_chimpanzees_Pan_troglodytes. Last accessed August 26, 2022.

Damerow, P., Englund, R. K., & Nissen, H. J. (1994). Die Entstehung der Schrift. In B. Riese (Ed.), *Schrift und Sprache* (pp. 90–101). Heidelberg: Spektrum akademischer Verlag.

Danks, J. H., & End, L. J. (1987). Processing strategies for reading and listening. In R. Horowitz, & S. J. Samuels (Eds.), *Comprehending oral and written language* (pp. 271–294). San Diego: Academic Press.

Dawkins, R. (1976). *The selfish gene.* Oxford: Oxford University Press.

De Saussure, F. (1922). *Cours de linguistique générale.* Paris: Payot.

Deuchar, M. (1990). Are the signs of language arbitrary? In H. Barlow, C. Blakemore, & M. Weston-Smith (Eds.), *Images and understanding* (pp. 168–179). Cambridge: Cambridge University Press.

van Dijk, T. A., & Kintsch, W. (1983). *Strategies of discourse comprehension.* New York: Academic Press.

Duncker, K. (1935). *Zur Psychologie des produktiven Denkens.* [*On psychology of productive thinking.*] Berlin: Springer.

Eimas, P. D., Siqueland, E. R., Jusczyk, P., & Vigorito, J. (1971). Speech perception in infants. *Science, 171,* 303–306.

Eitel, A., Scheiter, K., Schüler, A., Nyström, M., & Holmqvist, K. (2013). How a picture facilitates the process of learning from text: Evidence for scaffolding. *Learning and Instruction, 28,* 48–63.

Ellis, A. W., & Young, A. W. (1996). *Human cognitive neuropsychology.* London: Taylor & Francis.

Engelkamp, J., & Zimmer, H. D. (1994). *The human memory. A multi-modal approach.* Toronto: Hogrefe.

Ericsson, K. A., & Kintsch, W. (1995). Long-term working memory. *Psychological Review, 102*(2), 211–245.

Fabrikant, S. I., & Montello, D. R. (2008). The effect of instructions on distance and similarity judgments in information spatializations. *International Journal of Geographic Information Science, 22*(4), 463–478.

Ferreira, F., & Anes, M. (1994). Why study spoken language? In M. A. Gernsbacher (Ed.), *Handbook of psycholinguistics* (pp. 34–36). San Diego: Academic Press.

Fiorella, L., & Mayer, R. E. (2022). Principles for reducing extraneous processing in multimedia learning: Coherence, signaling, redundancy, spatial contiguity and temporal contiguity principles. In R. E. Mayer, & L. Fiorella (Eds.), *The Cambridge handbook of multimedia learning* (pp. 185–198). Cambridge: Cambridge University Press.

Fletcher, C. R. (1984). Markedness and topic continuity in discourse processing. *Journal of Verbal Learning and Verbal Behavior, 23,* 487–493.

Gardner, B. T., & Gardner, R. A. (1975). Evidence for sentence constituents in the early utterances of child and chimpanzee. *Journal of Experimental Psychology: General, 104,* 244–267.

Gardner, R. A., Gardner, B. T., & Van Cantfort, T. E. (Eds.) (1989). *Teaching sign language to chimpanzees.* Albany: State University of New York Press.

Garrod, S. C., & Sanford, A. (1983). Topic dependent effects in language processing. In G. B. Flores d'Arcais, & R. J. Jarvella (Eds.), *The process of language understanding* (pp. 271–296). Chichester: Wiley.

Gentner, D. (1983). Structure-mapping: A theoretical framework for analogy. *Cognitive Science, 7,* 155–170.

Gibson, J. J. (1954). The visual perception of objective motion and subjective movement. *Psychological Review, 61*(5), 304–314.

Givón, T. (Ed.) (1983). *Topic continuity in discourse: A quantitative cross-language study*. Amsterdam: Benjamins.

Goethe, J. W. von (1833). *Theoretische Schriften, Maximen und Reflexionen*. Stuttgart: Cotta'sche Buchhandlung.

Graesser, A. C., Millis, K. K., & Zwaan, R. A. (1997). Discourse comprehension. *Annual Review of Psychology, 48*, 163–189.

Graesser, A. C., Singer, M., & Trabasso, T. (1994). Constructing inferences during narrative text comprehension. *Psychological Review, 101*, 371–395.

Graesser, A. C., & Zwaan, R. A. (1995). Inference generation and the construction of situation models. In C. A. Weaver III, S. Mannes, & C. R. Fletcher (eds.), *Discourse comprehension. Essays in honor of Walter Kintsch* (pp. 117–139). Hillsdale, NJ: Lawrence Erlbaum.

Green, R. (1981). Remembering ideas form text: The effect of modality of presentation. *British Journal of Educational Psychology, 51*, 83–89.

Greer, B., De Bock, D., & Van Dooren, W. (2009). The Isis problem as an experimental probe and teaching resource. *The Journal of Mathematical Behavior, 28*(4), 237–246.

Grice, M. P. (1967). *Logic and conversation*. The William James Lectures. Cambridge, MA: Harvard University Press.

Guthrie, J. T., Taboada, A., & Shular Coddington, C. (2007). Engagement practices for strategy learning in concept-oriented reading instruction. In D. S. McNamara (Ed.), *Reading comprehension strategies. Theories, interventions, and technologies* (pp. 241–266). New York: Lawrence Erlbaum.

Gyselinck, V., Jamet, E., & Dubois, V. (2008). The role of working memory components in multimedia comprehension. *Applied Cognitive Psychology, 22*, 353–374.

Halliday, M. A. K. (1994). *An introduction to functional grammar*, 2nd ed. London: Hodder Arnold.

Harp, S. F., & Mayer, R. E. (1998). How seductive details do their damage: A theory of cognitive interest in science learning. *Journal of Educational Psychology, 90*(3), 414–434.

Hatano, G., & Inagaki, K. (1986). Two courses of expertise. In H. Stevenson, H. Azuma, & K. Hakuta (Eds.), *Child development and education in Japan* (pp. 262–272). New York: W. H. Freeman.

Hildyard, A., & Olson, D. R. (1978). Memory and inference in the comprehension of oral and written discourse. *Discourse Processes, 1*, 91–117.

Hochpöchler, U., Schnotz, W., Rasch, T., Ullrich, M., Horz, H., McElvany, N., Schroeder, S., & Baumert, J. (2013). Dynamics of mental model construction from text and graphics. *European Journal of Psychology of Education, 28* (4), 1105–1126.

Hoffmann, D. L., Standish, C. D., García-Diez, M., Pettitt, P. B., Milton, J. A., Zilhão, J., Alcolea-González, J. J., Cantalejo-Duarte, P., Collado, H., de Balbín, R., Lorblanchet, M., Ramos-Muñoz, J., Weniger, G.-Ch., & Pike, A. W. G. (2018). U-Th dating of carbonate crusts reveals Neandertal origin of Iberian cave art. *Science, 359*(6378), 912–915.

Johnson-Laird, P. N. (1983). *Mental models. Towards a cognitive science of language, inference, and consciousness.* Cambridge: Cambridge University Press.

Johnson-Laird, P. N., & Byrne, R. M. J. (1991). *Deduction.* Hove: Lawrence Erlbaum.

Kalyuga, S., Chandler, P., & Sweller, J. (2000). Incorporating learner experience into the design of multimedia instruction. *Journal of Educational Psychology, 92*, 126–136.

Kalyuga, S., & Sweller, J. (2022). The redundancy in multimedia learning. In R. E. Mayer, & L. Fiorella (Eds.), *The Cambridge handbook of multimedia learning* (pp. 212–220). Cambridge: Cambridge University Press.

Kamermans, K., Pouw, W., Fassi, L., Aslanidou, A., Paas, F., & Hostetter, A. B. (2019). The role of gesture as simulated action in reinterpretation of mental imagery. *Acta Psychologica, 197*, 131–142.

Kanizsa, G. (1955). Margini quasi-percettivi in campi con stimolazione omogenea. *Rivista di psicologia, 49*(1), 7–30. [English translation (1987): Quasi-perceptual margins in homogeneously stimulated fields. (With a 1986 addendum.) In G. E. Meyer and S. Petry (Eds.), *The perception of illusory contours* (pp. 40–49). New York: Springer.

(1968). Percezione attuale, esperienza passata e l'"esperimento impossibile" [Actual perception, past experience and the "impossible experiment"]. In G. Kanizsa & G. B. Vicario (Eds.), *Ricerche sperimentali sulla percezione [Experimental investigations on perception]* (pp. 10–47). Trieste, Italy: Università degli studi di Trieste. Republished in the March–June 2019 issue of *Giornale Italiano di Psicologia, 46*, 299–323.

King, A. (2007). Beyond literal comprehension: A strategy to promote deep understanding of text. In D. S. McNamara (Ed.), *Reading comprehension strategies. Theories, interventions, and technologies* (pp. 267–290). New York: Lawrence Erlbaum.

Kintsch, W. (1988). The role of knowledge in discourse comprehension: A constructive-integration model. *Psychological Review, 95*, 163–182.

Kintsch, W., & van Dijk, T. A. (1978). Toward a model of text comprehension and production. *Psychological Review, 85*, 363–394.

Kita, S. (Ed.) (2003). *Pointing: Where language, culture, and cognition meet.* Mahwah, NJ: Lawrence Erlbaum.

Knauff, M., & Johnson-Laird, P. N. (2002). Visual imagery can impede reasoning. *Memory & Cognition, 30*(3), 363–371.

Köhler, W. (1969). *The task of Gestalt psychology.* Princeton, NJ: Princeton University Press.

Kosslyn, S. M. (1994a). *Elements of graph design.* New York: W. H. Freeman & Co.

(1994b). *Image and brain. The resolution of the imagery debate.* Cambridge, MA: MIT Press.

Kulhavy, R. W., Stock, W. A., & Caterino, L. C. (1994). Reference maps as a framework for remembering text. In W. Schnotz & R. W. Kulhavy (Eds.), *Comprehension of graphics* (pp. 153–162). Amsterdam: Elsevier Science.

Kürschner, C., & Schnotz, W. (2008). Das Verhältnis gesprochener und geschriebener Sprache bei der Konstruktion mentaler Repräsentationen. *Psychologische Rundschau, 59*(3), 139–149.

Kürschner, C., Schnotz, W. & Eid, M. (2006). Konstruktion mentaler Repräsentationen beim Hör- und Leseverstehen. *Zeitschrift für Medienpsychologie, 18*(2), 48–59.

Larkin, J. H., & Simon, H. A. (1987). Why a diagram is (sometimes) worth ten thousand words. *Cognitive Science, 11*, 65–99.

Leahy, W., Chandler, P., & Sweller, J. (2003). When auditory presentations should and should not be a component of multimedia instruction. *Applied Cognitive Psychology, 17*, 401–418.

Levie, W. H., & Lentz, R. (1982). Effects of text illustrations: A review of research. *Educational Communication and Technology, 30*(4), 195–232.

Levin, J. R., Anglin, G. J., & Carney, R. N. (1987). On empirically validating functions of pictures in prose. In D. M. Willows & H. A. Houghton (Eds.), *The psychology of illustration*, Vol. 1 (pp. 51–86). New York: Springer.

Levin, J. R., & Mayer, R. E. (1993). Understanding illustrations in text. In B. K. Britton, A. Woodward, & M. R. Binkley (Eds.), *Learning from textbooks: Theory and practice* (pp. 95–113). Mahwah, NJ: Lawrence Erlbaum Associates, Inc.

Liu, K., & Jiang, Y. (2005). Visual working memory for briefly presented scenes. *Journal of Vision, 5*, 650–658.

Lowe, R. K. (1996). Background knowledge and the construction of a situational representation from a diagram. *European Journal of Psychology of Education, 11*, 377–397.

Lowe, R. K., & Boucheix, J. M. (2011). Cueing complex animations: Does direction of attention foster learning processes? *Learning and Instruction, 21* (5), 650–663.

Lowe, R. K., Schnotz, W., & Boucheix, J. M. (2022). The animation composition principle in multimedia learning. In R. E. Mayer, & L. Fiorella (Eds.), *The Cambridge handbook of multimedia learning* (pp. 313–323). Cambridge: Cambridge University Press.

Luria, A. (1973). *The working brain*. Harmondsworth: Penguin.

Marey, E. J. (1895). *Movement*. New York: Appleton.

Markman, A. B. (1999). *Knowledge representation*. Mahwah, NJ: Lawrence Erlbaum Associates.

Marr, D. (1982). *Vision. A computational investigation into the human representation and processing of visual information*. San Francisco, CA: Freeman.

Mastropieri, M. A., & Scruggs, T. E. (1989). Constructing more meaningful relationships: Mnemonic instruction for special populations. *Educational Psychology Review, 1*, 83–111.

Mayer, R. E. (1997). Multimedia learning: Are we asking the right questions? *Educational Psychologist, 32*, 1–19.

(2005). Cognitive theory of multimedia learning. In R. E. Meyer (Ed.), *The Cambridge handbook of multimedia learning* (pp. 31–49). New York: Cambridge University Press.

(2009). *Multimedia learning*, 2nd ed. Cambridge: Cambridge University Press.

(2011). Instruction based on visualizations. In R. E. Mayer, & P. A. Alexander (Eds.), *Handbook of research on learning and instruction* (pp. 427–445). New York: Routledge.

(Ed.) (2014). *Cambridge handbook of multimedia learning*, 2nd ed. New York: Cambridge University Press.

Mayer, R. E., & Fiorella, L. (Eds.) (2022). *Cambridge handbook of multimedia learning*, 3rd ed. New York: Cambridge University Press.

Mayer, R. E., & Gallini, J. K. (1990). When is an illustration worth ten thousand words? *Journal of Educational Psychology*, *82*, 715–726.

Mayer, R. E., & Johnson, C. I. (2008). Revising the redundancy principle in multimedia learning. *Journal of Educational Psychology*, *100*(2), 380–386.

Mayer, R. E., & Moreno R. (1998). A split-attention effect in multimedia learning: Evidence for dual processing systems in working memory. *Journal of Educational Psychology*, *90*, 312–320.

Mayr, E. (1976). *Evolution and the diversity of life*. Cambridge, MA: Harvard University Press.

McCloud, S. (1993). *Understanding comics: The invisible art*. New York: Harper Collins.

McCrudden, M. T., & Schraw, G. (2007). Relevance and goal-focusing in text processing. *Educational Psychology Review*, *19*, 113–139.

McKoon, G., & Ratcliff, R. (1992). Inference during reading. *Psychological Review*, *99*, 440–466.

(1995). The minimalist hypothesis: Directions for research. In C. A. Weaver III, S. Mannes, & C. R. Fletcher (Eds.), *Discourse comprehension. Essays in honor of Walter Kintsch* (pp. 97–116). Hillsdale, NJ: Lawrence Erlbaum.

Miller, J. (1990). Moving pictures. In H. Barlow, C. Blakemore, & M. Weston-Smith (Eds.), *Images and understanding* (pp. 180–194). Cambridge: Cambridge University Press.

Millis, K. K., & King, A. (2001). Rereading strategically: The influences of comprehension ability and a prior reading on the memory for expository text. *Reading Psychology*, *22*, 41–65.

Millis, K. K., Simon, S., & TenBroek, N. S. (1998). Resource allocation during the rereading of scientific text. *Memory & Cognition*, *26*(2), 232–246.

Montgomery, H. (1984). Mental models and problem solving: Three challenges to a theory of restructuring and insight. *Scandinavian Journal of Psychology*, *29*, 85–94.

Moreno, R., & Mayer, R. E. (1999). Cognitive principles of multimedia learning: The role of modality and contiguity. *Journal of Educational Psychology*, *91*, 358–368.

Mousavi, S. Y., Low, R., & Sweller, J. (1995). Reducing cognitive load by minimizing auditory and visual presentation modes. *Journal of Educational Psychology*, *87*, 319–334.

Murai, C., Kosugi, D., Tomonaga, M., Tanaka, M., Matsuzawa, T., & Itakura, S. (2005). Can chimpanzee infants (Pan troglodytes) form categorical representations in the same manner as human infants (Homo sapiens)? *Developmental Science, 8*(3), 240–254.

Ogden, L. K., & Richards, J. A. (1923). *The meaning of meaning*. London: Routledge & Kegan Paul.

Ohlsson, S. (1992). Information processing explanations of insight and related phenomena. In M. Keane, & K. Gilhooly (Eds.), *Advances in the psychology of thinking* (pp. 1–44). London: Harvester-Wheatsheaf.

Oliva, A., & Torralba, A. (2006). Building the gist of a scene: The role of global image features in recognition. *Progress in Brain Research, 155,* 23–36.

Orrill, C. H., Sexton, S., Lee, S.-O., & Gerde, C. (2008). *Mathematics teachers' abilities to use and make sense of drawn representations.* Paper presented at the Eighth International Conference for the Learning Sciences – ICLS 2008 in Utrecht.

Paivio, A. (1986). *Mental representations: A dual coding approach*. Oxford: Oxford University Press.

Palmer, S. E. (1978). Fundamental aspects of cognitive representation. In E. Rosch, & B. B. Lloyd (Eds.), *Cognition and categorization* (pp. 259–303). Hillsdale, NJ: Lawrence Erlbaum.

Peirce, C. S. (1932). *Collected papers, II. Elements of logic*. Cambridge, MA: Harvard University Press.

Peterson, D. (1996). *Forms of representation*. Exeter: Intellect.

Pinker, S. (1990). A theory of graph comprehension. In R. Freedle (Ed.), *Artificial intelligence and the future of testing* (pp. 73–126), Hillsdale, NJ: Lawrence Erlbaum.

(1994). *The language instinct*. New York: William Morrow.

Povinelli, D. J., Bering, J. M., & Giambrone, S. (2003). Chimpanzees' "Pointing": Another error of the argument by analogy. In S. Kita (Ed.), *Pointing: Where language, culture, and cognition meet* (pp. 35–68). Mahwah NJ: Lawrence Erlbaum.

Rasch, R. (2003). *42 Denk- und Sachaufgaben. Wie Kinder mathematische Aufgaben lösen und diskutieren*. Stuttgart: Klett, Kallmeyer, Kaulis.

Rieben, L., & Perfetti, C. (1991). *Learning to read: Basic research and its implications*. Hillsdale, NJ: Lawrence Erlbaum.

Robin, H. (1992). *The scientific image: From cave to computer*. New York: Harry N. Abrams Inc.

Rosch, E., & Lloyd, B. B. (1978). *Cognition and categorization*. Hillsdale, NJ: Lawrence Erlbaum.

Rouet, J.-F., & Britt, M. (2022). Multimedia learning from multiple documents. In R. E. Mayer, & L. Fiorella (Eds.), *The Cambridge handbook of multimedia learning* (pp. 521–536). Cambridge: Cambridge University Press.

Rouet, J.-F., Britt, M. A., & Durik, A. M. (2017). RESOLV: Readers' representation of reading contexts and tasks. *Educational Psychologist, 52*(3), 200–215.

Rubin, D. L., Hafer, T., & Arata, K. (2000). Reading and listening to oral-based versus literate-based discourse. *Communication Education, 49*(2), 121–133.

Rummer, R., Schweppe, J., Fürstenberg, A., Seufert, T., & Brünken, R. (2010). Working memory interference during processing texts and pictures: Implications for the explanation of the modality effect. *Applied Cognitive Psychology, 24,* 164–176.

Sanchez, C. A., & Wiley, J. (2006). An examination of the seductive details effect in terms of working memory capacity. *Memory & Cognition, 34*(2), 344–355.

Sanders, J. R. (1973). Retention effects of adjunct questions in written and oral recall. *Journal of Educational Psychology, 65,* 181–186.

Savage-Rumbaugh, S., & Lewin, R. (1994). *Kanzi: The ape at the brink of the human mind.* New York: John Wiley & Sons.

Schmalhofer, F., & Glavanov, D. (1986). Three components of understanding a programmer's manual: Verbatim, propositional, and situational representations. *Journal of Memory and Language, 25,* 279–294.

Schnotz, W. (2005). An integrated model of text and picture comprehension. In R. E. Mayer (Ed.), *The Cambridge handbook of multimedia learning* (pp. 49–69). Cambridge: Cambridge University Press.

(2011). Colorful bouquets in multimedia research: A closer look at the modality effect. *Zeitschrift für Pädagogische Psychologie, 25,* 269–276.

(2014). Integrated model of text and picture comprehension. In R. E. Mayer (Ed.), *The Cambridge handbook of multimedia learning,* 2nd ed. (pp. 72–103). Cambridge: Cambridge University Press.

(2022). Integrated model of text and picture comprehension. In R. E. Mayer, & L. Fiorella (Eds.), *The Cambridge handbook of multimedia learning* (pp. 82–99). Cambridge: Cambridge University Press.

Schnotz, W., & Bannert, M. (1999). Einflüsse der Visualisierungsform auf die Konstruktion mentaler Modelle beim Bild- und Textverstehen [Effects of the visualization form on the construction of mental models in picture and text comprehension]. *Zeitschrift für Experimentelle Psychologie, 46,* 216–235.

(2003). Construction and interference in learning from multiple representations. *Learning and Instruction, 13,* 141–156.

Schnotz, W., & Kürschner, C. (2008). External and internal representations in the acquisition and use of knowledge: Visualization effects on mental model construction. *Instructional Science, 36*(3), 175–190.

Schnotz, W., & Lowe, R. K. (2008). A unified view of learning from animated and static graphics. In R. K. Lowe, & W. Schnotz (Eds.), *Learning with animation. Research implications for design* (pp. 304–356). New York: Cambridge University Press.

Schnotz, W., Mengelkamp, C., Baadte, C., & Hauck, G. (2014). Focus of attention and choice of text modality in multimedia learning. *European Journal of Psychology of Education, 29*(3), 483–501.

Schnotz, W., & Wagner, I. (2018). Construction and elaboration of mental models through strategic conjoint processing of text and pictures. *Journal of Educational Psychology, 110*(6), 850–863.

Schraw, G., & Lehman, S. (2001). Situational interest: A review of the literature and directions for future research, *Educational Psychology Review, 13,* 23–25.

Schüler, A., Scheiter, K., & Schmidt-Weigand, F. (2011). Boundary conditions and constraints of the modality effect. *Zeitschrift für Pädagogische Psychologie*, *25*, 211–220.

Sidner, C. L. (1983). Focusing and discourse. *Discourse Processes*, *6*, 107–130.

Silveira, J. (1971). Incubation: The effect of interruption timing and length on problem solution and quality of problem processing. Unpublished doctoral dissertation. University of Oregon, USA.

Stiller, K. D., Freitag, A., Zinnbauer, P., & Freitag, C. (2009). How pacing of multimedia instructions can influence modality effects: A case of superiority of visual texts. *Australasian Journal of Educational Technology*, *25*, 184–203.

Stringer, C. B. (1992). Replacement, continuity and the origin of *Homo sapiens*. In G. Bräuer, & F. H. Smith (Eds.), *Continuity or replacement. Controversies in Homo sapiens evolution* (pp. 9–24). Rotterdam: Balkema.

Sweller, J., Ayres, P., & Kalyuga, S. (2011). *Cognitive load theory*. New York: Springer.

Tomasello, M. (2008). *Origins of human communication*. Cambridge, MA: MIT Press.

Torralbo, A., Santiago, J., & Lupiáñez, J. (2006). Flexible conceptual projection of time onto spatial frames of reference. *Cognitive Science*, *30*, 745–757.

Tufte, E. R. (1983). *The visual display of quantitative information*. Cheshire, CT: Graphics Press.

(1990). *Envisioning information*. Cheshire, CT: Graphics Press.

(1997). *Visual explanations. Images and quantities, evidence and narrative*. Cheshire, CT: Graphics Press.

Vidal-Abarca, E., Mañá, A., & Gil, L. (2010). Individual differences for self-regulating task-oriented reading activities. *Journal of Educational Psychology*, *102*(4), 817–826.

Visalberghi, E., Fragaszy, D. M., & Savage-Rumbaugh, S. (1995). Performance in a tool-using task by common chimpanzees (*Pan troglodytes*), bonobos (*Pan paniscus*), an orangutan (*Pongo pygmaeus*), and capuchin monkeys (*Cebus apella*). *Journal of Comparative Psychology*, *109*(1), 52–60.

Wainer, H. (1997). *Visual revelations. Graphical tales of fate and deception from Napoleon Bonaparte to Ross Perot*. Mahwah, NJ: Lawrence Erlbaum.

Wertheimer, M. (1938). *Laws of organization in perceptual forms in a source book for Gestalt Psychology*. London: Routledge & Kegan Paul.

Winn, W. D. (1994). Contributions of perceptual and cognitive processes to the comprehension of graphics. In W. Schnotz, & R. Kulhavy (Eds.), *Comprehension of graphics* (pp. 3–27). Amsterdam: North-Holland.

Zelazny, G. (1985). *Say it with charts*. Homewood, IL: Dow Jones-Irwin.

Zhao, F., Schnotz, W., Wagner, I., & Gaschler, R. (2020). Texts and pictures serve different functions in conjoint mental model construction and adaptation. *Memory & Cognition*, *48*(1), 69–82.

Zwaan, R. A., Langston, M. C., & Graesser, A. C. (1995). The construction of situation models in narrative comprehension: An event-indexing model. *Psychological Science*, *6*, 292–297.

Index

CPSIA information can be obtained
at www.ICGtesting.com
Printed in the USA
BVHW052122140223
658501BV00012B/216